F. VON HÜGEL'S
PHILOSOPHY OF RELIGION

BIBLIOTHECA EPHEMERIDUM THEOLOGICARUM
LOVANIENSIUM

LXII

BARON FRIEDRICH VON HÜGEL'S
PHILOSOPHY OF RELIGION

BY

JAMES J. KELLY

LEUVEN
UNIVERSITY PRESS

UITGEVERIJ PEETERS
LEUVEN

1983

CIP-GEGEVENS

Kelly, James J.

Baron Friedrich von Hügel's philosophy of religion / by
James J. Kelly. – Leuven : Peeters : Leuven University Press. –
(Bibliotheca ephemeridum theologicarum lovaniensium ; 62)

ISBN 90-6186-146-2
SISO 202 UDC 230.1
Trefw.: Hügel, Friedrich von ; godsdienstfilosofie.

ISBN 90 6186 146 2

D/1983/1869/9

Leuven University Press/Presses Universitaires de Louvain
Universitaire Pers Leuven
Krakenstraat 3, B-3000 Leuven-Louvain (Belgium)

Uitgeverij Peeters, Bondgenotenlaan 153, B-3000 Leuven (Belgium)

FOREWORD

On his death in 1925 Friedrich von Hügel, affectionately known to his friends as "the baron", bequeathed his personal library, his philosophical and theological books and papers along with his extant correspondences to the Scottish Presbyterian University of St. Andrews[1]. However, because of the modernist scare which pervaded the Roman Catholic ecclesiastical and theological milieu a protective screen was thrown up around von Hügel and his unpublished papers and letters by sympathisers who feared a posthumous condemnation and the repercussions of such action on the baron's elderly, strictly orthodox widow[2]. Bernard Holland who published the first major selection of von Hügel letters portrayed him as a thoroughly sound and orthodox Catholic. Anything controversial implicating the baron in the modernist movement was modified or deleted. Whether this "historiographical" tradition had its origins with von Hügel himself is not of primary concern. More important is the fact that a small number of the baron's works and a great deal of his correspondence remained unpublished or when published were usually presented in such a highly *selected* form that no impartial judgment or balanced conclusions could be drawn from them. When one adds to this the often questionable textual-critical work of some of the more recent editions of the baron's papers one becomes convinced of the necessity for any student of von Hügel to return to the original sources and not base his research on selected and often biased secondary documents.

Our two year research Fellowship on the von Hügel archives at St. Andrews provided us with this unique opportunity. It allowed us to employ for the first time, along with all the published works of and about von Hügel, the baron's study library, over 3,000 books and articles, usually bearing the date and reason for purchase on the inside cover, the date of reading, what are termed *notanda*, *admiranda* and *criticanda* on the fly-leaf and critical notes and personal comments

---

1. Since the acquisition the University Library has made considerable important additions to the von Hügel collection.

2. For example, three weeks after von Hügel's death we find Dom Cuthbert Butler writing to Friedrich Heiler: "Thanks for your article. There are very good and true things in it. But I hope such articles are not going to lead to any denunciation at Rome that would cause his writings to be put on the Index. I have no doubt you would deplore such a result as really as I would — and it would break his wife's heart. Still I cannot help fearing it is a very possible issue of your article". E. C. Butler to Friedrich Heiler, 26 February 1925, Butler's handwritten note to verso of Heiler's letter of 17 February 1925, Downside.

throughout the work. Alongside this, one could study the 43 volumes
of the baron's diaries containing his reading lists on the memoranda
pages at the front and back of each diary. From 1884 onwards these
are accompanied by von Hügel's proposed study programme for each
year. And from 1887 we have chronological summaries of the
baron's work for each year at the end of the diary, while the diary
itself gives the detailed day to day account of all von Hügel's readings,
personal contacts and activities, including his letter writing and the
mail he received. Add to this the mass of unpublished manuscript
letters to and from the baron available at St. Andrews and the
other known correcpondences in various libraries and personal archives
in Britain and throughout the world, and the further possibility of
tracing hitherto unknown letters of the baron from information
discovered in the diaries and of allowing each and all of these
disparate sources to elucidate, correct, broaden and deepen each other,
and one has a unique and comprehensive basis, not only for articulating
von Hügel's religious philosophy, but also for concretely illuminating
the various influences on the baron's mind from youth to old age. The
present work is the first to utilise all these sources in such a
comprehensive and dialectical fashion in an effort to discover the
fundamental motivating forces of von Hügel's thought and consequently
to portray a more critical analysis and new constructive synthesis of
his religious philosophy.

Structurally the book[3] is divided into two parts. While Part I sketches
the biography of von Hügel as a religious philosopher, the Second
Part examines his religious philosophy. The First Part should not be
regarded as a biography in the strict sense of the word[4] but rather
an attempt to investigate and portray the baron's development as a
religious philosopher and so historically ground what is systematically
elaborated in the Second Part. The significance of Part I lies in the fact
that it detects and documents a major evolution in von Hügel's thought
away from the neo-Kantianism of Johannes Volkelt (1848-1930) in
the direction of a radically empirical conception of experience along the
lines of the Cambridge psychologist, James Ward (1843-1925). Although
this transition had been taking place in the baron from the turn of the
century through the influence of such men as William James, Henri
Bergson and Henry Jones, the decisive breakthrough only came about

---

3. This book is a revised version of a much larger dissertation entitled *The
Reality of God: A Critical and Constructive Analysis of the Religious Philosophy
of Baron Friedrich von Hügel*, 3 vols., LXXI-461 pp., Appendix 86 pp., presented for
the degree of Doctor in Sacred Theology in the Faculty of Theology of the
Catholic University of Louvain (Leuven) in 1978.
4. For a biography please consult M. DE LA BEDOYÈRE, *The Life of Baron von
Hügel*, London, 1951.

in October 1905 when von Hügel was forced to postpone the conclusion of his *Mystical Element* to revise an earlier paper "Experience and Transcendence"[5] for publication in Wilfrid Ward's *Dublin Review*. While revising the paper the baron was compelled to send the following unpublished letter to Ward on 24 October 1905 : "on carefully studying it [the 1903 Synthetic paper] these last days, I have come to feel, *quite clearly and finally*, that I have — evidently gradually and, up to now, all but unconsciously, — *seriously changed my own views* on the important matter in question. Just exactly the most emphatic passages, and indeed the general drift and emotional tone of the whole, no more represent what I believe to be true. So that I could not let you have it without, practically, producing a new paper, of a different tone and drift, in which I could incorporate parts of *this* article, — but these parts would perform different functions from those allotted to them in their present positions. — I find that it has been James Ward's criticism and the study of Höffding's *Kierkegaard* and Caird's *Theology in the Greek Philosophers* (these books were only finished by me with the end of my holiday, 4 weeks ago) which have produced this change in me"[6]. Subsequently von Hügel drafted a new article, also entitled "Experience and Transcendence"[7], in which a wider, more radical empirical notion of experience as a basis and framework for man's religious and mystical experience was explicated for the first time.

Probably the main reason why this decisive shift in the baron's thought has passed unnoticed by scholars is because the epistemological sections of his *magnum opus*, *The Mystical Element of Religion*, which still mainly espoused the neo-Kantian Volkelt, were completed before the appearance of the seemingly insignificant 1906 article "Experience and Transcendence". And as von Hügel never revised *The Mystical Element* in the light of his new insights nor developed them systematically elsewhere, commentators have been content to restate the main trend of the epistemology of this major work. The present book uncovers this decisive transition in the baron's thought and proceeds in its Second Part to construct a new synthesis of his religious philosophy on this basis. The first three chapters of this Second Part develop von Hügel's radically empirical conception of experience, i.e. as sensational, emotional, cognitional, volitional in which reality is immediately given. The two subsequent chapters investigate the specifically religious, mystical and Christian dimensions of experience. In the light of this the Sixth Chapter examines the vital relationship between God, man, society and the world. The final chapter on Personal Religion forms a culminating point for most of the important themes developed throughout the work.

5. Read before the Synthetic Society on 28 May 1903.
6. Von Hügel to W. Ward, 24 October 1905, St. Andrews University Library.
7. *The Dublin Review*, 138, 1906, 357-79.

ACKNOWLEDGMENTS

   I can only acknowledge my gratitude to a few of the very many
people who contributed in their varied ways to the realisation of this
work. Furthest back and up to the present I have been fortunate to
receive the continual support and understanding of my parents.
   During my early philosophy years in Ireland I was skilfully initiated
and guided into philosophy by Dr. Patrick Brady. For my further
philosophical, theological and psycho-analytical training I owe a
profound debt of gratitude to the Katholieke Universiteit te Leuven
(Belgium). To the Faculties of Philosophy, Psychology and more
especially the Faculty of Theology in which I was formed in the
best Louvain traditions and to the distinguished members of the staffs
who were so kind and friendly to me both as a student and colleague
I extend my deepest gratitude. A special word of thanks goes to Professors
Marc Caudron, Piet Fransen and most especially Maurits Sabbe whom
I count a friend. My gratitude is also extended to Professor Frans
Neirynck for accepting this work into the *Bibliotheca Ephemeridum
Theologicarum Lovaniensium* and also for his personal help and advice
during the final revision of my manuscript. To my doctoral director
and promotor, Professor Magister Jan H. Walgrave this work owes
most. It was Professor Walgrave who first introduced me to von
Hügel and radical empiricism and so allowed me the possibility of
discovering the radical empirical treads in von Hügel's thought. A word
of gratitude also goes to the Senate of the University of St. Andrews
for the two year St. Leonard's College Fellowship they awarded me
to research their von Hügel archives, to Mr. R. N. Smart, the
archivist at St. Andrews, and Mr. E. D'Hondt of the Theology
Library, Leuven. Last and most important of all my deepest and most
heart-felt thanks goes to my wife, Annemie, who encouraged me to
prepare this work for publication and who undertook the unrewarding
task of typing the successive drafts. To her and our son, Fionn, I dedicate
the book.

   14 October 1982   James J. KELLY

TABLE OF CONTENTS

PART I

THE BIOGRAPHY OF A RELIGIOUS PHILOSOPHER :
FRIEDRICH VON HÜGEL (1852-1925)

PART II

BARON FRIEDRICH VON HÜGEL'S
RELIGIOUS PHILOSOPHY

BIBLIOGRAPHY

ABBREVIATIONS

BEDOYÈRE   Michael DE LA BEDOYÈRE, *The Life of Baron von Hügel*, London, 1951.

BM   British Museum.

BOA   Birmingham Oratory Archives.

C.E.   Du Christ éternel et de nos christologies successives. — *La Quinzaine* 58 (1 June, 1904).

D.C.D.   Petite consultation sur les difficultés concernant Dieu. — in *Crisi modernista e rinnovamento cattolico in Italia* by P. SCOPPOLA, Bologna, 1961.

Diary   Baron Friedrich von Hügel's manuscript diaries, 43 volumes.

E.A.I, II   *Essays and Addresses on the Philosophy of Religion*, First and Second Series, London, 1921, 1926.

E.L.   *Eternal Life: A Study of Its Implications and Applications*, Edinburgh, 1912.

E.T.I   Experience and Transcendence (23 May, 1903). — *Papers Read Before the Synthetic Society, 1896-1908*, presented by A.J. BALFOUR, London, 1909.

E.T.II   Experience and Transcendence. — *The Dublin Review* 138 (April, 1906).

G.S.   *The German Soul in Its Attitude towards Ethics and Christianity, the State and War*, London, 1916.

L.N.   Gwendolen GREENE, *Letters from Baron von Hügel to a Niece*, London, 1928.

M.E.I, II   *The Mystical Element of Religion as Studied in Saint Catherine of Genoa and Her Friends*, volume I, II, London, 1908.

R.G.   *The Reality of God and Religion and Agnosticism*, edited by Edmund G. GARDNER, London, 1931.

S.L.   *Baron Friedrich von Hügel: Selected Letters 1896-1924*, edited by Bernard HOLLAND, London, 1927.

SAUL   St. Andrews University Library.

T.L.S.   *The Times Literary Supplement.*

VHB   Von Hügel Bibliography.

PART I

ARCHIVES AND MANUSCRIPT COLLECTIONS

A. VON HÜGEL ARCHIVES, St. Andrews University Library (= SAUL)

1. Diaries of F. von Hügel, 43 vols, 1877-79, 1884-1900, 1902-24.
2. F. von Hügel's will. MS. B3280.H8.

3. Boxes containing von Hügel's manuscripts, papers and miscellaneous articles of other writers (uncatalogued).
4. Two documents relating to admission of Johann Alois Baron von Hügel to consortium of imperial nobles in 1803. MSS.5579-5580.
5. Papers relating to the *Weekly Register*, 1899-1902. MS.36363.

6. Letters of von Hügel to :

Blondel, Maurice (55),	1895-1924	MS.B3280.H8B6 (Typed copies).
Bremond, Henri (64)	1899-1923	MS.30284.
Chapman, Adeline (20)	1901-1921	MS.37194.
Clutton, Mr & Mrs M. (2)	1912-1913	MS.30994-5.
Delehaye, Hippolyte (15)	1905-1922	MS.37016 (Microfilm).

Containing von Hügel's 7 page memoir of Charles de Smedt.

Ehrhard, Albert (5)	1898-1922	MS.37017 (Photocopies).
Eucken, Rudolf (7)	1897-1906	MS.37019 (Microfilm).
Guest, Mrs (1)	1897	MS.37194.
Herford, Vernon (2)	1906,1920	MSS.30410, 30494.
Holiday, Mr & Mrs H. (3)	1893-1911	MS.36349.
Kraus, Franz Xaver (7)	1895-1900	MS.36364 (Photocopies).
Lilley, Alfred Leslie (70)	1903-1925	MSS.30513-30580.

The Lilley papers also include 1 letter of Mary Catherine von Hügel, the baron's wife, to Lilley, 30 January 1925, MS.30628. For references to von Hügel among Lilley's other correspondences cf. MSS.30587, 30588, 30593, 30601, 30603/1, 30748, 30753/1, 30625, 30628, 30631/6, 30639, 30662, 30663, 30667, 30669, 30675, 30697, 30701, 30740, 30757, 30758, 30766, 30778, 30779, 30789, 30790, 30796, 30799, 30804, 30805, 30809, 30820, 30821, 30822, 30824, 30827, 30828, 30839, 30840, 30843, 30847, 30849, 30862, 30865, 30866, 30873.

Mansel, Juliet (28)	1910-1921	MS.37194.

Contains also numerous papers by von Hügel on the history and archaeology of Rome and a number of photographs of the baron and his family.

Mansel, Mildred (3)	1910-1915	MS.37194.
Mignot, Eudoxe-Irénée (29)	1893-1903	MS.30306 (Photocopies).
Osborne, Charles Edward (5)	1906-1910	MS.37018/1-5.

With reference to the modernist crisis the Osborne papers also contain the following letters to Osborne from Quin, M. (1), Petre, M.D. (1), Shelley, N. (1), Tyrrell, G. (10), MS.37018/6-18.

Smith, Norman Kemp (37)	1919-1924	MS.30420.
Underhill, Evelyn (15)	1921-1924	MS.5552.
Ward, James (13)	1902-1923	MS.30498.
Ward, Wilfrid (203)	1882-1916	MS.21,VII,143 : I-VII.
Ward, Mrs W. (6)	1890-1918	MS.21,VII,143 : I-VII.

The Ward papers also contain von Hügel's three page manuscript dated 30 April 1896 entitled : "Note on Mr. R.H. Hutton's Paper, Why is the Universe intelligible to us?"; 5 copies or drafts of letters from Ward to von Hügel; a copy by Mrs Ward of a letter of von Hügel to Cardinal Vaughan, 27 September 1896; an extract by Ward of 1 letter of von Hügel to a Mrs Cave, 2 February 1888. The Papers also include letters to Ward from Baroness Eliza von Hügel, the Duke of Norfolk, R.H. Hutton, Cardinal Vaughan, David Fleming etc. All uncatalogued.

Young, Charles Edward (21)	1904-10	MS.30499-30512.

The Young papers also contain the following letters to Young from : Miss Katherine Clutton (1), 1907-08, MS.30500; Henry C. Corrance (2), 1904-10, MS.30502; Alfred Fawkes (1), 1905, MS.30503; Pierre Jay (2), 1906-09, MS.30505; Augustin Leger (2),

1908, MS.30506; A.L. Lilley (19), 1903-09, MS.30507; Alfred Loisy (7), 1905-09, MS.30508; Joseph Rickaby (1), 1908, MS. 30510/1; George Tyrrell (1), 1908, MS. 30510/2; Giovanni Semeria (2), 1905-09, MS.30511; Charles John Shebbeare (1), 1908, MS.30512.

7. Letters to von Hügel from :

Alfieri, Ajace A. (1)	1909	MS.2200.
Balfour, Arthur J. (7)	1908-1916	MSS.2201-2207.
Batiffol, Pierre (1)	n.d.	MS.2208.
Bergson, Henri (1)	1911	MS.2209.
Bishop, Edmund (25)	1904-1913	MSS.2210-2234.
Blondel, Maurice (55)	1895-1924	MSS.2235-2289.
Boutroux, Etienne (9)	1907-1918	MSS.2290-2298.
Bremond, Henri (56)	1899-1923	MSS.2299-2384.
Buonaiuti, Ernesto (4)	1907-1910	MSS.2355-2358.
Butler, Edward Cuthbert (14)	1895-1924	MSS.2359-2373.
Casati, Giovanni (1)	1909	MS.2374.
Cochin, Henry (1)	1906	MS.2375.
Deissmann, Gustav A. (1)	1923	MS.2376.
Delehaye, Hippolyte (12)	1905-1922	MSS.2377-2388.
Desjardins, Paul (1)	1909	MS.2389.
Dessoulavy, Charles (1)	1909	MS.2390.
De Vere, Aubrey (4)	1874	MSS.2391-2394.
Dickinson, Albert (10)	1915-1923	MSS.2395-2404.
Driver, Samuel Rolles (6)	1895-1907	MSS.2405-2410.
Duchesne, Louis (56)	1885-1920	MSS.2411-2466.
Ellis, Robinson (5)	1885-1894	MSS.2467-2471.
Eucken, Irene (1)	n.d.	MS.2472.
Eucken, Rudolf (93)	1896-1914	MSS.2473-2565.
Federici, Mattia (1)	1909	MS.2566.
Fogazzaro, Antonio (14)	1902-1910	MSS.2567-2580.
Fogazzaro, Maria (3)	1913-1921	MSS.2581-2583.
Fracassini, Umberto (1)	1909	MS.2584.
Gallarati-Scotti, Tommaso (1)	1909	MS.2585.
Gardner, Percy (16)	1902-1915	MSS.2586-2601.
Gasquet, Francis A. (1)	1892	MS.2602.
Genocchi, Giovanni (8)	1898-1916	MSS.2603-2610.
Gillis, John (1)	1922	MS.2611.
Gooch, George P. (1)	1892	MS.2612.
Gore, Charles (3)	1898-1909	MSS.2613-2615.
Grandmaison, Léonce de (1)	1910	MS.2616.
Green, Everard (1)	1909	MS.2617.
Guillaume, Alphonse (1)	n.d.	MS.2618.
Harnack, Adolf von (1)	1911	MS.2619.
Hastings, James (12)	1903-1917	MSS.2610-2631.
Hebert, Marcel (8)	1897-1902	MSS.2632-2639.
Heiler, Friedrich (7)	1920-1923	MSS.2640-2646.
Holland, Bernard (1)	1903	MS.3233.
Holtzmann, Heinrich (18)	1901-1910	MSS.2657-2674.
Hort, Fenton J.A. (2)	1885-1886	MSS.2676-2677.

Houtin, Albert (8)	1903-1911	MSS.2678-2685.
Hutton, Richard H. (4)	1888-1894	MSS.2686-2689.
Huvelin, Henri (16)	1884-1904	MSS.2690-2704.
Inge, William Ralph (6)	1911-1923	MSS.2705-2710.
James, John G. (1)	1909	MS.2711.
Jung, Gertrud (1)	1923	MS.2712.
Laberthonnière, Lucien (36)	1897-1924	MSS.2713-2748.
Lathbury, Daniel C. (1)	1909	MS.2749.
Le Roy, Edouard (10)	1906-1920	MSS.2750-2759.
Lilley, Alfred L. (2)	1909	MSS.2760-2761.
Lyall, Sir Alfred C. (9)	1902-1910	MSS.2762-2770.
Martineau, James (2)	1887-1888	MSS.2771-2772.
Maturin, Basil W. (1)	1912	MS.2773.
Mignot, Eudoxe-Irénée (54)	1893-1917	MSS.2774-2827.
Montefiore, Claude J. (55)	1894-1921	MSS.2828-2883.
Newman, John Henry (20)	1874-1884	MSS.2884-2900.
Osborne, Charles E. (2)	1909	MSS.2901-2902.
Paley, Frederick A. (7)	1882-1885	MSS.2903-2909.
Petre, Maude D. (1)	1883	MS.2910.
Pollock, Sir Frederick (3)	1915-1917	MSS.2911-2913.
Postgate, John P. (1)	1883	MS.2914.
Prenner, Joseph (1)	1909	MS.2915.
Rawlinson, Gerald C. (18)	1906-1912	MSS.2916-2933.
Reinach, Salomon (2)	1905-1908	MSS.2934-2935.
Robinson, Frederick O. (1)	n.d.	MS.2936.
Sabatier, Charles Paul (22)	1895-1912	MSS. 2937-2958.
Sanday, William (3)	1894-1896	MSS.2959-2961.
Sauer, Joseph (1)	1909	MS.2962.
Schweitzer, Albert (2)	1922	MSS.2963-2964.
Scott-Hope, Josephine (1)	1916	MS.2965. (Mrs. Wilfrid Ward).
Selwyn, Gordon (1)	1909	MS.2966.
Seth, Andrew (8)	1899-1915	MSS.2967-2974.
(afterwards Andrew Seth Pringle-Pattison).		
Sidgwick, Henry (2)	1891-1900	MSS.2975-2976.
Smith, Norman Kemp (89)	1914-1925	MSS.2977-3066.
Söderblom, Nathan (5)	1910-1922	MSS.3067-3071.
Talbot, Edward S. (1)	1909	MS.3072.
Thomas, J.M. Lloyd (1)	1909	MS.3073.
Thorin, Ernest (1)	1886	MS.3074.
Troeltsch, Ernst (23)	1901-1923	MSS.3075-3098.
Troeltsch, Marta (2)	1923	MSS.3099-3100.
Tucker, Vincent (1)	1892	MS.3101.
Vaihinger, Hans (8)	1904-1920	MSS.3102-3109.
Waggett, Philip N. (1)	1909	MS. 3110.
Walker, James A. (1)	1909	MS.3111.
Ward, James (25)	1900-1922	MSS.3112-3136.
Ward, Maisie (2)	1916	MSS.3137-3138.
Ward, Wilfrid Philip (28)	1884-1916	MSS.3139-3166.
Ward, William George (6)	1875-1879	MSS.3167-3172.

Webb, Clement J. (48)　　　　1904-1923　　MSS.3173-3220.
Wood, Charles Lindley (10)　　1895-1911　　MSS.3221-3231. (Lord Halifax).

B. OTHER VON HÜGEL ARCHIVES

1. *Aberdeen.*
Cairns, David S.
Three manuscript letters from von Hügel. Including a 10 page manuscript of von Hügel entitled "Notes on Dr. David S. Cairns' Draft Chapter 'Evangelism'". In possession of Dr. David Cairns, 1 St. Swithin St., Aberdeen, Scotland.

2. *Bath*, Downside Abbey Archives.
Bishop, Edmund (Papers).
When the present writer visited Downside in July 1974 the letters of von Hügel to Edmund Bishop were believed lost, cf. also Barmann, p. 1. I was informed in 1978 that the letters were recovered and are now among the Bishop Papers. The entire von Hügel/Bishop correspondence, twenty-two letters (1897-1913), published by Abercombie, cf. VHB, no. 85.
Butler, Edward C. (Papers), MS.36998.
Six letters from von Hügel (1905-1924) and one from Lady Mary von Hügel (1925), all published by the present writer. Included also is a pencilled critique by von Hügel of an outline of the history of christian mysticism prepared by Butler for his book *Western Mysticism.*

3. *Birmingham*, Oratory Archives. Von Hügel to :
Newman, John H. (7)　　　　1874-1886　　MS.AML　(2),　(100a),　(83),
　　　　　　　　　　　　　　　　　　　　　VC.50(12),(16), (37); AVC22(43).
Ryder, Henry I.D. (12)　　　1890-1893　　MS.VC.20, PC205-6.

4. *Cambridge*, University Manuscripts Dept. Von Hügel to :
Hort, Fenton J.A. (1)　　　　1885　　　Add.6597 p.719.
Jackson, Henry (1)　　　　　1902　　　Add.5944.

5. *Harvard University*, The Haughton Library. Von Hügel to :
James, William (1)　　　　　1909　　　bMs.AM.1092.I.

6. *London.*
　a. *The British Museum*. Von Hügel to :
Petre, Maude D. (103)　　　1899-1922　　Add.MSS.45361-2.
With one letter from Miss Petre to von Hügel, MS.45361 f.97.
Tyrrell, George　　　　　　1897-1909　　Add.MSS.44927-44931.
Complete correspondence Tyrrell-von Hügel.
　b. *Mr. Tom Burns*. Von Hügel to :
Greene, Gwendolen.
The originals of the published *Letters from Baron Friedrich von Hügel to a Niece*, including also a selection of spiritual advice given to von Hügel by the Abbé Henri Huvelin in 1886 and 1893 and published by the present writer. In the possession of Mr. Tom Burns, 48 Great Peter St., London.
　c. *Franciscan Library*. Von Hügel to :
Fleming, David (2)　　　　　1897-1902　　Uncatalogued.
　d. *Westminster, Archdiocese Archives*. Von Hügel to :
Vaughan, Card. Herbert (1)　　1896　　　VI/17(XXI)MSS.1-54.

e. *William, Dr. (Library)*.
One volume of the manuscript minutes of the *London Society for the Study of Religion*, 1904-1925, MS.WL80, ED.17.

7. *Melbourne*, University Archives. Von Hügel to :
Gibson, W. R. Boyce (1)   1906   Uncatalogued.

8. *Oxford*
  a. *Balliol College Library*. Von Hügel to :
Caird, Edward (1)   1902   Uncatalogued.
Includes also a copy of Caird's reply dated 25 Dec. 1902.
  b. *Bodleian Library*. Von Hügel to :

Dawson, Albert (1)	1914	MS.Eng.Lett.c.196 f.62.
Gardner, Percy (12)	1902-1915	MS.Eng.Lett.c.55 fs.195-229.
Hopkins, Gerard M. (1)	1889	MS.Eng.Misc.a.8 f.68.
Marvin, Francis S. (7)	1916-1920	MS.Eng.Lett.c.265 f.29; c.266 fs. 71-73; c.267 fs.2,8-9.
Sanday, William (2)	1896-1897	MS.Eng.Misc.d.123 (2) fs.610-11; 612-13.

9. *Uppsala*, University. Söderblom Stiftelsen. Von Hügel to :
Söderblom, Nathan (10)   1910-1922   Uncatalogued.

10. *York*, Archives of the Wood Family of Hickleton and Garrowby. Von Hügel to :
Wood, Charles L. (13)   1895-1911   MSS.A4.
Included within "The General Church Papers, 1861-1933" of the Second Viscount Halifax, MSS.A4.

PART II

VON HÜGEL BIBLIOGRAPHY

A. PUBLISHED WORKS OF FRIEDRICH VON HÜGEL (1883-1924)

    1. Carl VON HÜGEL, The Story of the Escape of Prince Metternich. — *The National Review* 1:4 (June, 1883), 588-605.
       Introduction and translation by Friedrich von Hügel.
    2. Chronique. — *Bulletin critique* 6:2 (1 May, 1885), 175-8; 7:6 (15 March, 1886), 117-8; 7:7 (1 April, 1886), 135; 7:24 (15 December, 1886), 477-8; 12:6 (15 March, 1891), 119-20; 12:24 (15 December, 1891), 478-9.
    3. The Spiritual Writings of Père Grou, S.J. — *The Tablet* 74:2589-90 (21 & 28 December, 1889), 990-1, 1029-31.
    4. Notes Addressed to the Very Reverend H.I.D.R. upon the Subject of Biblical Inspiration and Inerrancy. — Privately printed, London, July, 1891, 15 pp.
    5. Wilfrid WARD, *William George Ward and the Catholic Revival*, London, 1893.
       Consult especially chapter V : "The Catholic Revival and the New Ultramontanism", pp. 82-129. Along with providing much of the data von Hügel's ideas guided Ward throughout this chapter. Confer also von Hügel's appreciation of W. G. Ward, pp. 365-75. And finally chapter XVI : "An Epilogue", pp. 419-33. The baron contributed so much to this chapter that Ward publically acknowledged it "as a joint production", p. XII.

6. The Papal Encyclical and Mr. Gore. — *The Spectator* 3438 (19 May, 1894), 684-5.

7. Fénelon's 'Spiritual Letters'. — *The Tablet* 83:2821 (2 June, 1894), 857-8.

8. The Roman Catholic View of Inspiration. — *The Spectator* 3440 (2 June, 1894), 750.

9. The Church and the Bible: The Two Stages of Their Inter-Relation. — *The Dublin Review* 115:231 (October, 1894), 313-41; 116:233 (April, 1895), 306-37; 117:235 (October, 1895), 275-304.

10. L'Abbé Duchesne and Anglican Orders. — *The Tablet* 84:2845 (17 November, 1894), 776.

11. H. E. MANNING, Obstacles à l'expansion de l'Eglise Catholique en Angleterre. — *Revue Anglo-Romaine* 2 (9 May, 1896), 241-51.
Translated by von Hügel and Fernand Portal from chapter 27, vol. II of Purcell's *Life of Cardinal Manning*, London, 1895.

12. Bulletin. — *Revue biblique internationale* 5:3 (1 July, 1896), 470-2.
Summary of: Quelques transpositions de faits que l'on remarque dans l'évangile de saint Luc. — von Hügel's communication to the Roman Society of Biblical Studies, 5 March, 1896).

13. Professor Eucken on the Struggle for Spiritual Life. — *The Spectator* 3568 (14 November, 1896), 679-81.

14. The Comma Johanneum. — *The Tablet* 89:2978 (5 June, 1897), 896-7.

15. Impressions of Elizabeth Rundle Charles (1827-1896). — *The Hampstead Annual* (1897), 52-62.

16. M.-J. Lagrange, Sources of the Pentateuch. — *The Catholic University Bulletin* (4 January, 1898), 115-22.
Von Hügel's English précis of Lagrange's *Les sources du Pentateuque*, in *Compte rendu*, pp. 179-200, cf. no. 17 below.

17. La méthode historique et son application à l'étude des documents de l'Hexateuque. — *Compte rendu du quatrième congrès scientifique international des Catholiques tenu à Fribourg (Suisse) du 16 au 20 août 1897, deuxième section, sciences exégétiques*, 1, Fribourg, 1898, 231-65.
Revised English version: The Historical Method and the Documents of the Hexateuch. — *The Catholic University Bulletin*, Washington D.C., (4 April, 1898), 198-226+ VII appendices).

18. Caterina Fiesca Adorna, the Saint of Genoa, 1447-1510. — *The Hampstead Annual* (1898), 70-85.

19. A Proposito dell'Abate Loisy. — *Studi Religiosi* 1 (July-August, 1901), 348-50.

20. Alfred von REUMONT, *Charles von Hügel, April 25, 1795 — June 2, 1870*, privately printed, Cambridge, 1903.
A biographical sketch of Carl von Hügel, pp. 31-49. Edited by Anatole von Hügel and translated from German by Friedrich von Hügel.

21. The Case of the Abbé Loisy. — *The Pilot* 9:199 (9 January, 1904), 30-1.

22. The Case of M. Loisy. — *The Pilot* 9:201 (23 January, 1904), 94.

23. The Abbé Loisy and the Holy Office. — *The Times* 37331 (2 March, 1904), 15. (Signed Romanus).

24. Storia, Fede e Chiesa. — *Il Giornale d'Italia* (11 March, 1904), 1.

25. Introduction to letters by Bailey Saunders and Loisy. — *The Times* 37382 (30 April, 1904), 6.

26. Du Christ éternel et de nos christologies successives. — *La Quinzaine*
    58:231 (1 June, 1904), 285-312.
    Important introductory section excised by the editor.
27. Correspondance. — *La Quinzaine* 60:238 (16 September, 1904), 276-7.
    Letter reply to Abbé J. Wehrlé.
28. Discussions: M. Loisy's Type of Catholicism. — *The Hibbert Journal*
    3:3 (April, 1905), 599-600.
29. Experience and Transcendence. — *The Dublin Review* 138 : 24 (April, 1906),
    357-79.
30. *The Papal Commission and the Pentateuch*, London, 1906, 64 pp.
    With Rev. Charles A. BRIGGS.
31. The Relations Between God and Man in *The New Theology* of the
    Rev. R.J. Campbell. — *The Albany Review* 1:6 (September, 1907), 650-68.
32. The Abbé Loisy. — *The Tablet* 3:3539 (7 March, 1908), 378-9.
33. Review, *Les Evangiles Synoptiques*. — *The Hibbert Journal* 6:4 (July, 1908),
    926-30.
34. *The Mystical Element of Religion as Studied in Saint Catherine of Genoa
    and her Friends*, 2 vols, London, New York, 1908, XXIV, 466+ VI, 422 pp.
    Second edition 1923, additional 13 page preface.
35. L'Abate Loisy e il problema dei Vangeli Sinottici. — *Il Rinnovamento*
    3 (January-June, 1908), 209-34; 4 (July-December, 1908), 1-44; 5 (January-
    June, 1909), 229-72, 396-423. (Signed H.).
36. Selbstanzeigen. — *Kantstudien* 14:1 (1909), 138-9.
    Von Hügel's own review of *The Mystical Element of Religion*.
37. Obituary notice for George Tyrrell. — *The Times* 39013 (16 July, 1909), 13.
    Written with Maude Petre but not signed by von Hügel. The identical notice
    appeared also, on the same day, in *The Daily Mail*, p. 9.
38. Una lettera del barone von Hügel sulla morte di Tyrrell. — *Corriere
    della Sera* (27 July, 1909).
    Translated into English by von Hügel and printed in the *Daily Graphic* 79:627
    (31 July, 1909), 12.
39. The Death-Bed of Father Tyrrell. — *The Tablet* 114 : 3612 (31 July, 1909),
    182.
40. Notes on Wilfrid Ward's "Authority a Reasonable Ground for Religious
    Belief" (27 January, 1899). — *Papers Read Before the Synthetic Society,
    1896-1908*. For private circulation, 235-9.
    Presented to the Members of the Synthetic Society by the Rt. Hon. Arthur
    James Balfour, August, 1909, London, 1909.
41. Experience and Transcendence (28 May, 1903). — *Papers Read Before
    the Synthetic Society, 1896-1908*. Cf. no. 40, 425-43.
42. The Late Father Tyrrell and the Faith. — *The Tablet* 114:3626
    (6 November, 1909), 738.
43. Father Tyrrell: Some Memorials of the Last Twelve Years of His Life. —
    The Hibbert Journal 8 : 2 (January, 1910), 233-52.
44. Religione ed illusione. — *Coenobium* 5 (March-April, 1911), 5-59. Reprinted
    in no. 68 below.
45. John, The Apostle. — *The Encyclopaedia Britannica*, 11th edition 15
    (1911), 432-3.
46. John, Gospel of St. — *The Encyclopaedia Britannica*, 11th edition 15 (1911),
    452-8.

47. Loisy, Alfred Firmin. — *The Encyclopaedia Britannica*, 11th edition 16 (1911), 926-8.
48. *Eternal Life: A Study of Its Implications and Applications*, Edinburgh, 1912, L, 443 pp.
   Second edition, 1913.
49. The Religious Philosophy of Rudolf Eucken. — *The Hibbert Journal* 10:3 (April, 1912), 660-77.
50. Father Tyrrell. — *The Tablet* 120: 3786 (30 November, 1912), 866-7.
51. The Essentials of Catholicism. — *Liddon House Occasional Paper* (July, 1913).
   Reprinted in no. 68 below.
52. The Real Germany and the False. How a Great Scholar Regards the War. — *The Christian Commonwealth* 34 (26 August, 1914), 309-10.
53. On the Specific Genius and Capacities of Christianity, Studied in Connection with the Works of Professor Ernst Troeltsch. — *The Constructive Quarterly* 2:5 & 8 (March & December, 1914), 68-98, 673-701.
   Reprinted in no. 68 below.
54. Christianity in Face of War: Its Strength and Difficulty. — *The Church Quarterly Review* 79:158 (January, 1915), 257-88.
   Reprinted in no. 56 below.
55. The German Soul and the Great War. — *The Quest* 6:3 (April, 1915), 401-29; 7:2 (January, 1916), 201-35.
   Reprinted in no. 56 below.
56. *The German Soul in Its Attitude towards Ethics and Christianity, the State and War*, London, 1916, 223 pp.
57. Progress in Religion. — *In Progress and History*, Oxford, 1916, 96-133.
   Edited by F. S. MARVIN. Reprinted in no. 68 below.
58. What do we mean by Heaven? What do we mean by Hell? A Synthetic Attempt. — *The Church Quarterly Review* 84:167 (April, 1917), 50-82.
   Reprinted in no. 68 below.
59. The Convictions Common to Catholicism and Protestantism. — *Homiletic Review* (April, 1917).
   Reprinted in no. 68 below.
60. Julius Wellhausen. — *The Times Literary Supplement* 842 (7 March, 1918), 117.
61. Religion and Illusion. — *The Quest* 9:3 (April, 1918), 353-82.
   Reprinted in no. 68 below.
62. Eudoxe Irénée Mignot. — *The Contemporary Review* 113 (May, 1918), 519-26.
63. Religion and Reality. — *The Quest* 9:4 (July, 1918), 529-62.
64. Christianity and the Supernatural. — *The Modern Churchman* 10:3 (June, 1920), 101-21.
   Reprinted in no. 68 below.
65. Cardinal Manning. — *The Times Literary Supplement* 1001 (24 March, 1921), 195.
66. A Great Book on Prayer. — *International Review of the Missions* 10:38 (April, 1921), 266-70.
   A Review of F. Heiler's *Das Gebet*, München, 1920.
67. Morals and Religion: A Symposium. — *The Hibbert Journal* 19:4 (July, 1921), 605-10.
   Reprinted in no. 77 below.

68. *Essays and Addresses on the Philosophy of Religion. First Series*, London, 1921, XIX, 308 pp. Along with containing the previously published articles, n°s 44 (20-41), 51 (227-41), 53 (144-94), 57 (67-97), 58 (195-224), 59 (242-53), 61 (20-41), 63 (42-66), 64 (278-98), the following hitherto unpublished essays and addresses also appear :
Preliminaries to Religious Belief (98-116).
Written to a friend, January, 1914.
Institutional Christianity (254-77).
Address to Executive Committee of the Christian Student Movement, October, 1918, substantially altered for publication.
The Apocalyptic Element in the Teaching of Jesus (119-43).
An address delivered before the Birmingham Clerical Society — Anglican —, October, 1919.
Responsibility in Religious Belief (3-19).
Paper read before the Secretaries of the British branches of the Christian Student Movement, March, 1920.

69. Apologist of Religion. — *The Times Literary Supplement* 1040 (22 December, 1921), 860.

70. Louis Duchesne. — *The Times Literary Supplement* 1062 (25 May, 1922), 342.

71. Note. — *The Times Literary Supplement* 1063 (1 June, 1922), 364.
Correcting slight error in his obituary notice on Louis Duchesne in the previous number.

72. The Rev. G.C. Rawlinson. — *The Church Times* 89:3133 (9 February, 1923), 158.

73. Ernst Troeltsch. — *The Times Literary Supplement* 1106 (29 March, 1923), 216.

74. E. TROELTSCH, *Christian Thought, Its History and Application*, London, 1923, XXXVI+179 pp. Prefatory Note and Introduction by F. von Hügel, V-VII, XI-XXXI.
German edition : *Der Historismus und seine Überwindung*. Fünf Vorträge. Eingeleitet von F. von Hügel. Berlin, XIII, 108 pp.

75. Der Mystiker und die Kirche aus Anlass des Sâdhu. — *Das Hochland* 22:1 (December, 1924), 320-30.

B. POSTHUMOUS PUBLICATIONS

76. F.R. LILLIE, *Some Letters of Baron von Hügel*, privately printed, Chicago, 1925, 64 pp.
Contains a reprint of E.R. Bevan's obituary notice of von Hügel from *The Times* (28 January, 1925); a reprint of ch.4 of E.A.I; 7 letters of the baron to Mrs. Lillie (later included in S.L.); one short unpublished letter along with two pages of Mrs. Lillie's notes of her final conversation with von Hügel in October, 1924 and three pictures of the baron.

77. Edmund G. GARDNER, *Essays and Addresses on the Philosophy of Religion, Second Series*, London, 1926. IX, 287 pp.
Incorporating the following essays and addresses :
Official Authority and Living Religion (3-23).
Written in 1904.
The Place and Function of the Historical Element in Religion (27-55).
Address delivered at the London Society for the Study of Religion, 5 May, 1905.

On the Place and Function, within Religion, of the Body, of History, and of Institutions (57-88).
Address delivered at the Religious Thought Society, July, 1913.
On Certain Central Needs of Religion, and the Difficulties of Liberal Movements in Face of the Needs: as Experienced within the Roman Catholic Church during the Last Forty Years (91-131).
Address delivered at Edinburgh, 7 July, 1914.
The Idea of God (135-54).
Revised address to the Anglican Fellowship, delivered at Oxford, August, 1918.
Morals and Religion (155-64).
Cf. no. 67 above.
Suffering and God (167-213).
Address to the London Society for the Study of Religion, May, 1921.
The Facts and Truths concerning God and the Soul which are of most Importance in the Life of Prayer (215-42).
Address delivered at Beaconsfield, 26 October, 1921. Reprinted separately as *The Life of Prayer*, London, 1927.
The Catholic Contribution to Religion 245-51).
Published in *The Student Movement*, December, 1921.
The Difficulties and Dangers of Nationality (255-76).
Published in the *Challenge*, 4 & 11 August, 1922.

78. Bernard HOLLAND, *Baron Friedrich von Hügel: Selected Letters 1896-1924*, London, 1927, VII + 377 pp. (with memoir).

79. Gwendolen GREENE, *Letters from Baron von Hügel to a Niece*, London, 1928, 201 pp.

80. F. VON HÜGEL, *Some Notes on the Petrine Claims*, London, 1930, VIII, 103 pp.
Composed in 1893.

81. Edmund G. GARDNER, *The Reality of God and Religion and Agnosticism*, London, 1931, 264 pp.
Being the literary remains of Baron Friedrich von Hügel.

82. Hazard A. DAKIN, *Von Hügel and the Supernatural*, London, 1934, 255-62.
Excerpts from the correspondence of Baron Friedrich von Hügel with the Reverend Canon George E. Newsom — later Master of Selwyn College, Cambridge.

83. Juliet MANSEL, A Letter from Baron von Hügel. — *The Dublin Review* 222: 452 (July, 1951), 1-11.

84. Georg K. FRANK, Die Briefe Friedrich von Hügels an Friedrich Heiler. — Ökumenische Einheit 3:2 (1952), 29-52.
Selection of thirteen letters of von Hügel to Heiler, 1920-1924.

85. Nigel ABERCROMBIE, Friedrich von Hügel's Letters to Edmund Bishop. — *The Dublin Review* 227:459-62 (January-October, 1953), 68-78, 179-89, 285-98, 419-38.

86. Pietro SCOPPOLA, Petite consultation sur les difficultés concernant Dieu in *Crisi modernista e rinnovamento cattolico in Italia*, Bologna, 1961, 367-97.
Written by von Hügel between 31 October and 20 November 1912. Cf. also M. NÉDONCELLE, A Recently Discovered Study of von Hügel on God. — *International Philosophical Quarterly* 1 (1962), 5-24.

87. J. Derek HOLMES, Von Hügel's (!) Letter to Ryder on Biblical Inspiration and Inerrancy. — *Historical Magazine of Protestant Episcopal Church* 38 (1969), 153-65.

88. Joseph P. WHELAN, Friedrich von Hügel's Letters to Martin D'Arcy. — *The Month*, new series 42:1-3 (July-August, 1969), 23-36.
   Five letters from 1919-1921.

89. Joseph P. WHELAN, The Parent as Spiritual Director : A Newly Published Letter of Friedrich von Hügel. — *The Month*, second new series 231 (August-September, 1970), 52-7, 84-7.

90. F. TURVASI & M. JUNGO, Der Höhepunkt der Modernistischen Kirche: Ein Briefwechsel von Hügel-Genocchi. — *Civitas*: Monatsschrift des Schweizerischen Studentenvereins 25 (April, 1970), 622-43.
   German translation of four letters of von Hügel to Giovanni Genocchi from 1898-1904.

91. Maurice NÉDONCELLE, Une lettre inédite de Friedrich von Hügel à William James. — *Studi Internazionali di Filosofia* 1 (Summer-Autumn, 1970), 117-30.

92. Duncan MACPHERSON, Von Hügel on George Tyrrell. — *The Month*, second new series 4:6 (1971), 178-80.
   A letter of 10 January 1911 to Mrs. Catherine Holiday.

93. E. GOICHOT, En marge de la crise moderniste : la correspondance Bremond-von Hügel. — *Revue des sciences religieuses* 48 (July, 1974), 209-34; 49 (July, 1975), 202-33; 53 (April, 1979), 124-46.

94. James J. KELLY Counselling von Hügel. — *The Tablet* 228 (July, 1974), 693-5. (Cf. also p. 702).

95. ID., Von Hügel to a friend. — *The Tablet* 229 (January, 1975), 78-9.

96. ID., Von Hügel on Religion. — *The Month* 236 (July, 1975), 212-15.

97. ID., A von Hügel memoir. — *The Tablet* 231 (October, 1977), 949-51.

98. ID., Von Hügel on Authority. — *The Tablet* 232 (May, 1978), 445-46.

99. ID., On the Fringe of the Modernist Crisis : The Correspondence of Baron Friedrich von Hügel and Abbot Cuthbert Butler. — *The Downside Review* 97 (October, 1979), 275-303.

100. Thomas M. LOOME, Letter of von Hügel to Joseph Sauer, 16 July 1904; A.L. Lilley, Maundy Thursday 1911; Wilfrid Ward, 2 October 1911 and 23 November 1911. — *Liberal Catholicism – Roman Catholicism – Modernism*, Mainz, 1979, 392-6; 392-6; 405-8; 408-10.

101. James L. ADAMS, Letter from Friedrich von Hügel to William James. — *The Downside Review* 98:332 (July, 1980), 214-36.

102. James J. KELLY, The Modernist Controversy in England : The Correspondence between Friedrich von Hügel and Percy Gardner, I & II. — *The Downside Review* 99:334, 335 (January, April, 1981), 40-58, 119-36.

C. ANTHOLOGIES OF VON HÜGEL'S WRITINGS (In chronological order)

103. Algar THOROLD, *Readings from Friedrich von Hügel*, London, 1928, 359 p.

104. Franklin P. CHAMBERS, *Baron von Hügel: Man of God*, London, 1945, 181 pp. Second edition issued in paperback by Fontana. Cf. no. 112 below.

105. Maria SCHLÜTER-HERMKES, *Friedrich von Hügel: Religion als Ganzheit*, Düsseldorf, 1948. Ausgewählt und übersetzt von Maria Schlüter-Hermkes, 480 pp.

106. Maria SCHLÜTER-HERMKES, *Andacht zur Wirklichkeit: Schriften in Auswahl*, München, 1952. Ausgewählt, übersetzt und eingeleitet von Maria Schlüter-Hermkes, 261 pp.

107. Franklin P. CHAMBERS, *Friedrich von Hügel: Selected Writings*, London, 1964, 192 pp.
108. Douglas V. STEERE, *Spiritual Counsels and Letters of Baron Friedrich von Hügel*, London, 1964, 186 pp.

D. UNPUBLISHED THESES ON VON HÜGEL

BEATIE, William J., *The Sense of the Infinite in the Philosophy of Religion of Friedrich von Hügel*, Ph. D. (Philosophy) dissertation, University of Louvain (U.C.L.), 1969.

BUCKLEY, Mary I., *Experience and Transcendence*: The Experience and Knowledge of God in the Writings of Friedrich von Hügel, Münster, 1968.

CLASPER, Paul D., *The Interpretation of Christian Mysticism in the Life and Writings of Baron von Hügel*, Ph.D. dissertation, Union Theological Seminary, New York, 1953.

DISSAMAYEKE, Hilarian C., *Christianity and Other Religions in the Thought of Baron Friedrich von Hügel*, Pontificia Universitas Gregoriana, 1971.

EMRICH, Richard, *The Conception of the Church in the Writings of Friedrich von Hügel*, Marburg, 1936.

FOLEY, James Thomas, *L'expérience du Mal et la Transcendance dans la Pensée Religieuse du Baron Friedrich von Hügel*, Ph.D. (Sciences Religieuses) dissertation, University of Strasbourg, 1972.

FRANK, Georg, *Der schottisch-deutsche Geisteslehrer Friedrich von Hügel (1852-1925): Eine Studie über seine Leben und seine Phänomenologie der religiösen Erfahrung*, Marburg, 1950.

FURSE, Margaret Lewis, *A Critique of Baron von Hügel and Emil Brunner on Mysticism*, Ph.D. dissertation, Columbia University, 1969 and Ph.D. dissertation, Union Theological Seminary, New York.

GENTILI, Antonio, *Le lettere del barone F. von Hügel a padre Giovanni Semeria, barnabita (1895-1912)*, Università di Pavia, 1972.

HEANEY, John J., *Exegesis, Authority and the Nature of the Church in the Life and Writings of Friedrich von Hügel*, S.T.D. dissertation, Institut Catholique de Paris, 1963.
Heaney's book, *The Modernist Crisis: von Hügel*, London, 1969 is based on this dissertation.

HULTSCH, G. E., *Kreuz und Vernunft bei Friedrich von Hügel: Untersuchungen zur Darstellung und Deutung seiner Werkes*, Vienna, 1970.

HUNTER, Doris Leehoutz, *The Interpretation of Religious Experience in the Thought of Baron Friedrich von Hügel and Frederick Robert Tennant*, Ph.D. dissertation, Boston University, 1958.

JOHNSON, M. C., *Baron Friedrich von Hügel's Appraisal of Asceticism*, M. A. thesis, Northwestern University, Evanston III, 1932.

KELLY, James J., *The Religious Philosophy of Friedrich von Hügel*, S.T.L. dissertation, Catholic University of Louvain (Leuven), 1972.

KELLY, James J., *The Reality of God: A Critical and Constructive Analysis of the Religious Philosophy of Baron Friedrich von Hügel*, S.T.D. dissertation, Catholic University of Louvain (Leuven), 1978.

KLASS, Walter Kottler, *The Idea of the Supernatural in the Writings of Friedrich von Hügel*, M.A. (Theology) thesis, Northwestern University, Evanston III, 1935.

LOOME, Thomas Michael, *Liberal Catholicism — Reform Catholicism — Modernism. A Contribution to a New Orientation in Modernist Research*, Tübingen, 1974.

LUCKOW, M., *Baron von Hügels Religionsphilosophie*, Jena, 1920.

MACHLE, Edward Johnstone, *Mysticism and Realism in the Philosophical Systems of Nyaya-Vaisesika, James Bissett Pratt, and Friedrich, Baron von Hügel*, Ph.D. dissertation, Columbia University, 1952.

MACPHERSON, Duncan M., *The Three Elements of Religion: A Study in the Thought of Baron Friedrich von Hügel*, University of Birmingham, 1967.

MICHALSON, Gordon E., *Baron von Huegel and Søren Kierkegaard: Similarities and Differences in their expositions of the Christian Faith*, Ph.D. dissertation, Drew University, 1947.

O'CONNELL, Lawrence, *Religious Experience in the Philosophy of Religion of Baron Friedrich von Hügel*, S.T.L. dissertation, Catholic University of Louvain (Leuven), 1972.

PEETERS, Godelieve, *Friedrich von Hügel en Gwendolen Greene: Themata uit Letters to a Niece*, Licence dissertation, Faculteit der Godgeleerdheid, Catholic University of Louvain (Leuven), 1970.

ROBERT, Wills J., *The Understanding of Man in the Writings of Baron von Huegel, Nicholas Berdyaev, John Wood Oman*. With a concluding critical and constructive statement toward the Christian Understanding of Man, Ph.D. dissertation, Union Theological Seminary, New York, 1948.

RUDDLE, Patrick J., *Unity in Multiplicity in the Ecclesiology of Baron Friedrich von Hügel*, S.T.D. dissertation, Catholic University of Louvain (Leuven), 1974.

STEERE, Douglas V., *Critical Realism in the Religious Philosophy of Baron Friedrich von Hügel*, Ph.D. dissertation, Harvard University, Cambridge, Mass., 1931.

VELLARINGATT, Chacko, *La notion de la Vie Eternelle d'après le Baron Friedrich von Hügel*, Ph.D. (Sciences Religieuses) dissertation, University of Strasbourg, 1965.

ZIELINSKI, C., *Der Begriff der Mystik in Baron Friedrich von Hügels Werke The Mystical Element of Religion*, Jena, 1913.

PART III

GENERAL BIBLIOGRAPHY

Works present in von Hügel's library are marked with an asterisk.

ABERCROMBIE, Nigel, *The Life and Work of Edmund Bishop*, London, 1959.

*ALIOTTA, Antonio, *The Idealistic Reaction against Science*, London, 1914.

AUBERT, Roger, Recent Publications on the Modernist Movement. — *Concilium* 7 (1966), 47-55.

—, Modernisme et intégrisme, deux étiquettes équivoques. — *Revue Nouvelle* 50 (1969), 15-38.

—, La crise moderniste. — Course Notes at the Catholic University of Louvain (U.C.L.), 1973-4.

BAILLIE, John, *Our Knowledge of God*, Oxford, 1943.

*BALFOUR, Arthur J., *The Foundations of Belief*, London, 1895.

BARMANN, Lawrence F., The Heresy of Orthodoxy. — *Theology* 71 (1968), 456-62.

—, *Baron Friedrich von Hügel and the Modernist Crisis in England*, Cambridge, 1972.

—, Baron Friedrich von Hügel as a Religious Genius. — *The Ampleforth Journal* 77 (1972), 64-8.

—, Von Hügel's Idea of Ecclesiastical Authority. — *The American Ecclesiastical Review* 168 (1974), 268-82.

BERGERON, Richard, *Les abus de l'Eglise d'après Newman : Etude de la Préface à la troisième édition de "La Via Media"*, Tournai, 1971.
(Cf. especially "L'Influence de la Préface sur Friedrich von Hügel", 207-19).

*BERGSON, Henri, *Essai sur les données immédiates de la conscience*, Paris, 1898.

*—, *L'évolution créatrice*, Paris, 1907.

BIESEN, Christian van den, The Authorship and Composition of the Hexateuch. — *The Dublin Review* 112 (1893), 40-65.

*BLONDEL, Maurice, *L'Action : Essai d'une critique de la vie, et d'une science de la pratique*, Paris, 1893.

*—, Histoire et dogme : Les lacunes philosophiques de l'exégèse moderne. — *La Quinzaine* 58 (1904), I : 145-67 ; II : 349-73 ; III : 433-58. (English translation *The Letter on Apologetics and History and Dogma* by A. Dru & I. Trethowan, London, 1964).

*BOSSUET, Jacques Bénigne, *Instruction sur les états d'oraison. Second traité. Principes communs de l'oraison chrétienne*, Paris, 1897.

*—, *Oeuvres. Revues sur les manuscrits originaux et les éditions les plus correctes*, Versailles, 1815-19. (Ed. by P. H. d'Aubérive, A. P. P. Caron and J. E. A. Gosselin, 43 vols).

*BOUTROUX, Emile, *Pascal*, Paris, 1900.

BRASNETT, B. R., *The Suffering of the Impassible God*, London, 1928.
(Especially "Baron von Hügel : Suffering and God", 115-40).

*BREMOND, Henri, *Apologie pour Fénelon*, Paris, 1910.

*—, *Histoire littéraire du sentiment religieux en France depuis la fin des guerres de religion jusqu'à nos jours*, 6 vols, Paris, 1916-22.

BROWNE, R. K., Newman and von Hügel : A Record of an Early Meeting. — *The Month*, new series 26 (1961), 24-33.

BROWNING, Robert, *The Poetical Works of Robert Browning*, 2 vols, London, 1906.

BUTLER, B. C., In Praise of von Hügel. — *The Tablet* 222 (1968), 537-8.

*BUTLER, E. C., *Western Mysticism*, London, 1922.

*CAIRD, Edward, *The Evolution of Religion*, 2 vols, Glasgow, 1893.

*—, *The Evolution of Theology in the Greek Philosophers*, 2 vols, Glasgow, 1904.

*—, *Hegel*, Edinburgh, 1909.

*CAMPBELL, R. J., *The New Theology*, London, 1907.

*CATHERINA ADORNI, Saint of Genoa, *Vita ed Opere di Santa Caterina da Genova*, Genova, 1877.

CAUSSADE, Jean-Pierre de, *Self-Abondonment to Divine Providence*, Glasgow, 1972.

CHAMBERS, Franklin P., *Stewards of the Mysteries of God : Friedrich von Hügel and William Medley of Rawdon : A Study in Spiritual Catholicity*, London, n.d. (Especially 3-23).

COCK, Albert A., Baron Friedrich von Hügel and His Work. — *Theology* 12 (1926), 316-31.

—, Friedrich von Hügel and His Work. — *Speculum Religionis*, Oxford, 1929. (Ch. 9, 195-213).

—, *A Critical Examination of von Hügel's Philosophy of Religion*, London, 1953.

CROPPER, Margaret, *Evelyn Underhill*, London, 1958.

DAKIN, Hazard A., Jr., *Von Hügel and the Supernatural*, London, 1934.

DALY, Gabriel, *Transcendence and Immanence : A Study in Catholic Modernism and Integralism*, Oxford, 1980. (Especially Ch.6 "Experience and Transcendence" on von Hügel).

DANTINE, W., Friedrich von Hügel. — *Tendenzen der Theologie im 20. Jahrhundert : Eine Geschichte in Porträts*, Stuttgart, 1966. (Especially 50-55, ed. H.J. Schultz).

D'ARCY, Martin C., The Mystical Element of Religion. — *The Catholic World* 20 (1925), 744-52.

DE LA BEDOYÈRE, Michael, *The Life of Baron von Hügel*, London, 1951.

*DENIFLE, Heinrich Suso, *Luther und Luthertum in der ersten Entwicklung*, 2 vols, Mainz, 1904-09.

*DESCARTES, René, *Oeuvres*, Paris, 1865. (Nouvelle édition, collationée sur les meilleurs textes et précédé d'une introduction par M. Gules Simon).

*DÖLLINGER, Johann Joseph Ignaz von, *Kirche und Kirchen, Papsthum und Kirchenstaat. Historisch-politische Betrachtungen*, München, 1861.

*—, *Christenthum und Kirche in der Zeit der Grundlegung*, Regensburg, 1868.

DOSH, Mark B., *The Notion of the Experience of God in the Religious Philosophy of Friedrich von Hügel*, Rome, 1961.

DRU, Alexander, *The Church in the Nineteenth Century : Germany 1800-1918*, London, 1963.

DUMOULIN, Heinrich, Soichi Iwashita und Friedrich von Hügel. — *Das Hochland* 45 (1952), 131-38.

*EHRHARD, Albert, *Stellung und Aufgabe der Kirchengeschichte in der Gegenwart*, Stuttgart, 1898.

*—, *Der Katholizismus und das zwanzigste Jahrhundert im Lichte der Kirchlichen Entwicklung der Neuzeit*, Stuttgart, 1902.

ELIOT, T.S. [An anonymous biographical notice on von Hügel]. — *Encyclopaedia Britannica* 2, 13th ed. (1926), 384.

—, An Emotional Unity. — *Dial* 84 (1928), 109-12.

EMRICH, Richard S., *The Conception of the Church in the Writings of the German-English Philosopher Baron Friedrich von Hügel : A Contribution to the Sociology of Religion*, Munich, 1939.

*EUCKEN, Rudolf, *Die Philosophie des Thomas von Aquino und die Kultur der Neuzeit*, Halle,, 1886.

*—, *Die Einheit des Geisteslebens in Bewusstsein und That der Menschheit : Untersuchungen*, Leipzig, 1888.

*—, *Die Lebensanschauungen der grossen Denker : Eine Entwicklungsgeschichte des Lebensproblems der Menschheit von Plato bis zur Gegenwart*, Leipzig, 1890.

*—, *Die Grundbegriffe der Gegenwart : Historisch und kritisch Entwickelt*, Leipzig, 1893.

*—, *Der Kampf um einen geistigen Lebensinhalt: Neue Grundlegung einer Welt-anschauung*, Leipzig, 1896.

*—, *Der Wahrheitsgehalt der Religion*, Leipzig, 1905. (English translation by W. T. Jones: *The Truth of Religion*, London, 1911).

*FALCKENBERG, Richard, *Geschichte der neueren Philosophie von Nikolaus von Kues zur Gegenwart*, Leipzig, 1898.

*FAWKES, Alfred, Modernism: A Retrospect and a Prospect. — *The Hibbert Journal* 8 (1909), 67-82.

*—, *Studies in Modernism*, London, 1913.

—, Baron Friedrich von Hügel. — *The Modern Churchman* 14 (1925), 662-6.

*FECHNER, Gustav Theodor, *Die Drei Motive und Gründe des Glaubens*, Leipzig, 1863.

*FÉNELON, Francis de Salignac de la Mothe, *Oeuvres de Fénelon, archevèque de Cambrai, publiées, d'après les manuscrits originaux avec un grand nombre de pièces inédites*, 22 vols, Versailles, 1820-24. (Vol. IV, 1820, contains "Analyse raisonnée de la controverse du quiétisme" by the Abbé Jean Gosselin, LXXIX-CCXXXIV).

FENTON, Joseph C., Von Hügel and Ecclesiastical Authority. — *The American Ecclesiastical Review* 133 (1955), 35-52.

—, Von Hügel and His Spiritual Direction. — *The American Ecclesiastical Review* 133 (1955), 190-27.

FEUERBACH, Ludwig, *The Essence of Christianity*, New York, 1957.

FOGAZZARO, Antonio, *The Saint*, London, 1908. (Translated from the Italian by M. Prichard-Agnetti).

*FRANCIS DE SALES, St, Bp of Geneva, *Oeuvres. Edition complète*, 16 vols, Annecy, 1892-1910.

*FRASER, Alexander Campbell, *Thomas Reid*, Edinburgh, 1898.

GALLAGHER, Kenneth T., *The Philosophy of Knowledge*, New York, 1964.

GARDNER, Charles, The Late Baron von Hügel. — *The Spectator* 134 (1925), 197-98.

GARDNER, Percy, Selected Letters of Baron von Hügel. — *The Modern Churchman* 17 (1927), 233-40.

—, The Literary Remains of Baron von Hügel. — *The Modern Churchman* 21 (1931), 195-200.

GOODIER, Alban, Baron Friedrich von Hügel's Spiritual Outlook. — *The Month* 153 (1929), 11-21.

—, Baron Friedrich von Hügel. — *The Dublin Review* 196 (1935), 73-84.

*GOUT, Raoul, *John Henry Newman*, Anduze, 1906.

GRANDMAISON, Léonce de, L'Evangile et L'Eglise. — *Etudes* 94 (1903), 145-74.

—, L'élément mystique dans la Religion. — *Recherches de science religieuse* 1 (1910), 180-208.

—, Review of B. Holland's *Selected Letters*. — *Revue d'histoire ecclésiastique* 23 (1927), 163 & 653-4.

GREEN, Martin, *Yeats's Blessings on von Hügel*, London, 1967.

GREENE, Gwendolen Plunket, Some Recollections of Baron von Hügel. — *The Spectator* 143 (1929), 148-9.

—, *Two Witnesses: A Personal Recollection of Hubert Parry and Friedrich von Hügel*, London, 1930.

—, Thoughts from Baron von Hügel. — *The Dublin Review* 188 (1931), 254-60.

GROU, John Nicolas, *Spiritual Maxims*, London, 1961. (With an appreciation by Baron Friedrich von Hügel).

*—, *Manuel des âmes intérieures*, Paris, 1847.

*—, *Ecole de Jésus-Christ*, Paris, 1885.

HANBURY, Michael, Baron von Hügel : *Letters to a Niece*. — *The Month*, new series 25 (1961), 13-22.

—, Newman and von Hügel, Reply to R. Browne. — *The Month*, new series 26 (1961), 240.

—, Baron von Hügel and the Ecumenical Movement. — *The Month*, new series 29 (1963), 140-50.

—, Von Hügel and Tyrrell. — *The Month*, new series 32 (1964), 323-26.

—, Von Hügel Today : A Forerunner of Vatican II. — *The Tablet* 219 (1965), 1291-3.

*HASTINGS, James (Ed.), *Encyclopaedia of Religion and Ethics*, Edinburgh, 1908-1921.

*HAUCK, Albert, *Kirchengeschichte Deutschlands*, 4 vols, Leipzig, 1898-1903.

HEANEY, John J., The Enigma of the Later von Hügel. — *The Heythrop Journal* 6 (1965), 145-59.

—, *The Modernist Crisis : von Hügel*, London, 1969.

*HEILER, Friedrich, *Das Gebet : eine religionsgeschichtliche und religionspsychologische Untersuchung*, München, 1920.

*—, *Sâdhu Sundar Singh, ein apostel des Ostens und Westens*, Basel, 1924.

—, Ein katholischer Laientheologe : Zum Tode Friedrich von Hügels — *Münchener Neueste Nachrichten*, February 14, (1925).

—, Friedrich von Hügel †27 Januar 1924 [sic]. — *Im Ringen und die Kirche* 2 (1931), 160-73.

*HOCKING, William Ernest, *The Meaning of God in Human Experience : A Philosophical Study of Religion*, New Haven, 1922.

*HÖFFDING, Harald, *Søren Kierkegaard als Philosoph*, Stuttgart, 1896.

*—, *Religionsphilosophie*, Leipzig, 1901.

*HOLTZMANN, Heinrich J., *Lehrbuch der neutestamentlichen Theologie*, 2 vols, Freiburg i.B., 1897.

*—, *Richard Rothe's speculatives System*, Freiburg i.B., 1899.

—, Review of *The Mystical Element of Religion*. — *Theologische Literaturzeitung* 34 (1909), col. 390-92.

*HOUTIN, Albert, *La question biblique chez les catholiques de France au XIXè siècle*, Paris, 1902.

*—, *La question biblique au XXe siècle*, Paris, 1906.

*—, *Histoire du modernisme catholique*, Paris, 1913.

HUBER, Wolfgang, Religiöse Erfahrung bei Friedrich von Hügel. — *Der Modernismus : Beiträge zu seiner Erforschung*, Wien, 1974, 83-103.

*HUVELIN, Henri, *Bossuet, Fénelon, le quiétisme*, 2 vols, Paris, 1912.

—, *Some Spiritual Guides of the Seventeenth Century*, London, 1927.

*INGE, William R., *Christian Mysticism*, London, 1899.

*JAMES, William, *The Principles of Psychology*, 2 vols, London, 1891.

*—, *The Will to Believe, and Other Essays in Popular Philosophy*, New York, 1897.

*—, *The Varieties of Religious Experience : A Study in Human Nature*, London, 1902.

*JANNSEN, Johannes, *Friedrich Leopold Graf zu Stolberg*, 2 vols, Freiburg i.B., 1877.

*JOHN OF THE CROSS, St, *The Works of St. John of the Cross*, 2 vols, London, 1889-91. (Translated from the Spanish with a life of the Saint by D. Lewis).

JOHNSON, Humphrey J.T., Baron von Hügel and the Catholic Religion. — *Studies* 39 (1950), 373-84.

—, Letters to the Editor : Baron von Hügel. — *The Tablet* 197 (1951), 484.

*JOLY, Henri, *The Psychology of the Saints*, London, 1898. (With preface and notes by G. Tyrrell).

*JONES, Henry, *A Critical Account of the Philosophy of Lotze*, Glasgow, 1895.

*—, *Browning as a Philosophical and Religious Teacher*, Glasgow, 1902.

*JONES, Rufus Matthew, *Studies in Mystical Religion*, London, 1909.

JUNG, Carl G., *Modern Man in Search of a Soul*, London, 1970.

*KANT, Immanuel, *Sämmtliche Werke*, 8 vols, Leipzig, 1867-68. (Ed. G. Hartenstein).

*—, *Kants gesammelte Schriften*, 15 vols, Berlin, 1902-13.

KELLY, James J., The Abbé Huvelin's Counsel to Baron Friedrich von Hügel. — *Bijdragen, Tijdschrift voor Filosofie en Theologie* 39 (1978), 59-69.

—, The Modernist Controversy : Von Hügel and Blondel. — *Ephemerides Theologicae Lovanienses* 55 (1979), 297-330.

—, Leergezag en theologie in het denken van baron Friedrich von Hügel. — *Communio* 5 (1980), 342-59.

—, Experience and Transcendence : An Introduction to the Religious Philosophy of Baron von Hügel. — *The Downside Review* 99 (1981), 172-89.

—, Religious Experience. — *Louvain Studies* 8 (1981), 244-57.

KERLIN, Michael J., *Historical Religion in the Thought of Friedrich von Hügel and George Tyrrell : a comparative study in the light of their General Philosophy of Religion*, Rome, 1966.

KLEIN, Felix, *Vie du père Hecker*, Paris, 1896.

*KRAUS, Franz Xaver, *Über das Studium der Theologie sonst und jetzt*, Freiburg i.B., 1890.

KRAUSS, Erna, Über das Verhältnis Gott und Mensch nach Friedrich von Hügel, in *Der Mensch vor Gott : Beiträge zum Verständnis der menschlichen Gottbegegnung*, Düsseldorf, 1948, 278-90.

*LABERTHONNIÈRE, Lucien, *Essais de philosophie religieuse*, Paris, 1903.

*—, *Le réalisme chrétien et l'idéalisme grec*, Paris, 1904.

LAING, R.D., *The Politics of Experience and The Bird of Paradise*, Middlesex, 1970.

LASH, Nicholas, Modernism, aggiornamento and the night battle, in *Bishops and Writers : Aspects of the Evolution of Modern English Catholicism*, Cambridge, 1977, 51-79.

*LEIBNIZ, Gottfried Wilhelm von, *Die philosophischen Schriften*, 7 vols. Berlin, 1875-90. (Herausgegeben von C.I. Gerhardt).

*LE ROY, Edouard, Essai sur la notion du miracle. — *Annales de philosophie chrétienne*, 4th series 3 (1906), 533, 166-91, 225-59.

LESLIE, Shane, *Henry Edward Manning : His Life and Labours*, London, 1921.

LESTER-GARLAND, L.V., Von Hügel's Three Laws of the Growth of Religious Biography. — *Theology* 25 (1932), 319-25.

—, *The Religious Philosophy of Baron F. von Hügel*, London, 1933.

Lettres Romaines. — *Annales de philosophie chrétienne*, 3rd series 3 (1904), 349-59,
    473-88, 601-20.
LILLEY, Alfred L., A Roman Catholic Protest Against the Recent Vatican Policy. —
    The Commonwealth 11 (1906), 216-20.
*—, *The Programme of Modernism*, London, 1908.
*—, *Modernism: a Record and Review*, London, 1908.
—, A Real Catholicism. — *The Interpreter* 6 (1910), 264-77.
*—, Modernism. — *Encyclopaedia of Religion and Ethics* 8 (1915), 763-8.
—, The Religious Philosophy of von Hügel. — *The Modern Churchman* 15
    (1925), 37-46.
—, Roman Catholic Modernism. — *The Modern Churchman* 17 (1927), 333-44.
*LINDSAY, Thomas M., *A History of the Reformation*, 2 vols, Edinburgh, 1915.
*LOISY, Alfred Firmin, *Histoire du canon de l'Ancien Testament*, Paris, 1890.
*—, *Histoire du canon du Nouveau Testament*, Paris, 1891.
*—, Le développement chrétien d'après le Cardinal Newman. — *Revue du clergé
    français* 17 (1898), 5-20.
*—, *Etudes évangéliques*, Paris, 1902.
*—, *L'Evangile et l'Eglise*, Paris 1902.
*—, *The Gospel and the Church*, London, 1903.
*—, *Quelques lettres sur des questions actuelles et sur des événements récents*,
    Ceffonds, 1908.
*—, Remarque sur le volume "Jésus ou le Christ". — *The Hibbert Journal* 8 (1909-
    10), 473-87.
—, *Mémoires pour servir à l'histoire religieuse de notre temps*, 3 vols, Paris,
    1930-1.
LONERGAN, Bernard, *Insight: A Study of Human Understanding*, London, 1967.
—, *Collection*, London, 1967.
—, *The Subject*, Milwaukee, 1968.
—, Natural Knowledge of God. — *The Proceedings of the American Philosophical
    Association* 44 (1970), 26-39.
—, *Method in Theology*, London, 1972.
—, *Philosophy of God, And Theology. The Relationship between Philosophy of
    God and the Functional Speciality, Systematics*, London, 1973.
—, *A Second Collection*, London, 1974.
LOOME, Thomas M., The Enigma of Baron Friedrich von Hügel - As
    Modernist I, II, III. — *The Downside Review* 91 (1973), 13-34, 123-40, 204-30.
—, "Die Trümmer des liberalen Katholizismus" in Grossbritannien und Deutsch-
    land am Ende des 19. Jahrhunderts (1893-1903): Die Kirchenpolitische
    Grundlage der Modernismuskontroverse (1903-1914). — *Kirchen und
    Liberalismus im 19. Jahrhundert*, Göttingen, 1976, 197-214.
—, *Liberal Catholicism – Reform Catholicism – Modernism*, Mainz, 1979.
*LOTZE, Rudolf H., *Mikrokosmos: Ideen zur Naturgeschichte und Geschichte
    der Menschheit: Versuch einer Anthropologie*, Leipzig, 1880-85.
*—, *Grundzüge der Religionsphilosophie*, Leipzig, 1884.
LOUIS-LEFÈBVRE, M.T., *Un Prêtre: L'Abbé Huvelin*, Paris, 1956. (English
    translation by the Earl of Wicklow: *Abbé Huvelin, Apostle of Paris*,
    Dublin, 1967.
LUNN, H.S., Review of von Hügel's *Mystical Element of Religion*. — *Review
    of the Churches* 1 (1924), 95-9.

MACPHERSON, Duncan, Baron von Hügel on Celibacy. — *The Tablet* 223 (1969), 757-58.

MAEDER, Michael, Being Human : A Study of Friedrich von Hügel. — *Sisters Today* 44 (1972), 183-97.

*MAISTRE, Joseph Marie de, *Du Pape*, 2 vols, Lyon, 1819.

MANSON, Aelfric & WEBB, Clement, The Faith of Baron von Hügel. — Review of Nédoncelle's book *Baron Friedrich von Hügel : A Study of his Life and Thought, Blackfriars* 18 (1937), 286-89. (Along with reply by Clement Webb, 539-40 and response of Aelfric Manson, 540-42 in the same issue of the periodical).

MARLÉ, René, *Au cœur de la crise moderniste : Le dossier inédit d'une controverse*, Paris, 1960.

*MARTINEAU, James, *Types of Ethical Theory*, 2 vols, Oxford, 1886.

*MARVIN, Francis S. (Ed.), *Progress and History*, London, 1916.

MEULENBERG, L., De betekenis van de frictie bij Fr. von Hügel. — *Tijdschrift voor Theologie* 12 (1972), 61-94.

*MICHELIS, Friedrich, *Kant vor und nach dem Jahre 1770 : Eine Kritik der gläubigen Vernunft*, Braunsberg, 1871.

*MILL, John Stuart, *Autobiography*, London, 1875.

*MIVART, St. George, Modern Catholics and Scientific Freedom. — *The Nineteenth Century* 18 (1885), 30-47.

*—, The Catholic Church and Biblical Criticism. — *The Nineteenth Century* 22 (1887), 31-51.

—, Letter from Dr. Mivart on the Bishop of Newport's Article in Our Last Number. — *The Dublin Review*, 3rd series 19 (1888), 180-7.

*MOEHLER, Johann Adam, *Gesammelte Schriften und Aufsätze*, 2 vols, Regensburg, 1839-40. (Herausgegeben von J. J. I. Döllinger).

*—, *Symbolik oder Darstellung der dogmatischen Gegensätze der Katholiken und Protestanten nach ihren öffentlichen Bekenntnisschriften*, Regensburg, 1913.

MUTH, Carl, Begegnung : Paul Huber, Friedrich von Hügel. — *Das Hochland* 46 (1953-1954), 235-40.

NÉDONCELLE, Maurice, *La philosophie religieuse en Grande-Bretagne de 1850 à nos jours*, Paris, 1934.

—, *La pensée religieuse de Friedrich von Hügel*, 1852-1925, Paris, 1935. English translation : *Baron Friedrich von Hügel : A Study of His Life and Thought*, London, 1937.

—, "Histoire et dogme", ou l'exigence de tradition active. — *Giornale di Metafisica* 16 (1961), 576-90.

—, Un texte peu connu de F. von Hügel sur le problème de Dieu. — *Revue des sciences religieuses* 36 (1962), 154-73. English translation : A Recently Discovered Study of von Hügel on God. — *International Philosophical Quarterly* 2 (1962), 5-24.

—, L. F. Barmann, *Baron Friedrich von Hügel and the Modernist Crisis in England*. Review. — *Revue des sciences religieuses* 48 (1974), 271-73.

NEUNER, Peter, Friedrich von Hügel's Bild von der Kirche : Kirchenvorstellungen im Modernismus und moderne Kirchenreform. — *Stimmen der Zeit* 189 (1972), 25-42.

—, Friedrich von Hügel der "Laienbishof der Modernisten". — *Aufbruch ins 20. Jahrhundert zur Streit um Reformkatholizismus und Modernismus*. Göttingen, 1976, 9-22.

—, *Religion zwischen Kirche und Mystik : Friedrich von Hügel und der Modernismus*, Frankfurt a.M., 1977.

—, *Religiöse Erfahrung und geschichtliche Offenbarung : Friedrich von Hügels Grundlegung der Theologie*, München, 1977.

* NEWMAN, John Henry, *An Essay on the Development of Christian Doctrine*, London, 1846.

—, *Fifteen Sermons Preached before the University of Oxford between A.D. 1826 & 1843*, London, 1872.

*—, *Two Essays on Biblical and on Ecclesiastical Miracles*, London, 1873.

*—, *The Idea of a University Defined and Illustrated*, London, 1873.

*—, *A Letter Addressed to His Grace the Duke of Norfolk on Occasion of Mr. Gladstone's Recent Expostulation*, London, 1875.

*—, *The Via Media of the Anglican Church*, 2 vols, London, 1877.

*—, *Apologia Pro Vita Sua : Being a History of his Religious Opinions*, London, 1879.

*—, On the Inspiration of Scripture. — *The Nineteenth Century* 15 (1884), 185-99.

—, *Certain Difficulties Felt by Anglicans in Catholic Teaching*, 2 vols, London, 1892.

—, *Tracts Theological and Ecclesiastical*, London, 1899.

—, *Loss and Gain : The Story of a Convert*, London, 1904.

—, *An Essay in Aid of a Grammar of Assent*, London, 1906.

NEWSOM, George E., Baron von Hügel. — *Theology* 11 (1925), 146-56.

O'BRIEN, B., Baron von Hügel on the Transcendence of God. — *The Dublin Review* 205 (1939), 221-35.

O'CONNOR, Francis M., Hügel, Friedrich von. — *New Catholic Encyclopaedia* 7, New York, 1967, 187-8.

*OLLÉ-Laprune, Léon, *De la certitude morale*, Paris, 1880.

*—, *La philosophie et le temps présent*, Paris, 1894.

*—, *Le prix de la vie*, Paris, 1894.

OSBORNE, Charles, Father Tyrrell : Some Impressions by an Anglican Friend. — *The Church Times* 62 (1909), 121.

—, George Tyrrell : A Friend's Impressions. — *The Hibbert Journal* 8 (1910), 253-63.

PASCAL, Blaise, *Pensées*, Middlesex, 1966. (Translation by A. J. Krailsheimer).

*PAULSEN, Friedrich, *Einleitung in die Philosophie*, Berlin, 1896.

*PETRE, Maude D., *The Soul's Orbit or Man's Journey to God*, London, 1904.

*—, *Autobiography and Life of George Tyrrell*, 2 vols, London, 1912.

*—, *Modernism : Its Failure and Its Fruits*, London, 1918.

—, Friedrich von Hügel : Personal Thoughts and Reminiscences. — *The Hibbert Journal* 24 (1925), 77-87.

—, George Tyrrell and Friedrich von Hügel in Their Relation to Catholic Modernism. — *The Modern Churchman* 17 (1927), 143-54.

—, Von Hügel and the Great Quest. — *The Modern Churchman* 21 (1931), 475-83.

—, *My Way of Faith*, London, 1937.

—, *Von Hügel and Tyrrell : The Story of a Friendship*, London, 1937.

PIUS X, *Pascendi dominici gregis*. — *Acta Apostolicae Sedis*, vol. 50, 1907. Facsimile reprint of official translation by Carraig Books, Dublin, 1971, 3-69.

—, *Lamentabili sane exitu*. — *Acta Apostolicae Sedis*, vol. 50, 1907.

POLANYI, Michael, *Personal Knowledge : Towards a Post-Critical Philosophy*, New York, 1964.

POULAT, Emile, Index bio-bibliographique, in *Alfred Loisy: sa vie et son œuvre*, Paris, 1960, 325-409.

—, *Histoire, dogme et critique dans la crise moderniste*, Paris, 1962.

*PRATT, James, *The Religious Consciousness: A Psychological Study*, New York, 1921.

*PRINGLE-PATTISON, (previously Andrew Seth), *Man's Place in the Cosmos and Other Essays*, Edinburgh, 1897.

*—, *The Idea of God*, London, 1917.

RABY, F. J. E., Baron von Hügel. — *Great Christians*, London, 1934.

RANCHETTI, Michele, *The Catholic Modernists: A Study of the Religious Reform Movement 1864-1907*, London, 1969. (Translated by Isabel Quigly).

REARDON, Bernard M. G., *Liberal Protestantism*, London, 1968.

—, The Modernist Movement in Retrospect. — *The Ampleforth Journal* 75 (1970), 213-21.

—, *Roman Catholic Modernism*, London, 1970.

REID, Thomas, *The Works of T. Reid*, 2 vols, Edinburgh, 1872. (Preface, Notes and Supplementary Dissertations by W. Hamilton).

RIVIÈRE, Jean, *Le modernisme dans l'Eglise*, Paris, 1929.

*ROHDE, Erwin, *Psyche*, Freiburg i.B., 1898.

ROLLMAN, Hans, Troeltsch, von Hügel and Modernism. — *The Downside Review* 93 (1978), 35-60.

*ROYCE, Josiah, *The World and the Individual*, 2 vols, London, 1900-01.

RUDDLE, Patrick J., The Ecumenical Dimension in the Work of Baron Friedrich von Hügel. — *Ephemerides Theologicae Lovanienses* 50 (1974), 231-54.

RUYSBROECK, Jan van, *Vier Schriften von J. Ruysbroeck in niederdeutscher Sprache*, Hannover, 1848. Ed. A. von Arnswaldt.

*SANDAY, William, *The Oracles of God: Nine Lectures on the Nature and Extent of Biblical Inspiration and on the Special Significance of the Old Testament Scriptures at the Present Time*, London, 1891.

*SCHELL, Hermann, *Katholische Dogmatik*, 4 vols, Paderborn, 1889-93.

*—, *Gott und Geist*, Paderborn, 1896.

*—, *Der Katholicismus als Princip der Fortschritts*, Würzburg, 1897.

*SCHILLER, Ferdinand C.S., *Humanism: Philosophical Essays*, London, 1903. (Especially ch. XII "Activity and Substances", 204-27).

*SCHLEIERMACHER, Friedrich, *Über die Religion: Reden an die Gebildeten unter ihren Verächtern*, Leipzig, 1880.

*—, *Der Christliche Glaube nach den Grundsätzen der evangelischen Kirche im Zusammenhange dargestellt*, 2 vols, Berlin, 1884.

SCHLÜTER-HERMKES, Maria, Friedrich von Hügel. — *Das Hochland* 22 (1924-25), 706-9.

—, Die geistige Gestalt Friedrich von Hügel. — *Das Hochland* 24 (1926-27), 52-63 and 197-214.

—, Ein Weltman als Meister der Spiritualität. — *Das Hochland* 43 (1950-51), 138-54.

—, Friedrich von Hügel Werke — *Oekumenische Einheit* 3 (1953), 25-8.

SCHMIDT, Paul W., *Die Geschichte Jesu*, Freiburg i.B., 1899.

SCHOENL, William J., George Tyrrell and the English Liberal Catholic Crisis, 1900-01. — *The Downside Review* 92 (1974), 171-84.

—, English Liberal Catholicism in the Early 1890's. — *The Clergy Review* 62 (1977), 92-105.

—, Von Hügel after the Modernist Controversy. — *The Clergy Review* 63 (1978), 211-9.

*SCHWEITZER, Albert, *Von Reimarus zu Wrede: Eine Geschichte der Leben-Jesu-Forschung*, Tübingen, 1906.

SCOPPOLA, Pietro, *Crisi modernista e rinnovamento cattolico in Italia*, Bologna, 1961.

*SETH, James, *A Study of Ethical Principles*, Edinburgh, 1894.

—, Review of *The Mystical Element of Religion* — *Mind* 18 (1909), 429-34.

*SIDGWICK, Henry, *Outlines of the History of Ethics*, London, 1886.

SIMON, Richard, *Histoire critique du Vieux Testament*, Paris, 1678.

*SMEDT, Charles de, *Principes de la critique historique*, Liège, 1883.

SMITH, John E., *Experience and God*, London, 1974.

*SMITH, Norman Kemp, *A Commentary to Kant's Critique of Pure Reason*, London, 1918.

*—, *Prolegomena to an Idealist Theory of Knowledge*, London, 1924.

*SMITH, William Robertson, *Lectures on the Religion of the Semites. 1st series: The Fundamental Institutions*, Edinburgh, 1889.

*SPINOZA, Benedictus de, *Benedicti de Spinoza Opera quae supersunt omnia*, Lipsiae, 1843-46.

STEDMAN, Ralph E., Baron Von Hügel's Literary Remains. — *The Contemporary Review* 140 (1931), 207-14.

STEINMANN, Jean, *Friedrich von Hügel: Sa vie, son œuvre et ses amitiés*, Paris, 1962.

*SURIN, Jean Joseph, *Oeuvres spirituelles de J.J. Surin ... publiées par M. Bouix*, 4 vols, Paris, 1879.

*—, *Dialogues spirituels choisis où la perfection chrétienne est expliquée pour toutes sortes de personnes*, Avignon, 1889.

STICHER, Urban, The Life of St. Catherine, 1752. — *Acta Sanctorum* Sept., ed. 1866, vol. 5, 123-95.

*TAYLOR, A. E., Review of *Eternal Life*. — *The Hibbert Journal* 12 (1913-14), 452-63.

*—, Review of *Essays and Addresses: First Series*. — *The Hibbert Journal* 20 (1921-22), 576-81.

—, Review of B. Holland's *Selected Letters*. — *The Hibbert Journal* 25 (1926-27), 750-2.

—, Review of von Hügel's *Essays and Addresses: Second Series*. — *The Hibbert Journal* 25 (1927), 374-7.

*TIELE, Cornelis P., *Elements of the Science of Religion*, 2 vols, Edinburgh, 1897-99.

THOROLD, Algar, The Religious Philosophy of Friedrich von Hügel. — *Edinburgh Review* 235 (1922), 340-56.

TRISTRAM, Henry, Cardinal Newman and Baron von Hügel. — *The Dublin Review* 240 (1966), 295-302.

*TROELTSCH, Ernst, *Gesammelte Schriften*, 2 vols, Tübingen, 1912-22.

*—, *Der Historismus und seine Überwindung*, Berlin, 1924. (Eingeleitet von F. von Hügel).

TURVASI, Francesco, *Giovanni Genocchi e la controversia modernista*, Roma, 1974.

*TYRRELL, George, *Nova et Vetera : Informal Meditations for Times of Spiritual Dryness*, London, 1897.

*—, *Hard Sayings : A Selection of Meditations and Studies*, London, 1898.

*—, *The Faith of the Millions : A Selection of Past Essays*, 2 vols, London, 1901.

—, *Religion as a Factor of Life*, Exeter, 1902. (Signed Dr. Ernest Engels).

*—, *A Much-Abused Letter*, London, 1906.

—, *Through Scylla and Charybdis : or, The Old Theology and the New*, London, 1907.

*—, *Oil and Wine*, London, 1907.

*—, *Medievalism : A Reply to Cardinal Mercier*, London, 1908.

*—, *Christianity at the Cross-Roads*, London, 1909.

—, The Mystical Element of Religion (Review). — *The Quarterly Review* 211 (1909), 101-26.

*—, The Mystical Element of Religion (Review). — *The Hibbert Journal* 7 (1909), 687-89.

*—, *The Church and the Future*, London, 1910.

*UNDERHILL, Evelyn, *Mysticism : A Study in the Nature and Development of Man's Spiritual Consciousness*, London, 1911.

—, *Man and The Supernatural*, London, 1927.

VEIGA COUTINHO, Lucio da, *Tradition et histoire dans la controverse moderniste*, Rome, 1954.

VIDLER, Alec R., *The Modernist Movement in the Roman Church, Its Origin and Outcome*, Cambridge, 1934.

—, *A Variety of Catholic Modernists*, Cambridge, 1970.

—, An Abortive Renaissance : Catholic Modernists in Sussex. — *Renaissance and Renewal in Christian History*, vol. 14 of *Studies in Church History*, Oxford, 1977, 377-92. (Ed. Derek Baker).

VOEGELIN, Eric, *Order and History*, Vol. I : *Israel and Revelation*, Baton Rouge, 1956; Vol. II : *The World of the Polis*, Baton Rouge, 1957; Vol. III : *Plato and Aristotle*, Baton Rouge, 1957; Vol. IV : *The Ecumenic Age*, Baton Rouge, 1974.

—, Immortality : Experience and Symbol. — *Harvard Theological Review* 60 (1967), 235-79.

—, *The New Science of Politics : An Introduction*, Chicago & London, 1971.

—, On Hegel - A Study in Sorcery. — *Studium Generale* 24 (1971), 335-68.

—, On Classical Studies. — *Modern Age* 4 (1973), 2-8.

—, *Anamnesis : Zur Theorie der Geschichte und Politik*, München, 1966.

—, *From Enlightenment to Revolution*, Durham, North Carolina, 1975.

*VOLKELT, Johannes, *Immanuel Kant's Erkenntnistheorie nach ihren Grundprincipien analisiert : Ein Beitrag zur Grundlegung der Erkenntnistheorie*, Leipzig, 1879.

WALGRAVE, Jan H., *Newman : Le développement du dogme*, Tournai, 1957. English translation by A. V. Littledale : *Newman the Theologian : The Nature of Belief and Doctrine as Exemplified in His Life and Works*, London, 1960.

—, *Geloof en theologie in de crisis*, Kasterlee, 1966.

—, Religious Experience. — Course Notes at the Catholic University of Louvain (K.U.L.), 1970-71.

—, *Unfolding Revelation : The Nature of Doctrinal Development*, London, 1972.

—, Man's Self-understanding in Christian Theology. — *Louvain Studies* 5 (1974), 48-58.

*WARD, James, Psychology. — *Encyclopaedia Britannica*, 9th & 10th editions, Edinburgh, 1886-1902, 37-85, 54-70.
*—, *Naturalism and Agnosticism*, 2 vols, London, 1899.
*—, Psychological Principles. — *Mind: A Quarterly Review of Psychology and Philosophy* (April, October 1883), 1-22, 3-19.
*—, Philosophical Orientation and Scientific Standpoints. — *The University Chronicle* (California) September 1904, 1-24. Offprint among von Hügel's miscellaneous papers, *SAUL*.
*—, The Present Problems of General Psychology. —*Philosophical Review* (American) 13 (1904), 603-21.
*—, Mechanism and Morals : The World of Science and the World of History. — *The Hibbert Journal* 4 (1905-6), 79-99.
*—, *The Realm of Ends, or Pluralism and Theism*, Cambridge, 1912.
*—, *Psychological Principles*, Cambridge, 1918.
WARD, Maisie, *The Wilfrid Wards and the Transition*, London, 1934.
*WARD, Wilfrid, *William George Ward and the Oxford Movement*, London, 1889.
*—, *The Life of John Henry Newman*, 2 vols, London, 1912.
WEBB, Clement C. J., *The Mystical Element of Religion* (Review). — *The Journal of Theological Studies* 11 (1910), 84-94.
—, *A Study of Religious Thought in England from 1850*, Oxford, 1933.
—, Von Hügel, Friedrich. — *Dictionary of National Biography: 1922-1930*, London, 1937. (Ed. J. R. H. Weaver).
—, Baron Friedrich von Hügel and His Contribution to Religious Philosophy. — *Harvard Theological Review* 42 (1949), 1-18.
*WELLHAUSEN, Julius, *Prolegomena zur Geschichte Israels*, Berlin, 1886.
WHELAN, Joseph P., *The Spirituality of Friedrich von Hügel*, London, 1971.
WHITEHEAD, Alfred North, *Adventures of Ideas*, Middlesex, 1948.
—, *Process and Reality : An Essay in Cosmology*, New York, 1967.
—, *Religion in the Making*, New York, 1972.
—, *Science and the Modern World*, London, 1975.
WINCHESTER, Bishop of, *The Army and Religion : An Enquiry and its Bearing upon the Religious Life of the Nation*, London, 1919. (With Preface by the Bishop of Winchester).
ZARI, Antonio, *Frederico von Hügel ed il suo pensiero religiosa*, Roma, 1935.
ZELLER, Eduard, *Die Philosophie der Griechen in ihrer geschichtlichen Entwicklung*, 3 vols, Leipzig, 1876-89.

PART I

THE BIOGRAPHY
OF A RELIGIOUS PHILOSOPHER:
FRIEDRICH VON HÜGEL (1852-1925)

CHAPTER I

THE EARLY FORMATIVE YEARS (1852-1892)

Frederick Maria Aloys François Charles von Hügel was born in Florence on 5 May 1852. His father, Baron Carl, was then Austria's Envoy Extraordinary and Minister Plenipotentiary at the Grand Ducal Court of Tuscany. His mother was a Presbyterian, Elizabeth Farquharson, daughter of the Scottish General Francis Farquharson of Allargue and of Margaret Outram[1]. Baron Carl was betrothed to Elizabeth at Verona on 10 August 1847[2] and the marriage took place at Florence on 28 June 1851. Friedrich was born in May the following year. Two years later, on 29 September, they had a second son, Anatole Andreas and a third child, a girl, Pauline, was born on 3 November 1858. With the outbreak of the revolution which ended Tuscany's separate statehood Baron Carl and his family left Florence with the Grand Duke and returned to Vienna on 27 April 1859. On 20 September of the following year Friedrich's father was appointed Austrian Envoy Extraordinary and Minister Plenipotentiary at the Belgian Court. The family moved to Brussels and remained there for almost seven years (1860-1867). During these years Friedrich and his brother were educated by a Protestant lady-friend of their mother, a certain Miss Redmayne, and their tutor was a Lutheran pastor. Their overall studies were supervised by the German Catholic historian, Alfred von Reumont who was then stationed in Brussels as Minister for Prussia.

Baron Carl retired in 1867 and moved with his family to Torquay in England. Here Friedrich studied geology under William Pengelly, a Quaker stonemason and self taught geologist. Later in life he returned to his early hobby as a means of escaping from the intricates of theology and the science's notion of proof as an accumulation of evidence was likewise to help him in his theological endeavours. With the approach of old age Baron Carl was seized with a longing for his native city of Vienna and on 31 May 1870 he left England for home. After great difficulty he reached Brussels but died there on 2 June in his seventy-sixth year. His wife and family conveyed the remains to Vienna for burial. While in Vienna the young Friedrich suffered a bad attack of typhus and as a side effect he was condemned to partial deafness and weak health for the remainder

1. Elisabeth became a Catholic shortly after her marriage.
2. Baron Carl was then just over 52 while his future bride was not yet 16.

of his life. During this period also he suffered a religious crisis which he passed through successfully thanks to the assistance of a Dutch Dominican, Fr. Raymond Hocking. Von Hügel's later view that without Hocking's help he would have ended up in a life of sin is probably exaggerated. However, it was under Hocking's influence that the young baron determined to set himself on a course of moral and religious training.

Back in London, at the age of twenty-one, Friedrich married Lady Mary Herbert, the daughter of Lord Herbert of Lea, a convert from Anglicanism, on 27 November 1873. The marriage was a very happy one and three daughters Gertrude, Hildegard and Thekla made the household one to be envied. Outside the family sphere, however, both the baron and his wife led two rather separate lives, she in the arts and he in philosophy and theology. Lady Mary in fact was a rather conservative Catholic who never fully shared nor really understood the baron's involvement in the movement for ecclesiastical and theological renewal. For three or four years following the marriage the couple had no permanent home, but lived partly abroad and partly in England. Even after securing a permanent home von Hügel had to spend many of the winter months on the Continent because of his wife's delicate health. Although this helped him make many foreign friends and achieve international recognition, it was not his ideal choice[3]. Through these visits abroad, however, the baron made the personal acquaintance of such men as Duchesne, Loisy, Blondel, Holtzmann, Troeltsch, Eucken and a number of ecclesiastic dignitaries in Italy. Needless to say his proficiency in the four major European languages, English, French, German and Italian was a great asset to him here. Because he was on such intimate terms with so many of the important thinkers who later became implicated in the modernist movement, he has been regarded as the centre, leader and even "the lay-bishop of the movement"[4]. However, for the present all this was far away. Real life had yet to begin for this young twenty-one year old who, with the security of a small income inherited from his father, set

---

3. Responding to a newspaper article praising his cosmopolitanism von Hügel wrote: "It is indeed true, that I am liable to move from land to land, — especially to your Italy, my birth-place, which I love so well, and that I am a man with his friends scattered across Europe and with his roots, apparently, deeply struck, in no place under heaven. But pray believe that this is, truly and indeed, one of the great trials of my life. My ideal has ever been, a strong rootedness in local and patriotic ties and obligations, and, through and in these, a deep sense of the unity in variety of that great organism ... humanity at large; and my horror, now as ever, is any and all mere cosmopolitanism". J.J. KELLY, Von Hügel to a friend, in The Tablet, 229, 1975, p. 78.

4. P. SABATIER, Les modernistes, Paris, 1909, p. LI.

out to devote his "life to the study of Biblical Criticism and Religious Philosophy"[5].

1. EARLY INFLUENCES (1874-1883)

There is very little evidence on which to build a picture of the baron's intellectual activities up to his marriage or over the next few years. A good source to begin with is a letter of his to John Henry Newman on 13 December 1874. The first paragraph of the letter deals with von Hügel's proposal to translate Bishop Joseph Fessler's moderate explanation of Vatican I's Decree on Papal Infallibility. The baron then takes advantage of the occasion to relate his indebtedness to Newman and in the process he gives us the first inkling of his early philosophical and theological formation. He writes : "how deeply, profoundly indebted I am to you, for all you have been to me by means of your books. The reading of *Loss and Gain*, *The Apologia*, *Anglican Difficulties* and *The Grammar of Assent* has, at different times and in different ways formed distinct epochs in my young intellectual and religious life. Such intellectual discipline as I have had, I owe it to your books"[6]. The influence of Newman can not be overestimated. And although very few explicit references to him may be found in the baron's writings, von Hügel had imbibed so much of the Cardinal during his early formative years and Newman had become so much a part of him that he was no longer explicitly conscious of his debt[7].

Another important influence on von Hügel's philosophical and theological development was William George Ward, commonly known since his Oxford days as "Ideal" Ward. The baron met Ward about the time of his marriage in 1873 and for the remaining nine years of "Ideal" Ward's life von Hügel learnt much from the various discussions in which they engaged[8]. Despite Ward's narrow and even bigoted position in theology, he guided the baron towards a notion of the supernatural which would ultimately break all religious ghettos since, as it was developed by the baron it stressed the fact that in their

5. F. VON HÜGEL, *The Relations Between God and Man in* The New Theology *of the Rev. R.J. Campbell*, in *The Albany Review*, 1, 1907, p. 651.
6. Von Hügel to Newman, 13 December 1874, BOA.
7. On Newman's death von Hügel wrote : "I talk Newman even oftener than I know". Von Hügel to Ryder, 18 August 1890, BOA.
8. Von Hügel tells us : "It was Dr. W.G. Ward, "Ideal" Ward, that brilliant Balliol lecturer, and later fervent, indeed partly extravagant, Roman Catholic — a great supernaturalist — who first taught me that the Supernatural should not be directly identified and measured by the amount of its conscious, explicit references to Christ or even simply to God, but by certain qualities which we shall attempt to trace later on, and of which heroism, with a keen sense of givenness and of 'I could not do otherwise', appear to be the chief". E.A.I., p. 280.

concrete humanity all men participate in God's love and receive His gift of grace.

In his reply to von Hügel's letter of 13 December 1874 Newman invited the young baron to visit him at the Oratory in Birmingham and enclosed a copy "With the respects of the author" of his *A Letter Addressed to His Grace The Duke of Norfolk*. Later in the month after reading this work the baron wrote to Newman : "I am ... so grateful to you for its publication ... I have ever longed for an authentic account of your views on this subject, when fighting my own battles (which I had the impudence to call yours) with Mr. Ward and others"[9]. Von Hügel clearly allies himself with the liberal-minded Newman against the intransigent Ward. And although he was friendly with both men, his mind was much more completely in tune with Newman than it ever was with Ward.

More than a year after Newman had issued his invitation von Hügel took up his offer and called on him in Birmingham. Newman's diary for 13 June 1876 reads : "Baron and Baroness von Hügel came"[10]. The baron's notebook[11] contains an account of the subjects discussed during the visit which lasted from the 13th to the 19th inclusive. It records that on the 14th, 16th and 18th there were "Talks with Fr. Newman". On the 14th they held discussions "About the vicariousness of Our Lord's suffering" and "On possibility of invincible ignorance in matters of natural religion". The third topic discussed was "As to Certainty" and the fourth "Scholastic Philosophy". Here Newman acknowledged that "the syllogism ignores the more and less and yet in moral evidence this is often the most important consideration". On 16 June they again discussed the notion of certainty and Newman made his famous remark that "A thousand objections don't make a doubt; if an objection is sufficient to constitute a doubt, we will never cease doubting". And he reminded von Hügel that "The question is not as to whether my view is dangerous or not ... but whether it is true or not". The second topic discussed on 16 June was "the Church's infallible teaching" and on the 18th this discussion shifted to infallibility itself. According to von Hügel, Newman maintained that since the Pope's infallibility was now defined it was really an obsolete question. While agreeing that earlier papal decisions "were not called infallible but irreformable", he held that "they would not be the latter without being the former". The visit concluded with a discussion on the temporal power of the papacy.

Von Hügel's diary of 1877 provides very little evidence which would

9. Von Hügel to Newman, 25 January 1875, BOA.

10. R. K. BROWN, *Newman and von Hügel : A Record of an Early Meeting*, in *The Month*, new series, 26, 1961, p. 26.

11. When consulted this notebook was in the strong room in St. Andrews uncatalogued.

allow us to trace the baron's intellectual development during this year.
A detailed examination shows that on 30 January he finished the
Autobiography of John Stuart Mill and on 21 February read on article
by Mark Pattison on the "Religion of Positivism". The diary for
27 March refers to "Baby, Gertrude, born at 7 a.m. — Dr. Black,
Mrs. Finn and I present". Gertrude was to become von Hügel's favourite
daughter and his constant companion. During August the baron had
many walks with a young Jesuit novice, Gerard Manley Hopkins who
called on him regularly. October and November were spent reading his
favourite poet, Robert Browning. The only really ecclesiastical contact
which occurred was, as we learn from Michael de la Bedoyère, "when
Cardinal Manning reopened the parish church on 5 May and the baron
sat next to him at the subsequent luncheon, thus seemingly considered
already the most notable parishioner"[12].

The diary for 1878 is somewhat more informative. Von Hügel
relates that on 22 January he began Blessed Raymond of Capua's
Life of St. Catherine. After a conversation with Fr. Addis two days later
about St. John's Gospel, he began a paper on the Gospel (which he
finished on 5 February) for a Miss Winscom. This, most probably the
first of his writings on St. John, was to culminate in his rather controversial articles in the eleventh edition of *The Encyclopaedia Britannica*
on "The Apostle John" and the "Gospel of St. John". February
the 4th found him writing out parts of de Torqueville's *L'Ancien Régime*
and on the 7th he finished his favourite work of Robert Browning
The Ring and the Book. The diary of the 7th also notes that "Pope
Pius IX died 2.30 p.m." while that of the 20th remarks "Cardinal
Giacchomo Pecci Pope Leo XIII".

Throughout March von Hügel read Newman's Preface to the Third
edition of the *Via Media*. This would become the most important source
for the notion of The Three Elements of Religion which the baron
later elaborated in *The Mystical Element of Religion*. On 24 April he
began Döllinger's *Kirche und Kirchen* but returned to Newman's Preface
on 16 May and to the second part of his *Anglican Difficulties* on
20 May. At the end of the following month the baron finished the
Life of St. Catherine of Sienna as spiritual reading. During July he read
Jowett's translation of Plato's *Republic* and on 4 August he began
Ernest Renan's *Essais de critique et de morale*. He again read Newman's Preface to the *Via Media* on 27 August and spent September
reading the poetry of Robert Browning. On 9 November he approached
Newman about translating some of his shorter writings. Among these
he included "the preface to the *Via Media* and the 5 lectures on the
Notes of the Church", i.e. Book II of the *Anglican Difficulties* and then
added "I have also thought of the Nine Discourses on University

12. BEDOYÈRE, p. 24.

Teaching"[13]. Although von Hügel received Newman's permission for this project on 12 November, he never carried it through. Nevertheless he continued reading the Cardinal's works. For example on 28 December he read the *Essay on the Development of Christian Doctrine* and on the 30th his essay on "Rationalism in Theology".

It is very difficult to give an account of von Hügel's work and development during 1879. All the pages of the diary up to 20 March have been torn out, after the 1st and 2nd all April is missing and also the pages after 8 October. In the Memoranda there is a two page list of "Books to get in 1879". The first refers largely to aids for scholarly research. The other page contains a list of the lives of saints including those of St. Gertrude, Hildegard, Gregory, Augustine, Justin Martyr, Irenaeus, etc. The list also contains a reference to Newman's book on *The Arians* and his *Theological Tracts*. Also a number of Aristotle's works are mentioned.

The diaries for 1880 to 1883 inclusive are missing. The only evidence of von Hügel's theological activity during 1880 is to be found in his notebook. It shows that von Hügel held discussions with "Ideal" Ward at his home in Hampstead between September 19-22 on the subject of Hell, specifically about the *poena sensus* of the damned. The discussion centred on the eternity of the pain of the damned which was being denied in theological circles at the time. Ward seemingly held for the eternity of the *poena sensus*. Newman is referred to as having "held all along, even when a Protestant, that the damned have a knowledge or consciousness of the eternity of their pain"[14]. The discussions with Ward also covered the problem of the "Invincible Ignorance of God". According to the notes, Ward believed that the possibility of invincible ignorance of the truths of Christianity rested on a different basis to that of the existence of God. The former, he maintained, would be a contingent truth, the latter a necessary one. The notes also relate Ward's admission that he could not "understand the meaning of Newman's repeated declaration that there is no logical halting place between Catholicism and Atheism"[15].

The next ten pages of the notebook contain extracts from the Review of Dr. Ward's Essay on the Church's Doctrinal Infallibility from the August 1880 issue of the *Irish Ecclesiastical Record*. And the following thirteen and a half pages contain extracts from "The Church's infallible Mysterium" by E. T. O'Dwyer, from the September 1880 issue of *The Irish Ecclesiastical Record*. There is no other available material for the baron's theological endeavours during this year.

The sources for 1881 are practically non-existent. The best we can do

13. Von Hügel to Newman, 9 November 1878, BOA.
14. Notebook, N.11.
15. Ibid.

is simply rely on the account de la Bedoyère gives from two letters of the baron's to "Ideal" Ward. At the time von Hügel and his family were on one of their regular trips abroad, in Germany, when he wrote: "We have settled to go to Westphalia; to move straight to Münster, stay there four of five weeks, and come straight home"[16]. The trip was eventually shortened because the baron's health, though never good at the best of times, was now at a particularly low ebb. From de la Bedoyère we also learn that during the year von Hügel wrote again to Ward advising him to get Jean-Pierre de Caussade's *Abandon à la providence divine*, saying "I hope so much you will confirm my admiration for, and deep interest, in the book"[17].

The material for 1882 is again quite sparse. The only indication we have of the baron's activities during this year comes from two letters to Wilfrid Ward. The first tells of von Hügel's efforts in finding a new house[18]. The second was sent to Wilfrid Ward on 17 December. In it the baron notes that since everyone starts with a rudimentary conscience which cannot be totally erased, no one can sincerely be without a consciousness of his dependence on a Lawgiver. Nevertheless, he admits that this consciousness would not involve everything which we associate with the word God. He further maintains that while he believes that the existence of God could be proved by reason, "the simpler arguments fall short of the proof of His Omnipotence"[19].

In June of 1883 von Hügel made his first journey into print in a very modest way. He translated some of his father's papers dealing with the escape of Prince Metternich during the Viennese Revolution of March 1848 adding a short introductory note of a little over a page which he signed "F. v. H." Much later we learn from von Hügel himself that in this year a friend faced him with "the religious problem raised by Anthony Trollope's Autobiography — that faithful account of a long life, so pure, truthful, modest, laborious, affectionate, and without one trace of hunger after God, the Other and the More". "The problem", he adds, "has never left me since then"[20].

16. BEDOYÈRE, p. 27.
17. Ibid.
18. The baron found a house in Hampstead at 4 Holford Road near Hampstead Heath where he walked practically every afternoon with his little Pekinese dog, Puck. He often arranged to meet his scholarly friends in the afternoon, so that they could accompany him on these walks. As he said: "A walk on the Health is the best form of interview". Later in 1903 he moved house for the last time to 13 Vicarage Gate, close to Kensington Gardens. It is interesting to note that von Hügel never owned but simply rented both houses.
19. Von Hügel to W. Ward, 17 December 1882, SAUL.
20. F. VON HÜGEL, *Apologist of Religion*, in *T.L.S.*, 1040, 1921, p. 860.

2. VON HÜGEL'S DEVELOPMENT : THE SCHOLAR-SAINT (1884-1892)

In his diary under the pencilled heading "A.M.D.G. work for 1884" von Hügel gives a list of books and articles he intended to study during the coming year. But, in theology, with the exception of three of the works, e.g. Sanday on the New Testament, Newman on Inspiration and Abbot on the Gospels, the baron did not abide by this plan at all. He did, however, carry out his plan for English literature and proceeded to read nearly all the works of Jane Austen.

A detailed examination of the diary reveals that on 29 January 1884 he read the entry on the "Bible" in *The Catholic Dictionary* and on the 31st he sent a note to Wilfrid Ward accepting the dedication of his father's *Philosophical Essays* to himself[21]. The baron read Newman's article "On the Inspiration of Scripture" on 31 January and again the following day. Between 11 and 12 February he surveyed various articles in *The Catholic Dictionary*, among others the entries on Canon of Scripture, Church and Christ, Hell, God and Grace. He also read Leo XIII's Encyclical to the French Bishops on 16 February.

At the beginning of March von Hügel began *The Passion of Our Lord in His Sacred Heart* by Fr. S. Coleridge as spiritual reading. On the 6th he visited Fr. Coleridge for the first time to discuss Newman's article on Inspiration and the authority of the Vulgate. On the 13th he completed Mr. Healy's article "Cardinal Newman on Inspiration" in the *Irish Ecclesiastical Record* for March and that evening along with Gerard Manley Hopkins he was present at a lecture by Gerald

---

21. In his note von Hügel wrote: "to have my name associated with the greatest of contemporary theistic philosophers is a gratification to myself ... indeed your father's philosophical work stands too high to be damaged ... by its association with an name so unrepresentative as my own". Von Hügel to W. Ward, 31 January, 1884, SAUL. Lest Newman consider him a disciple of "Ideal" Ward, von Hügel wrote as follows to him concerning the dedication : "When, some months ago, Mr. Wilfrid Ward asked me to be allowed to dedicate to me the posthumous collection of his father's published Philosophical Essays, I was flattered but also somewhat surprised and certainly a little embarassed; for much as I always appreciated Mr. Ward's dialectical vigour and personal kindness, and fully as I agreed with his general philosophical principles (to which I was first won by the 'Grammar of Assent'), there was yet as complete a difference of temperament and of conclusion [on] such subjects as the Church's Infallibility, and indeed historico critical questions generally as could well obtain between faithful Catholics, and at the end of nine years intercourse such subjects were all but altogether tabood [sic], and quite absolutely disagreed upon between us. — It was only the consideration of the marked difference in his treatment of philosophical and of historico-theological subjects, and his general coincidence with the tone and conclusions of the 'Grammar' in the former which overcame my fear that the few who care about my views at all might misinterpret them by my acceptance, and allowed me to accept the honour of some association with a work in its chief features so much your own". Von Hügel to Newman, 1 July 1884, BOA.

Christopher Rawlinson[22] on the "Evidence of Christ". The baron began William Sanday's Inaugural Lecture on the Study of the New Testament on 18 March and a week later he received a copy of "Ideal" Ward's *Philosophical Essays* and began reading Wilfrid Ward's Introduction.

For the next seven weeks there is no evidence of any new philosophical or theological reading. Von Hügel travelled to Paris on 5 May where he visited the Abbé Louis Duchesne[23] for the first time on 12 May and returned again on the 23rd. It was during this visit that von Hügel agreed to write short chronicles about British scriptural publications and research for Duchesne's *Bulletin critique*. The baron again met Duchesne on the 24th, this time at the Institut Catholique and two days later, after listening to a lecture by M. Boissier at the *Collège de France*, he bought Duchesne's *cours*. On 5 June he read Newman's privately printed Postscript to his article on Inspiration[24] and at a soirée given by Mgr. Maurice d'Hulst, Rector of the Institut Catholique, that evening von Hügel spoke to Mgr. d'Hulst, Abbé Paul de Broglie and Abbé Duchesne about Newman's articles[25]. On 16 June the baron, accompanied by his wife and daughter Hildegard, paid his first visit to the Abbé Henri Huvelin[26]. If Duchesne can be said to have impressed von Hügel as a scholar, Huvelin personified the ideal of sanctity which was to remain with him throughout his life.

The diary pages for 3 to 9 July 1884 have been torn out. Von Hügel returned to London during this period. On the 29th Franz von Hummelauer, the Old Testament scholar, came to lunch and stayed the night. The next day the baron had a talk with Hummelauer about "Authenticity and Inspiration" but there are no more details of the

22. On Rawlinson's death von Hügel wrote an appreciation: cf. VHB, no. 72.

23. Louis Duchesne (1843-1922). For von Hügel's relationship with Duchesne cf. VHB, nos 70, 71.

24. The Inspiration article along with the Postscript have been published in a critical edition by J.D. HOLMES and R. MURRAY, *Newman — On the Inspiration of Scripture*, London, 1967.

25. For an "Index bio-bibliographique" of the relevant personages of the period cf. Emile POULAT, *Alfred Loisy : sa vie et son œuvre*, Paris, 1960, pp. 325-409.

26. Henri Huvelin (1838-1910), was, according to the baron, "A gentleman by birth and breeding, a distinguished Hellenist, a man of exquisitely piercing, humorous mind, he could readily have become a great editor or interpreter of Greek philosophical or patristic texts, or a remarkable Church historian. But this deep and heroic personality deliberately preferred 'to write in souls', whilst occupying, during thirty-five years, a supernumerary, unpaid post in a large Parisian parish. There, suffering from gout in the eyes and brain, and usually lying prone in a darkened room, he served souls with the supreme authority of self-oblivious love, and brought light and purity and peace to countless troubled sorrowing, or sinful souls". E.L., pp. 374-5. The Abbé Huvelin's importance in guiding von Hügel into the great Catholic tradition of French spirituality of the late seventeenth century cannot be overestimated. For further information cf. J. KELLY, *The Abbé Huvelin's Counsel to Baron Friedrich von Hügel*, in *Bijdragen Tijdschrift voor Filosofie en Theologie*, 39, 1978, pp. 59-69.

discussion. A reception was held for Cardinal Manning at von Hügel's house on 3 August with about eighty people attending and from 26 to 31 August von Hügel made a retreat with the Jesuits at Manresa House. Between 24 July and 2 September the baron payed eight visits to the British Museum to examine the Parthenon Sculptures and to study the coins of the period. There are no diary entries from October and we have no other evidence of von Hügel's activities during this period.

In the diary for 1885, under books "to be read in 1885" the baron noted Franz Hettinger *Apologia Vol. III-V*, Newman's *University Sermons*, Grou's *Avis pour la vie* and *Vie et œuvres*, Döllinger's *Christenthum und Kirche*, and he determined to study the teaching of Molinos along with the relevant sections in Denzinger, Gury and Schram. What he actually studied during this year can be ascertained only by a detailed examination of his diary.

On 6 February he attended a lecture by Mr. Newton at University College, London, on Greek inscriptions, the third of the course, but only the second heard by von Hügel. On the 23rd he journeyed to Oxford where he dined with John Wordsworth, the Oriel Professor of the Interpretation of Scripture. That evening he attended a lecture by Charles Gore of Pusey House on the fourth century African theologian, Victorinus Afer. The following day he examined Wordsworth's critical text of the first fifteen chapters of Matthew's Gospel in the Vulgate version. In the evening he dined with Samuel Rolles Driver at Christ Church in Pusey's old rooms and there he was shown the first two parts of the *Corpus Inscriptionum Semiticarum*, and books on the Phoenician language. On the 25th, after lunch with William Sanday at Exeter College, the baron returned home by the 4.05 express.

During March he attended Mr. Newton's fourth and last lecture on inscriptions during the reign of Alexander and on 5 April he sent off his first batch of notes for the "chronique" section of Duchesne's *Bulletin critique*, some of which dealt with Wordsworth's critical edition of the Vulgate version of the first fifteen chapters of Matthew. Bishop (later Cardinal) Herbert Vaughan dined with von Hügel on the 8th and they discussed *The Tablet* and the University question, i.e. the ban on Catholics attending Oxford and Cambridge[27]. After reading a review of Charles De Smedt's *Principes de la critique historique*

---

27. In a pencilled note on pages 142-3 of Andrew D. White's *A History of the Warfare of Science with Theology in Christendom*, Vol. 2, New York, 1903, Hüg. BL245.W5, SAUL, the baron indicates Vaughan's attitude on the University question: "Cardinal Vaughan, sometime before giving way about the frequentation by Catholics of Oxford-Cambridge Universities, declared to me, in answer to my argument from the large percentage of good results amongst such Catholics as had, under obviously unfavourable circumstances, gone, up to then, to those universities, — that this was precisely what we ought to expect the Devil to do — he would, in this way, lull the Catholic and the Church authorities to sleep and into falling into his trap".

in Duchesne's *Bulletin* von Hügel turned to the work itself on 28 April. The *Bulletin critique* with the baron's first contribution came on 2 May and over the next three weeks von Hügel prepared three more notices and sent them off to Duchesne. The remainder of the year was spent mostly studying ancient coins, reading Head's *Coinage of Lydia and Persia* and visiting the coin room of the British Museum and the Fitzwilliam Museum (Cambridge).

Four memoranda pages of the 1886 diary contain long lists of "books to get". The most important among these for von Hügel's future development were the works of St. Catherine of Genoa (mentioned here for the first time), along with the works of Schleiermacher, Grou, Ritschl and Plato. Again it is only by a detailed examination of the diary with other relevant material that one gets a clear grasp of the actual work undertaken in the course of this year.

During the early part of 1886 the baron continued his study of Greek coins. On 25 May he left London for Paris and without contacting any of his other friends there he visited Huvelin for advice and spiritual direction on five occasions during his six day stay. Because he had been guided by Huvelin into the great Catholic tradition of French spirituality of the late seventeenth century, von Hügel was later able to steer an independent though lonely course through the rough seas and turbulent waves of liberal catholicism on the one side and neo-ultramontanism on the other. Being firmly anchored in this more authentic earlier tradition the baron was able, during the terrible years of the modernist crisis, to keep his sanity and balance while many about him were cast adrift.

After returning from Paris von Hügel finished Jean-Nicholas Gou's *Manuel des âmes intérieures* on 7 August and thereafter began his *Ecole de Jésus-Christ* also as spiritual reading. He completed four announcements for Duchesne's *Bulletin* and sent them away on 5 November. In a lighter vein he read Shakespeare's *Julius Caesar* on 23 September and on 13 November he brought Gertrude and Hildegard to visit Madame Tussaud's wax-works.

At the beginning of his diary for 1887 von Hügel indicates the most important books which he intended to buy during the coming year. These included the complete works of Fénelon, Kant's works (8 volumes), Friedrich Ueberweg's *Plato*, Friedrich Michelis' *Plato* and his French translation of Kant's works. Under "Reading done" von Hügel gives a list of the most important works he read during the current year. For a complete view of the baron's work during the year one must as usual make a detailed examination of the diary itself.

On 22 January 1887 von Hügel began Fénelon's *Lettres spirituelles* and later on in the month he read "Ideal" Ward's long letter to J. S. Mill, dealing with moral responsibility in intellectual matters. During February he read many of William Thackeray's novels. We have to wait until early June before he returned to serious study, first with Ueberweg's Kant on 13 June, then Whately's "The Errors of Romanism" on 2 July and finally St. George Mivart's article on "The Catholic Church and Biblical Criticism" on 27 July. In this last controversial but prophetic article Mivart forecast, as the baron would soon discover, that the future conflict in the Church would arise from the historical critical study of the Scriptures.

On 30 July von Hügel began Rudolf Eucken's *Die Philosophie des Thomas von Aquino und die Kultur der Neuzeit* and thereafter Schubert's biography of Kant. He then took a vacation and on 12 October he started a systematic study of Kant's works in Gustav Hartenstein's edition. This was continued until early December and on the 11th of the month he began reading the Abbé Gosselin's "Analyse raisonnée de la controverse du quiétisme". This was to become the baron's chief guide in analysing the quietist controversy, and his conclusions in the *Mystical Element* are in substantial agreement with those of Abbé Gosselin.

At the beginning of 1888 von Hügel prepared his study programme for the coming year. It was to include James Martineau's *Types of Ethical Theory* and *A Study of Religion*, Kant's *Grundlegung zur Metaphysik der Sitten* and his *Anthropologie*, Butler's *Sermons*, Pascal's *Pensées*, Epictetus' *Enchiridion* and his *Dissertationes* and finally the important works of Bossuet and Fénelon concerning the quietist and pure love controversy.

During January 1888 the baron visited James Martineau and had a two hour talk with him, presumably about his book *A Study of Religion* which interested von Hügel at the time. The morning of 28 January found him finishing some notes he was making on Whately's article "The Errors of Romanticism" and in the afternoon he began R. H. Hutton's essay on "Cardinal Newman". After completing this on the 29th he began reading an essay Wilfrid Ward had lent him on "R. H. Hutton as a Religious Thinker". Ward called to see him the next day and they discussed the essay. On the following day, 31 January, von Hügel began R. H. Hutton's essay "George Eliot as Author" and on the evening of February the 1st he dined at the Devonshire Hotel with R. H. Hutton and had a three hour talk with him. It is interesting to dwell on the mode of the baron's activities during this month. Along with reading the men's articles or books von Hügel always endeavoured to discuss the ideas with the authors themselves. Such a personal approach would characterise him throughout his life and probably it is the only fair way to become acquainted with a man's real thought.

During February the baron studied Fénelon's "Lettre sur la charité" and then returned to his study of Abbé Gosselin's "Avertissement" and his "Analyse raisonnée de la controverse du quiétisme". After finishing Fénelon's "Lettre" von Hügel turned to his "Letters to Clement XI" and then delved into Bossuet's *Oeuvres*. In April he read Fénelon's *L'Explication des maximes des saints sur la vie intérieure*. This completed the baron's first serious study of the important documents of the quietist and pure love controversy and the results were later to find their place in his *Mystical Element*[28].

For the remainder of April 1888 and the first half of May the baron read a number of the works of Jacob Grimm, including his *Selbstbiographie*. On 18 May he began arranging his study library under the following four divisions: "(1) Classical Literature and Antiquities; (2) Christian Literature and Antiquities; (3) General and Hellenic and Germanic Philosophy; (4) Philosophy and Scholastic and Mystical Theology"[29]. Dom Francis Aidan Gasquet lunched with him on 5 July and afterwards as they strolled together on the Heath they discussed "hypnotism, the Reformation; 5 century movements"[30]. November the 2nd saw von Hügel engaging in his first recorded reading of the *Vita di S. Caterina da Genoa* as spiritual reading. What had begun here as a simple devotional exercise was later to become the baron's *magnum opus*, *The Mystical Element of Religion as Studied in Saint Catherine of Genoa and her Friends* (1908).

In addition to the works proposed for study in 1888 but which had not been completed von Hügel also determined in 1889 to study Henry Sidgwick's *Outlines of the History of Ethics*, Thomas Hill Green's *Miscellaneous Writings* along with Richard Nettleship's *Memoir of T. H. Green*. In English poetry he decided to read the complete works of Milton and Tennyson and in literature the first and second part of Shakespeare's *King Henry IV* and *The Merry Wives of Windsor*. Finally, in German literature he wanted to read Jacob Grimm's *Kleine Schriften*.

On 9 January 1889 the baron went to the Haymarket Theatre to see Singer's production of *The Merry Wives of Windsor* and later in the month he read the play itself. In January he also began his study of the poems of Tennyson and Milton and set about reading *She Stoops to Conquer* by Oliver Goldsmith. Thereafter he commenced a detailed study of Henry Sidgwick's *Outlines of the History of Ethics* and continued this intermittingly until he dined with Mr. and Mrs. Sidgwick in Cambridge on 2 March. Throughout February and March he also

28. According to Maurice Nédoncelle, the positions taken by Bremond in his classical treatment of this controversy in *Histoire littéraire du sentiment religieux* were dictated by von Hügel. As Nédoncelle writes: "It was von Hügel who first suggested the solution to Bremond, even down to providing the vocabulary". M. NÉDONCELLE, *La Pensée religieuse de Friedrich von Hügel*, Paris, 1935, p. 165. English translation: *Baron Friedrich von Hügel: A Study of His Life and Thought*, London, 1937, p. 155.

29. Diary, 18 May 1888.

30. Diary, 5 July 1888.

continued his proof-reading of Wilfrid Ward's life of his father. In April he finished Nettleship's *Memoir of T. H. Green*, (started on 18 March), and began T. H. Green's *Miscellaneous Works*.

August found von Hügel reading his favourite poet, Robert Browning's *Transcendentalism* and during this month he resumed St. John of the Cross' *Ascent of Mount Carmel* as spiritual reading and on completion he turned to David Lewis' *Life of St. John of the Cross*, also as spiritual reading. The remainder of September was taken up with some light reading in Robert Browning and Sir Walter Scott and during October St. John of the Cross' *Obscure Night of the Soul* became his spiritual reading.

In November the baron decided to write an article on the spiritual writings of Jean Nicholas Grou. In preparation for this he began translating passages from Grou's *Manuel des âmes intérieures* on 3 November. The first draft of the article was completed a fortnight later and the final manuscript corrected and sent off to *The Tablet* on 7 December. Three day later he began the second part of his article which he completed and sent off on 17 December [31]. The scholar-saint ideal present in Grou's spirituality attracted the baron immensely. As he wrote in his first article Grou was: "Sober, silent, solid, simple; a solitary, laborious, claimless scholar, gentleman and saint; passing, with evergrowing serenity, through everthickening storms and sufferings, exterior and interior; driven back and pressed down upon the very foundations and mainsprings of faith and love" [32]. Written in December 1889 this offers a magnificent expression of the ideal which von Hügel's own life would concretise and bring to fruition.

The baron spent much of January and February 1890 proof-reading and attempting to interest various publishers in an English translation Mrs. Charles Greene was preparing of Fénelon's *Spiritual Letters*. When finally he finished correcting Mrs. Greene's first batch of proofs on 13 May von Hügel returned them to her and a week later he set off with his family for Wildbad (Germany).

Four days after his return, i.e. on 8 July, von Hügel started Hermann Lotze's *Grundzüge der Psychologie* and on the 26th he began Franz Xaver Kraus' *Das Studium der Theologie*, which he finished three days later. In his work Kraus emphasised the necessity of a strong

31. Von Hügel acknowledged his profound debt to Grou in a letter to Mrs. Margaret Clutton in 1912: "Grou has helped me greatly to acquire a spirituality that allows, and indeed requires, much freedom of research and of thought, considerable friction and tension yet all within a profound, radical devotedness". J. P. WHELAN, *The Parent as Spiritual Director: A Newly Published Letter of Friedrich von Hügel*, in *The Month*, second new series, 2, 1970, p. 56.

32. F. VON HÜGEL, *The Spiritual Writings of Père Grou, S.J.*, in *The Tablet*, 74, 1889, p. 900.

positive historical theology as one of the means for overcoming
scholastic theology and as part of the effort to break out of the ghetto
mentality, created by the politicisation of Catholicism with its narrow
absolutist neo-ultramontanism, he urged a return to a religious Catholicism.

The baron's diary for 11 August records the death of "Cardinal
Newman 4.45 p.m.". Six days later von Hügel was at work studying
Hermann Lotze's *Mikrokosmos*. Dr. Gustav Bickell, the well known
orientalist from Innsbruck, was visiting London during August so on the
22nd the baron sent him a card inviting him to Hampstead. Bickell
came on the evening of the 24th and they had their first discussion
together. Both men dined together two days later at von Hügel's
home and after "a good talk"[33] the baron resolved to read Kuenen and
Wellhausen. Another visit followed on the 29th, with a walk on the
Heath and a late supper together. At Bickell's instigation von Hügel
read Robertson Smith's *Religion of the Semites* and the following
day, after the baron had spent the afternoon with three children
bringing a stray dog they had found to the police station, he returned
home to study Julius Wellhausen's *Prolegomena zur Geschichte Israels*
in preparation for a visit Bickell was paying him later in the evening.
Von Hügel also studied Bickell's translation of Koheleth and when
Bickell arrived for his seventh visit at 5 p.m. on 9 September, he
commenced with Hebrew lessons for the baron. From now until
4 October Bickell gave him ten lessons in Hebrew and for his part von
Hügel introduced him to R.H. Hutton, Bishop John C. Hedley,
Walter H. Frere and Dom Francis A. Gasquet of Downside. Under
Bickell's influence the baron became aware of the terrible arrears which
had to be made up in Catholic scholarship and theology. Bickell
showed him that in the Catholic Church "more or less since Tridentine
times, but especially since the French Revolution, the spiritual life
indeed still remained something astonishingly deeper and richer than
what was correspondingly furnished by the various Protestant bodies;
but that, next to this spiritual life, ranked here not the life of the
mind but the things of, more or less political, policy and force. Thus we
understood and welcomed Nature only as visibly organized and con-
straining Order and Power; whereas, in a completely healthy and richly
fruitful life, the things of the mind would rank immediately after the
things of the spirit — the things of visible organisation, order and power
would rank third"[34].

Against the political Catholicism and the narrow, absolutist neo-
ultramontanism of his day, von Hügel became convinced that next to

33. Diary, 26 August 1890.
34. F. VON HÜGEL, *Eudoxe Irénée Mignot*, in *The Contemporary Review*, 113, 1918,
p. 521.

the things of the spirit in man (which would become for him the mystical element in religion), should come the life of the mind (the philosophical, theological and critical historical element), and only then the visible organisation (the institutional, traditional element of religion). With this vision he broke with the narrow static essentialism of the ecclesiology of his own time and recovered a dynamic organic conception of religion and the Church in which all the different elements would interact, modifying and being modified by each other. Within this conception also he would find a legitimate place and a relative autonomy for genuine historical, critical research and its results.

After Bickell left London the baron sent a note to the Jewish scholar, Julius Spira, engaging him as a Hebrew teacher and at 10 a.m. on 4 November he had his first Hebrew reading in Genesis with Spira. Over the next five years he had more than two hundred lessons from Spira. October the 16th saw von Hügel returning to his study of Robertson Smith's *Religion of the Semites*, probably in preparation for his meeting with Smith in Cambridge on 20 October. The day after this encounter he wrote a letter to Wilfrid Ward in praise of Loisy's *Histoire du canon de l'Ancien Testament*[35]. Here we come upon the first reference to the man whom von Hügel was to defend throughout his life, believing that the struggle for the establishment of biblical criticism and the autonomy of the historical critical method was personified in him.

During November and December the baron worked on his Hebrew with Spira and read Grou's *Maximes spirituelles* and St. John of the Cross' *A Spiritual Canticle* as spiritual reading. On 30 November he sent some notices off to the *Bulletin critique* and during December he busied himself with some light reading. For example, on 21 December he started reading Charles Dickens' *Christmas Carol* aloud for the family.

Von Hügel's Hebrew continued to progress and by February the 24th 1891 he had finished his third reading of Genesis up to chapter 19. Exactly one month later the Rev. Henry Ignatius Ryder, Newman's successor at the Birmingham Oratory, sent a manuscript of his "The Bible and Inspiration" for von Hügel's consideration[36]. The baron

35. Von Hügel wrote: "In these 250 pp. you have an extraordinary production: the very things we want. A series of lectures, as delivered at the Institut Catholique in Paris (directly and exclusively managed by a Committee of French Bishops), and dedicated, as such, to his pupils; and containing every date and composite authorship demanded by Wellhausen and Kuenen. You don't get that every day. I shall look out with interest as to the work's reception; it is a phenomenon, even if its history turns out to be that Loisy and d'Hulst the Rector of the Institut have quietly stolen a march on the Bishops". Von Hügel to W. Ward, 21 October 1890, SAUL.

36. The article was published as: *Scripture Inspiration and Modern Biblical Criticism*, in *The Catholic World*, 56, 1893, pp. 742-54; *Rival Theories on Scripture and Inspiration*, 57,

started reading this three weeks later and after drawing up a long critique sent it to Ryder. Later in July he revised these notes and had them privately printed. While this was in progress the baron visited Arthur Cook on 2 July and arranged for Greek philosophical readings with him. On 17 November von Hügel started these readings alone and on 10 December Arthur Cook came. Together they began their first Greek philosophy readings with Thales and continued with the Pre-Socratics for two hours three times a week over the next six weeks.

By the beginning of 1892 the thunderstorms, as von Hügel would later call them, were already gathering. Rumours abounded that Loisy's works were being denounced in Rome especially by the French Dominicans. The diary notes the death of Cardinal Manning [37] at 8 a.m. on 14 January and on the 22nd Bishop Herbert Vaughan, the future Archbishop and Cardinal of Westminster, came to see the baron who was ill in bed. On 16 January 1892 the baron finished his Pre-Socratic readings with Arthur Cook. By then he had read Heraclitus, Parmenides and Empedocles thoroughly in the original. His spiritual reading up to 26 January was Fénelon's "Third Letter to Clement" and the following day he turned to Fénelon's dissertation on pure love.

Von Hügel received his first visit from Fr. Christian van den Biesen, a professor of Scripture at St. Joseph's College, Mill Hill, on 11 February. Both men were to become good friends especially through their common interest in the composition of the Hexateuch. After van den Biesen's visit the baron began Loisy's *Histoire du canon du Nouveau Testament* and on 5 March he resumed his reading of Loisy's *Histoire du canon de l'Ancien Testament*, this time studying it systematically. On 11 March he completed a careful study with notes of Zeller's *Philosophie der Griechen* and on the 15th he commenced a second set of Greek philosophy readings with Arthur Cook. Between now and 22 April, when the tuition ceased, he had fifteen lessons. On 21 June von Hügel began his third series of readings with Arthur Cook, this time starting with Plato's *Timaeus*. Precisely one month later van den Biesen called to discuss an article he was preparing for the *Dublin Review* on "The Authorship and Composition of the Hexa-

1893, pp. 206-18; *The Proper Attitude of Catholics Towards Modern Biblical Criticism*, 57, 1893, pp. 396-406.

37. Many years later, in 1921, on the occasion of the publication of Shane Leslie's *Life of Cardinal Manning*, von Hügel wrote of his relationship with the Cardinal as follows: "Although my opportunities, through my marriage connections, were unusually great for getting to know the Cardinal well, I must not claim to have come to know him intimately. A man of action and of leadership, a man alarmingly certain and absolute on every point on which he cared at all, he could not really help men of scholarship and of investigation", F. VON HÜGEL, *Cardinal Manning*, in *T.L.S.*, 1001, 1921, p. 195.

teuch" and returned again for the same reason on 28 July. During August the baron read Richard Simon's inaugural work in the history of modern biblical criticism, *Histoire critique du Vieux Testament*, while at the same time correcting the proofs of van den Biesen's forth-coming articles. On 16 August he browsed through Jannsen's *Stolberg* and the following day he set off for a holiday in Ireland.

After returning from Ireland at the end of September von Hügel began revising the second volume of Mrs. Greene's English translation of Fénelon's letters and on 19 October he resumed reading *Stolberg*, finishing it on the 23rd. The next day he began Wörner's *J. A. Möhler*. The inscriptions on the inside cover of this book testify to an extremely careful reading by the baron. And while he broke off this study on the 26th to make a "roughdraft of new paragraph for Dr. van den Biesen"[38], he resumed it on 29 October and continued it through 5, 7, 8, 9 and 12 November. Later in the month, on the night of the 24th, von Hügel was unable to sleep because of a liver chill so he got up and, as the diary relates, "looked thro' Möhler's *Symbolik*".

Because he told Loisy that he had only studied the chapter on the church in the *Symbolik*, it has been assumed that Möhler exerted almost no influence on von Hügel or the modernists. A typical example of this view is expressed by J. J. Heaney when he writes: "The writings of the great Tübingen Catholic ecclesiologist, J. Möhler, exerted very little influence on von Hügel. In 1913 he told Loisy that, not only had Newman and Tyrell [sic] probably never read Möhler, but that he himself had read only the 'chapter on the Church', in *Symbolik*. This statement is somewhat important for our study. While we will show that the Baron found the contemporary treatment of the Church distastefully juridical, still he never quite achieved a picture of the Church that projected its full organic richness. His theory remained somewhat geometrical; the influence of Möhler might have helped here"[39]. As will become evident from our study of the baron's thought, his philosophy is organic throughout. Far from beginning with a geometrical pattern of a multiplicity of separate parts or elements, von Hügel's philosophy always begins with a dynamic whole, an organic unity within which the various elements have a vital function but apart from which they are simply abstractions. The failure to appreciate this basic principle in the baron's philosophy necessarily leads to a misrepre-sentation of his notion of the Church since his organic notion of the Church flows from his organic conception of all reality. Furthermore, to conclude simply from the fact that von Hügel only read the chapter on the church in the *Symbolik* that Möhler had very little

38. Diary, 26 October 1892.
39. J. J. HEANEY, *The Modernist Crisis: von Hügel*, London, 1969, p. 27.

influence on him is an unwarrented and completely fallacious assumption. Could he not have read a number of other works of or about Möhler? As a matter of fact an examination of the evidence shows that the baron was thoroughly acquainted with Möhler's thought. As we said, he read Wörner's *Johann Adam Möhler* very thoroughly between 23 October (when he bought the work) and 12 November and, as we shall see later, he returned to it again on 23 March 1894. On the inside cover of this book von Hügel has made the following inscription which testifies beyond doubt to the respect and esteem in which he held Möhler : "A very interesting dense pot pourri : a pity that basically so little of such a great man is preserved. With Newman, as a character (personality), even above Newman, the greatest Catholic of our century"[40]. Now that the dust is beginning to settle and passions are calmer, it must be admitted that the deepest thinkers at the turn of the century, e.g. von Hügel and Blondel, who were thought to be implicated in a new heresy, were aware of the parallels between themselves and the earlier Catholic tradition of the Tübingen school and were in fact the bearers of a more central Catholic tradition than the current nineteenth century neo-scholastic theology. As we shall see shortly, the real innovators in this period were the narrow absolutist politically minded neo-ultramontanes.

During November the baron continued to revise the proofs of the life of W.G. Ward. And, as the diary relates, on 10 December he "began Paper (writing) on W. G. Ward" which he finished on the 16th and after revision sent to Wilfrid Ward on 23 December for inclusion in the latter's life of his father to be entitled *Willian George Ward and the Catholic Revival*. This letter is most important because in it, at the close of his period of scholarly and saintly formation, von Hügel tries to delineate his position with respect to the absolutist ultramontane "Ideal" Ward and to specify the theological tradition in which he was to remain rooted throughout the modernist crisis.

In the letter sent on 23 December 1892 he wrote to Wilfrid Ward : "Personally, I have never been anything but an Ultramontane, in the old and definite sense of the word, ever since I have been a convinced Catholic at all"[41]. The baron's ultramontanism, however, was not of the extreme type as "Ideal" Ward's. Von Hügel's form of ultramontanism arose from a tradition which understood the term in the original, "very restricted sense of anti-Gallican"[42]. As such, ultramontanism entailed

40. Inside cover, Balthasar Wörner, *Johann Adam Möhler. Ein Lebensbild mit Briefen und kleinen Schriften Möhler's herausgegeven von P. B. Gams*, Regensburg, 1913, Hüg.BV150.M6F13, SAUL. Translation by the present writer.
41. W. Ward, *William George Ward and the Catholic Revival*, London, 1893, p. 371.
42. Von Hügel to W. Ward, 4 September 1888, SAUL.

breadth not narrowness, liberty not intolerance, universality not nationalism, spirituality and interiority not politics and external power. The narrowness associated with the word was in the baron's view a nineteenth century product. It had been engrafted on to the older ultramontanism by the quasi-political campaign of Joseph de Maistre. For example, de Maistre's *Du Pape* was in fact more concerned with increasing the power of the pope in society and politics than with the theological doctrine of ultramontanism as such. The baron rejected both liberal catholicism and neo-ultramontanism as being two sides of the one coin and to illustrate this he points to the example of Veuillot who moved from being a liberal Catholic to an extreme ultramontane without any great difficulty[43]. In his attempt to preserve what was best in both von Hügel realised that he had to seek out a position beyond the two[44]. To instal himself firmly within this older, more moderate and balanced ultramontanism von Hügel returned especially to François de Salignac de la Mothe Fénelon (1651-1715). He wrote to Wilfrid Ward on 28 December 1892: "Fénelon is, for all interests and purposes, a very genuine Ultramontane, of the older type"[45]. In Fénelon the baron found embodied, as he tells us quoting Möhler: "the interior beauty and glory of the Spirit of the Church" and "a rich treasury of Catholic piety, wisdom, and experience of life"[46]. Fénelon's spirituality was practical, active, with a constant attention to purity of intention and the importance of the present moment. It was a simple, homely yet utterly

---

43. As von Hügel wrote to W. Ward: "I was right in looking upon de Maistre as the founder of Modern Ultramontanism, and the earliest but one of the Traditionalists [de Bonald being the earliest]. The genealogical tree would be rightly the following:

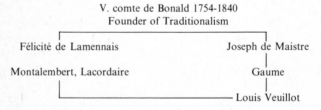

V. comte de Bonald 1754-1840
Founder of Traditionalism

Félicité de Lamennais   Joseph de Maistre

Montalembert, Lacordaire   Gaume

Louis Veuillot

You will see from this why and how it was easy, really, for Veuillot to forsake his liberal friends and become so violent a reactionary: the fact is both parties were really related: they were spiritual cousins". Von Hügel to W. Ward, 14 April 1892, SAUL.

44. As von Hügel wrote: "St. François de Sales and Fénelon in the past, Bishop Fessler, M. Foisset and Father Hilarius, Cardinal Newman and Father Ryder in our time, would, in various degrees and ways, represent this position". See n. 41, Ibid.

45. Von Hügel to W. Ward, 28 December 1892, SAUL. In an earlier letter to Ward on 8 December von Hügel wrote: "I find it is also Kraus' *idée fixe*, that we ought to push Fénelon to the front as our typical and ideal Ultramontane".

46. F. VON HÜGEL, *Fénelon's "Spiritual Letters"*, in *The Tablet*, 83, 1894, p. 858.

unworldly, childlike spirituality which recognised the advantages of hard
intellectual work and scholarship for the maintenance of the spiritual
life itself. It was as von Hügel said : "a piety bearing all about it the
marks of those spacious times which could develop within the
Church a Bossuet and a Richard Simon, a De Rancé and Mabillon"[47].

In these spacious times the baron discovered not only a deeper
tradition of spirituality and an authentic ultramontanism, but also the
first blossomings of historical-critical scholarship as witnessed, for
example, by Richard Simon and Jean Mabillon. The ideal of the scholar-
saint exemplified in this French spiritual tradition which von Hügel
made his own enabled him to cut through the party squabbles of
the liberal and ultramontane extremes and to occupy a unique but
isolated and little understood position above and beyond the current
fray. The baron recovered from the seventeenth century a tradition which
had been lost since the condemnation of Quietism and Fénelon (1699)
and Richard Simon and the historical-critical method (1682), both at
the instigation of Bossuet. Shortly after these condemnations the rout
of the saints and scholars took place and living religion headed towards
its inevitable decline. For now the mystical and interior element,
the germ of true religion was driven underground and replaced by
external devotions and rituals, and instead of sincere critical scholarship
and intellectual endeavour, uncritical submission and loyalty was
demanded to the decisions of an external authority. Such a situation
could continue so long as the Church clung to the old world and its
established position therein. But with the emergence of the modern
world the differences between Bossuet and Fénelon surfaced in the
split between the Theocrats and Traditionalists (Bonald and de Maistre)
and the romantic Liberals (Chateaubriand and Ballanche), the former
harking back to Bossuet, the latter to Fénelon. This breach quickly
narrowed and solidified into the neo-ultramontane party (Gaume and
Veuillot) and the liberals (Montalembert and Lacordaire). So long as
"the life of the mind" remained dormant within Catholicism and "the
things of, more or less political, policy and force"[48] were in the
ascendency, the conflict remained insoluable because its deeper implications were not appreciated and it was seen simply as a matter of policy,
even of party politics.

A partial recovery of the critical scholarly aspect of the tradition by
academic liberal catholicism (Döllinger) did not succeed because it
remained divorced from the deeper mystical, theological and philosophical aspects of religion. As von Hügel wrote to Wilfrid Ward in
April 1892 : "I have been thinking of how nearly right Erasmus and
Döllinger were (the latter until he broke away), apart from their

47. Ibid.
48. See n. 34, p. 521.

deficient devotional spirit"[49]. However, the recognition of all these dimensions of the problem began to emerge for the first time towards the end of 1892, when such men as von Hügel and Maurice Blondel began to take an active part in the philosophical and theological revival. In the hands of lesser men of both sides (the reformers and the authorities), the expected recovery would issue in the modernist crisis. And although the modernist revival was seemingly defeated in 1907 with the decrees *Lamentabili sane exitu* and more especially *Pascendi dominici gregis*, the deepest insights of the more solid thinkers of the time might be dampened but could not be silenced forever[50].

---

49. Von Hügel to W. Ward, 10 April 1892, SAUL.

50. As von Hügel wrote to René Guisan on 11 July 1921 : "You tell me that you love the Modernists; and I, I have had — I still have — among several who are so called, or who remain so labelled — very dear friends. Moreover those who love labels (I myself have a great fear of them) have not failed, very often, to classify me also as a modernist. But it seems clear to me that the whole history of christian theology could be grouped according as to whether one or other tendency or prevalent, more or less fixed idea, has prevailed — at least on the surface and in appearance — in the world of Christian thought. At one moment, it is Jansenism — everybody is Jansenist or is suspected of being such. Then it is quietism. Later it is liberalism. And finally modernism. — And then I notice how different, basically, the most solid thinkers of the same epoch, remain, even if they find themselves thus grouped under — basically — a sobriquet". S.L., p. 333.

CHAPTER II

THE MATURE ACTIVE YEARS (1893-1909)

VON HÜGEL'S ACHIEVEMENT

Von Hügel continued revising Wilfrid Ward's life of his father during January 1893. On 17 January, after reading the third edition of Henry Sidgwick's *Outlines of the History of Ethics*, he sent some notes to the author about the work. He made his first visit to Claude Montefiore on 23 January and so began a life long friendship with the great Jewish scholar. On the last day of the month the baron finished the fourteenth and last reading of his fourth set of Greek philosophy readings with Arthur Cook.

At the beginning of February von Hügel received a copy of Mgr. d'Hulst's "La question biblique" which had appeared in *Le Correspondent* on 25 January. On 18 March Wilfrid Ward forwarded the proofs of the Epilogue of his book and the baron commenced working on these immediately. As Ward admits in his foreword this epilogue was really a joint production of von Hügel and himself. The epilogue shows the baron at the beginning of this decisive year, 1893, quietly confident that the renewal which had been taking place within Catholicism in the spiritual, scholarly and institutional sphere would continue and blossom forth. As he wrote in Ward's book regarding the difficult question of the historical critical method: "the standards of works and criticism of the seventeenth century have again been taken up, after more than a century of theories"[51]. Von Hügel wrote to two of these critics, Mgr. d'Hulst on 19 April and to Abbé Loisy on the 30th, and on 3 May he received his first replies. Two days later he worked on some notes for Cardinal Vaughan who was to visit him that afternoon. While walking on the Heath both men discussed the biblical question and the Cardinal promised to allow him to write on the whole problem and on d'Hulst and Loisy in the *Dublin Review*.

May the 15th found von Hügel reading the *Jewish Quarterly Review* in preparation for a visit he intended to pay Claude Montefiore the following day. Two days later he wrote a note to Israel Abrahams[52] and on the 22nd he went to the Synagogue in Highbury St. with Mr. and Mrs. Spira (Spira was still teaching him Hebrew) where they

---

51. See n. 41, p. 373.
52. At this time both Montefiore and Abrahams were joint editors of the five year old *Jewish Quarterly Review*.

were in time for the second half of the service for the Second Day of the Feast of Weeks. During June the baron read a number of articles in the *Jewish Quarterly Review* and continued his Greek philosophy readings with Plato's *Laws*. July seems to have been a rather uneventful month. The only evidence of work is an insertion in the diary on the 8th of his having revised some Fénelon proofs for Mrs. Greene. During August he continued this revision for Mrs. Greene and managed some light reading. On the last day of August he began collecting material to refute some arguments the Rev. Walter Howard Frere had brought up to Rhoda von Schubert, a friend of the family, against her entering the Catholic Church. Von Hügel completed this and sent it to Rhoda on 7 September and six days later Rhoda came and spent three hours with him, presumably discussing the notes. The notes seemingly had the desired effect, for at 3 p.m. on the 27th Rhoda was received into the Catholic Church in the baron's presence [53].

During the first half of October von Hügel finished revising the proofs of Fénelon's *Spiritual Letters* and read the proofs of Purcell's *Life of Cardinal Manning*. On the 17th he left Hampstead for Paris where he arrived that evening and the next afternoon he visited the Abbé Loisy for the first time. The following day he called on Abbé Huvelin and went to see Loisy again on the 20th and afterwards called on Duchesne. Huvelin heard the baron's confession on the 21st and von Hügel returned two days later with his eldest daughter, Gertrude. The baron now commenced studying Ollé-Laprune's *La philosophie et le temps présent* and on 26 October Ollé-Laprune visited him and agreed to revise any philosophical papers he might write.

On 12 November von Hügel read Loisy's "La question biblique et l'inspiration des Ecritures" in the final issue of the *Enseignement biblique*. This controversial article was to be the occasion for Loisy's expulsion from the Institut Catholique. However, for the present the baron was more interested in religious philosophy and on 17 November, as the diary relates, he "began writing my Essays in Philosophy of Religion". On 20 November the thunderclouds burst with Loisy's announcement that he had lost his professorship of Semitic Languages at the Institut Catholique and that the Archbishop of Paris was suppressing the *Enseignement biblique*. After receiving the news von Hügel returned to writing his philosophical essays but on the 22nd he started a letter to Loisy. However, before finishing this he took a bus to Fréjus to see Mgr. Eudoxe Irénée Mignot, Bishop of Fréjus, for the first time [54].

53. These notes were published 37 years later as *Some Notes on the Petrine Claims*, London, 1930. Unless seen as a very early work of von Hügel, these notes can give a very misleading impression of the baron's views. Over the following ten years especially, the baron revised his scriptural opinions a great deal. Cf. BEDOYÈRE, pp. 63-4.

54. Many years later the baron recalled this first meeting with Mignot: "It was on

In Loisy's opinion this meeting marked the beginning of the modernist movement. Mgr. Mignot with his Vicar General, Abbé Ardoin, returned the baron's visit two days later and von Hügel's health was good enough to allow him to walk half way back to Fréjus with the two men. The baron continued his philosophical writing and his study of Greek philosophy during December. On the last day of the year he read Pope Leo XIII's encyclical "De Studiis scripturae sacrae", better known as *Providentissimus Deus*.

The Greek philosophical reading was continued until 13 January 1894 and on the 14th the baron started Rudolf Eucken's *Lebens-anchauung*. He finished his second reading of Gosselin's "Analyse du quiétisme" at the end of the month and thereafter began *Acte de la condamnation des quiétistes*. During February he read Bossuet's *Instruction sur les états d'oraison* and in March he finished Loisy's *Synoptiques* as far as printed and again took up Wörner's *J. A. Möhler*. On the 24th the baron began *Verhandlungen der Versammlung katholischer Gelehrten in München* (1863) which he completed on the 30th. His copy of this work is well annotated. On the inside cover of the book he makes the following remarks about Döllinger's "Rede über Vergangenheit und Gegenwart der katholischen Theologie" — the classic programmatic statement of liberal catholicism : "In Döllinger's Address many beautiful and great things : but his remarks about the Prophetic role in the Church and about the scientific gains of the Reformation and his despicable allusions about Pope are all painful and seductive ... Both the denial and even the ignoring of the fact that science also in its results is subject to the infallible teaching authority of the Church

November 22nd, 1893, that I first saw him, in circumstances vividly suggestive of his entire career. I had walked from the heaths and woods of the new health resort, Valescure, down to the ancient seaport townlet of Fréjus, where he had now been Bishop some eight years. He received me, a tall, erect, handsome man of fifty-one, a native of the Ile de France, with dark eyes and finely modulated voice, in his rambling old palace, in his study — a high up turret-chamber looking out on the sea. You looked down on the dried-up Roman harbour of Forum Julii, Caesar's foundation, whither Octavian, now soon to be Augustus, had sent some of Queen Cleopatra's galleys after their defeat at Actium. The Bishop sat there, environed by Bible editions and helps — Hebrew, Greek, Latin, French and English ; and every word he spoke revealed the man trained at S. Sulpice by M. Le Hir, that admirably thorough Hebrew scholar and teacher to whom Renan, Le Hir's pupil some twelve years earlier, admits owing his own, assuredly great, knowledge of Hebrew. The little sleepy, sun-baked, profoundly Southern town — the haunt of lizards and of fleas, of beggars and of much mouldering picturesqueness, thus environed a man full of mental activity and vigour — a mind rich in backward and in forward looking thought. He promptly plunged with me in to Old Testament questions as raised or renewed by Driver, Kirkpatrick, and other contemporary English scholars, or as suggested by the French critics or apologists — by Reuss or Loisy or Vigouroux — or as brought home to him by his own close personal study, especially of the Pentateuch". See n. 34, p. 519.

are both completely untenable. The whole account is very suggestive —
what is said about the scholastics never goes too far at all"[55].

At the end of March 1894 the baron resumed his philosophical
essay writing and continued this throughout the following month. He
visited Ollé-Laprune for two and a half hours on 25 April and
gave him the general outlines of fifteen essays he was preparing. Before
leaving Paris he paid three more visits to Loisy (receiving a loan of the
latter's memorandum containing his submission to the papal Encyclical)
and he also went to see Huvelin three times. The baron left Paris on
2 May and arrived home the next day. After finishing the Preface to
Ollé-Laprune's *Philosophie* on the 4th he began Blondel's *L'Action*.
However, he was drawn away from this by the current controversy on
Providentissimus Deus, for the following day he set about surveying the
various back numbers of *The Tablet* and *The Spectator* on what he
termed the "Biblical Encyclical". Four days later, on 9 May, von
Hügel began composing a letter to *The Spectator* concerning certain
views Charles Gore had put forward on the Encyclical. After completing
this on 14 May he sent it off to *The Spectator* and it appeared on the
19th under the title "The Papal Encyclical and Mr. Gore". In his note
von Hügel tried to interpret the encyclical as broadly as possible,
attempting to preserve a certain deference to papal teaching and at
the same time acknowledging the need of a certain autonomy in
biblical research[56].

On 16 May the baron began collecting material for a letter to *The
Tablet* on Fénelon's *Spiritual Letters*. In his letter which appeared on
2 June the baron pointed to the influence of Fénelon's spirituality
on both Stolberg and Möhler, and with reference to himself he
wrote: "Personally, I have been immensely helped by the St. Francis de
Sales-Fénelon-Grou type and hence have worked to help put those
helps within the reach of other also"[57]. On the day this letter appeared
von Hügel went to the Archbishop's house, Westminster, and had a
long talk over the biblical question with Cardinal Vaughan. Nine
days later he wrote to the Cardinal offering to write on the question.
As a result he received an invitation from Canon Moyes, the editor of the
Dublin Review to submit some articles on the Encyclical. The next day

55. *Verhandlungen der Versammlung katholischer Gelehrten in München von 28
September bis 1 October 1863*, Regensburg, 1863, Hüg.BX1536.V4, SAUL. Translation by
present writer.

56. As von Hügel wrote to W. Ward two days later: "You will have noticed
at once that I have gone as far as possible to the right as to the document's
doctrinal importance, as far as possible to the left as to its liberal interpretation.
This too, I think, the wiser course with an eye to Rome. They will either be
frightened at the quasi-finality with which the pronouncement gets treated, or pleased
and willing to pass a good deal of widening out". Von Hügel to W. Ward, 21 May 1894,
SAUL.

57. See n. 46, p. 858.

von Hügel wrote to Wilfrid Ward telling him that he intended his articles to be "neither a defence of the Encyclical nor an answer to Gore". And he continued : "The real question to my mind is whether there is or is not such a thing as a science of the Bible (as distinguished from its dogmatic and devotional use); and whether it is to be allowed to pursue its own method (as distinct from proclaiming any and every conclusion), and whether suppression of labour, or even of publication (again as distinct from broadcast dissemination), is not a danger as great as any that is attempted to be met"[58]. Here we catch a glimpse of what would become, in the coming years, the baron's preoccupation with obtaining acceptance and toleration within the Church for a science of the Bible with its own specific methods and partial autonomy within the theological process.

On 30 August von Hügel completed the first of his three articles on "The Church and the Bible : The Two Stages of Their Inter-Relation". In the articles the baron made a plea for a relative, functional autonomy of the historical-critical method. While admitting that the critic cannot conclusively demonstrate or even positively found the faith, he nevertheless affirms the important negative role the critic's results play in the determination of the faith. Soon after the appearance of his first article von Hügel set off for Paris where he arrived on 25 October. He immediately paid a visit to Loisy and Duchesne and the next day he went to see Abbé Huvelin. Two days later he began studying Fechner's *Die Drei Motive und Gründe der Glaubens*, a work which was to be of value when he came to articulate his conception of the three elements of religion. The baron prepared a rough draft of a letter about Louis Duchesne and the Anglican Orders issue for *The Tablet* on the 29th and after submitting the final draft to Duchesne on the 31st he sent it off to *The Tablet*.

On 1 November he returned again to the *Vita ed Opere di S. Caterina da Genova* as spiritual reading. Two days later he set off with his family for Rome, making a number of short stops on the way before arriving in Genoa on 8 November. The baron remained there for a full day and had confession, mass and communion at the *Ospedale di Pammatone* where St. Catherine worked for most of her life. A Capuchin showed the family around the hospital and they visited St. Catherine's two rooms and the Chapel with her shrine. In the afternoon von Hügel returned alone for a second guided tour with another Capuchin. On this occasion he spent three quarters of an hour praying before St. Catherine's shrine.

The next day the family set off for Rome where they arrived at 11.30 p.m. Four days later, on 14 November, von Hügel made his first acquaintance with the Barnabite scriptural scholar, Padre Giovanni

58. Von Hügel to W. Ward, 14 June 1894, SAUL.

Semeria, who was to become his life long friend. On 29 November
the baron had his first interview with Cardinal Rampolla, the
Secretary of State. Rampolla was so impressed with the baron that
he asked him to prepare a memorandum for the Pope on the subjects of
their discussion, i.e. Anglican Orders, the university question and the
scriptural situation in England after *Providentissimus Deus*. Von Hügel
began the memoir on 30 November and with the exception of a visit he
payed to Rampolla on 4 December, the whole of this month was
taken up with its preparation. The baron continued working on the
memorandum until he finished it on 9 January 1895. At 5 p.m. that
afternoon he took his 25 pp+ 12 pp (appendix) to Cardinal Rampolla
at the Vatican.

It was during this stay in Rome that von Hügel made his first
personal acquaintance with Maurice Blondel through the mediation
of Duchesne's predecessor at the *Ecole de Rome*, Paul Fabre. On
8 March the baron left his card at Blondel's and as the diary for the
following day recounts he returned from a visit to Cardinal
Rampolla (who was unable to see him because of ill-health) with
Maurice Blondel and Paul Fabre. While von Hügel now became more
interested in Blondel's philosophy he did not neglect his biblical studies
for on 3 April he arranged to learn biblical Aramaic from Professor
Ignazio Guidi of the Collegio Urbano and he resumed these lessons
when he returned to Italy the following December. In the meanwhile
he read a number of Blondel's articles and on 22 April he began a
systematic study of Blondel's *L'Action*.

Von Hügel's brother, Anatole, and his wife, Isy Froude, came to
Rome for a holiday in March so the baron spent most of the time
from now until he left on 8 May with them. The day after his
arrival in Paris, 18 May, von Hügel called on both Huvelin and Loisy
and after visiting both men twice more he left for home on 28 May.
The baron resumed his study of Blondel's *L'Action* on 8 June and
continued until he completed it on 1 July. On 4 July he began
collecting notes for his final article on "The Church and the Bible".
He worked on this article throughout July and when he finished it
on 21 August he sent it off to Canon Moyes. About this time von
Hügel completed Père Grou's *Oraison dominicale* as spiritual reading
and thereafter began Bossuet's *Etats d'oraison*.

During September the baron studied Hebrew with Spira and on
3 October 1895 he left London for Paris where he visited the Abbé
Duchesne, Fernand Portal and Loisy. A week later, after being joined
by his family, he journeyed to Genoa where he arrived on the 12th.
On the morning of the 13th von Hügel again heard mass and received
communion at St. Catherine's shrine and in the afternoon paid a
second visit. The following day he returned again and on the 15th,
after mass and communion at St. Catherine's shrine, he saw her

relic and visited her rooms in the hospital. The baron came back again in the evening accompanied by his wife and after visiting St. Catherine's shrine he attended benediction in the Church.

The family left for Florence on the 16th and travelled on to Assisi the following day. Von Hügel remained here for a month during which time he visited St. Francis' tomb and read his life. On 18 November he moved on to Rome where he renewed all his old friendships. However, within four days he had made a new acquaintance, F.X. Kraus. Kraus was the father of *Reformkatholizismus*, the movement which attempted to break out of the ghetto mentality of political Catholicism and replace it with religious Catholicism. Like Kraus, von Hügel felt that Catholicism had become imprisoned in the political edifice of the old world and that it would continue to decline until such time as it recovered its primary role as a religious institution. The baron visited Cardinal Rampolla on the 25th and the same evening Kraus called on his new friend. Kraus visited him again on 2 December and also on the 7th and 8th and the next day, as the diary relates, von Hügel "began setting prints of memoir for Cardinal Rampolla"[59]. This thirty-seven page memorandum on the attitude of English Catholics to Anglicans, when completed on 20 December, was presented by the baron personally to Rampolla.

During January 1896 von Hügel busied himself with the Anglican Orders issue, however, towards the end of the month he sent off two important letters: one to Rudolf Eucken on the 22nd and the second to Hermann Schnell on the 24th. Two days later he was introduced to Eugenio Pacelli (the future Pius XII), by Don Francesco Faberi and the baron took both men to see F.X. Kraus. On 1 February von Hügel received the first copy of Blondel's "Letter on Apologetics" from the author and began reading it immediately. At four o'clock on the 6th he attended a meeting of the *Società degli Studi Biblici* at the College of Propaganda at which Cardinal Lucido Parocchi presided and Don Francesco Faberi read a paper on specific passages from St. Paul. Don Eugenio Pacelli, by now a good friend of the baron, was also present and accompanied him home. Almost a month later, on 5 March, von Hügel himself presented a paper on some transpositions in St. Luke which was summarised in Lagrange's *Revue biblique* and noted as an important communication. The next day the baron learnt that he had been granted a papal audience. He immediately prepared

---

59. Diary, 20 December 1895. Later Lord Halifax wrote to the baron about this memorandum: "I am amused in looking over the correspondence to see that Cardinal Ledochowski evidently alluding to you, called your Memorandum upon the 'Orders' question 'un impertinenza' on the part of a layman. It passes my comprehension why the poor laity should not be allowed to have their opinions upon historical questions". C.L. Wood (Lord Halifax) to von Hügel, 5 September 1911, SAUL.

a little paper for the Pope and on the 7th, accompanied by Duchesne, he had a 22 minute audience with Pope Leo XIII.

During this time the Anglican Orders issue was the burning problem in Rome and von Hügel quite naturally became involved. The baron made some notes on English religious affairs for Duchesne in March and on 4 April he began translating Cardinal Manning's "Hinderances to the spread of Catholicism" with the Abbé Portal. After finishing half of this he left Rome on 7 April for Genoa where he again visited the shrine of St. Catherine. He remained in Genoa until 21 April when he left for Paris. As the diary relates the baron had a "long talk with Abbé Loisy at Neuilly" on the morning of the 23rd and at 4 o'clock in the afternoon he visited Huvelin for a talk and confession. He paid three more visits to Loisy and two to Huvelin and on 2 May he left Paris for home.

After finishing Eucken's *Lebensanschauungen* at the end of April von Hügel received a copy of Eucken's *Die Grundbegriffe der Gegenwart* from his wife as a birthday present and immediately began studying it. Lord Halifax visited him on 10 June and on the 16th both men went to Charing Cross Station to welcome Louis Duchesne and Samuel Berger, on their way to receive honorary doctorates at Cambridge. After the ceremony on the 18th the baron began reading Lord Acton's "The Study of History" and the next day he attended a luncheon-party at which Lord Acton was also present. Between 23 and 28 June von Hügel finished Eucken's *Der Kampf um einen geistigen Lebensinhalt* and on 9 July he began making notes for a review of the book. During August he studied Friedrich Paulsen's *Einleitung in die Philosophie* and thereafter Christoph Sigwart's *Vorfragen der Ethik*. On 19 September the baron's diary records "Telegram in *Standard* of Bull absolutely condemning Anglican Orders having appeared in Rome Previous Evening". Eight days later he wrote to Cardinal Vaughan accepting the Bull and proposing toleration of Portal's *Revue Anglo-Romaine*.

The baron left for Paris on 31 October and two days later he visited Loisy ("much very full talk on N.T. subjects"[60]) and the Abbé Huvelin. Von Hügel called on both men twice more and on 7 November Maurice Blondel came to see him. They met again the next day and "talked admirably about Scholastic Philosophy, fresh life for Theology, and on his conception of the place of the Incarnation (understood Franciscan-wise)"[61]. Von Hügel left Paris on the 9th and arrived in Genoa on the 11th. Much of his time in Genoa was spent with Semeria, but he paid a visit to the *Deposito di San Caterina* on the 14th. The baron

---

60. Diary, 2 November 1896.
61. Diary, 8 November 1896. Later in 1903-4 the baron was to disagree fundamentally with what he termed Blondel's Panchristocentricism. Cf. especially von Hügel's *Du Christ éternel* — VHB, no. 26.

arrived in Rome for his third winter stay on 23 November and immediately met his old circle of friends, Duchesne, Mignot, Ardoin, Guidi, Fabre, though when Eugenio Pacelli came to see him on the 29th the diary entry reads: "thought I noticed a change in his mind". A certain David Panziere called on him on 4 December and von Hügel engaged him for Hebrew readings commencing with Deuteronomy. The baron called on Enrico Gismondi, professor of exegesis at the Gregorian on 5 December and on the 22nd he visited Cardinal Rampolla for his first time during this visit.

During January 1897 the baron attended the annual meeting of the Biblical Society at Propaganda with Pacelli and Faberi and later on in the month he saw Cardinal Rampolla and put in "a word for Blondel"[62] who was now coming under criticism in Rome. February was taken up with his study and readings in Hebrew and in March the baron began Holtzmann's *Neutestamentliche Theologie* and resumed Wellhausen's *Israelitische und jüdische Geschichte*. The following month he read Lucien Laberthonnière's "Le problème religieux" and on the 23rd he left Rome for Florence to see Salvatore Minocchi and then travelled on to Genoa to visit Semeria. On 4 May he travelled to Paris and two days later he met Loisy and then Huvelin. On the 10th von Hügel made his first personal acquaintance with Lucien Laberthonnière and later in the evening the Abbé Hackspill accompanied by the Abbé Pierre Batiffol called on him. Hackspill brought the Abbé Touzard, professor of Old Testament at S. Sulpice, to see him on the 11th and after their discussions the baron left for a meeting with Ollé-Laprune. Von Hügel saw Loisy, Huvelin and Laberthonnière once again and on 15 May he left Paris for home.

Back in London the baron wrote to *The Tablet* protesting against the decision of the Holy Office in January 1897 affirming the authenticity of 1 Jn 5:7[63]. By the middle of June he had completed a detailed study of all the books of the Hexateuch in Hebrew so he agreed to accept an invitation to submit a paper to the fourth International Scientific Congress for Catholics to be held at Fribourg in August. He immediately began with the preparation of this paper and by 24 July he had already completed the English draft. After translating it into French he sent it off on 5 August to Semeria who was to read it to the Congress on the 16th. The paper entitled "La méthode historique et son application à l'étude des documents de l'Hexateuque" was well received, though Semeria's Italian accent did not facilitate its reception in French. The paper contained the results

62. Diary, 26 January 1897.
63. 1 Jn 5:7 "There are three witnesses in heaven: the Father, the Word and the Spirit and these three are one". For the decree of the Holy Office cf. *Acta Sanctae Sedis*, 29, 1896-7, p. 637.

of the best scholarly research on the Hexateuch over the previous 150 years and was regarded, with Père Lagrange's paper, as the best contribution in the scriptural section. As the *Revue critique* remarked: "Von Hügel has wished to show that the critical method is not arbitrary, that the difference in sources is based on literary evidence ... This difference is confirmed by the evolution of the ideas and institutions which allow us to date the sources approximatively... It is the first time that the opinions of modern criticism are defended so openly by a Catholic scholar"[64]. It is very likely that this display of advanced thought led to the scriptural section of the following Congress at Munich in 1900 being cancelled.

On 20 September von Hügel began a notice on Mrs. Elisabeth R. Charles for the *Hampstead Annual* and on the same day he wrote for the first time to George Tyrrell expressing agreement with the latter's *Nova et Vetera* and proposing a meeting[65]. Both men met on 9 October and came together once more before the baron left London on 30 October with Rome as his ultimate destination. As usual von Hügel stopped off at Paris to see Loisy, Huvelin, Laberthonnière, Ollé-Laprune, Marcel Hébert, Batiffol and during this visit he met the Abbé Félix Klein for the first time and read his *Vie du Père Hecker*. He left Paris on 9 November and proceeded to Genoa where he met Semeria and attended mass at the altar-shrine of St. Catherine. The baron arrived in Rome on the evening of the 18th and the following day, at the suggestion of Mgr. Denis O'Connell, Rector of the North American College in Rome, he began translating his Fribourg address on the Hexateuch into English for publication in *The Catholic University Bulletin* of Washington. Dr. Charles Augustus Briggs, the Hebrew and biblical scholar, was introduced to the baron by Mgr. O'Connell on the 19th. Three days later von Hügel began a précis of Père Lagrange's Fribourg article also for *The Catholic University Bulletin*. During the rest of November the baron met all his old Roman friends and on 14 December he had his first meeting with Dr. Albert Ehrhard, author of *Stellung und Aufgabe der Kirchengeschichte in der Gegenwart*. Ehrhard was absent when the baron went to visit him again on 19 December but in his place he found Dr. Sebastian Merkle.

Von Hügel continued the English translation of his Hexateuch paper throughout January 1898 and completed it on 13 February. F. X.

64. *Revue critique*, 43, 24 October 1898, pp. 276-7. Translation by present writer.

65. As the baron relates it: "It was I who began the correspondence, without ever having seen him, to thank him for the furtherance I had so abundantly found, in his *Nova et Vetera*, of 'ideas and tendencies' which had 'now, for so long, been part of my life's aim and combats'. He was then thirty-seven, and I was forty-five years of age. We first met on October 9, for one of many walks on Hampstead Heath". F. VON HÜGEL, *Father Tyrrell: Some Memorials of the Last Twelve Years of His Life*, in *The Hibbert Journal*, 8, 1910, p. 236.

Kraus arrived in Rome on 21 February and the following day he called
on von Hügel. That day the baron began the *Vita ed Opere di
S. Caterina da Genoa* once again as spiritual reading and over the
following two months his philosophical studies included the works
of Descartes, Spinoza and Fichte. Von Hügel left Rome on 26 April
breaking his journey at Genoa to visit Semeria and have photographs made of St. Catherine's portrait before continuing on by train
to Würzburg where he arrived on the evening of 8 May. The following
afternoon he visited Hermann Schnell and after their discussions
Albert Ehrhard collected him and both men had supper together. The
baron left Würzburg for Jena on 10 May and at 10 o'clock the next
morning Rudolf Eucken called on him at his hotel and brought him
home for lunch. In the afternoon both men began their first philosophical
discussion of the week. Another followed the next day and after their
third talk on 13 May Eucken took von Hügel "to a meeting of the
students' *Philosophische Gesellschaft*" at which, as the diary relates:
"Eucken said a few words and so did I". The baron attended a lecture
by Eucken "On Movement and Rest" on the 14th, had a fourth
discussion with him the following day and after their fifth philosophical
discussion on 16 May he prepared to leave Jena. Von Hügel
arrived in Brussels on 19 May and, after calling on Père Hippolyte
Delehaye, the Bollandist he set off for Ostend and arrived home on
20 May. Shortly afterwards he was admitted to hospital for a small
operation but was allowed home on 18 June. The baron then read
Arthur Balfour's *The Foundations of Belief* and thereafter began
Henri Joly's *The Psychology of the Saints*. On 26 July, the day he
completed this book, he received a letter from Genocchi "announcing
his destitution from Biblical Professorship"[66].

On 6 August von Hügel took the first positive steps which were to
lead to his *magnum opus*, *The Mystical Element of Religion*. He
began copying out references for an article on St. Catherine of
Genoa which he had promised Sydney Mayle, the publisher of *The
Hampstead Annual* and on 16 September his diary records: "began
writing my St. Catherine article". While working on this article on
3 October he wrote to George Tyrrell: "If I still could, I would
gladly get out of it altogether: I now incline to think I was rash and
mistaken in proposing to write on her, though it was, no doubt, only
as a substitute for the original proposal made to me, to write on
St. Catherine of Siena, or St. Teresa, or St. Francis Assisi"[67]. Within
three weeks the article was completed but on 30 October the baron had
to return to hospital for a second minor operation. Upon release, on

66. Diary, 26 July 1898.
67. M. D. Petre, *Von Hügel and Tyrrell: The Story of a Friendship*, London,
1937, pp. 41-2. Hereinafter referred to as *Von Hügel and Tyrrell*.

14 November, he visited Sydney Mayle and "accepted to expand St. Catherine article into a little book"[68]. As with many of von Hügel's endeavours the final result vastly overstretched the limits of the initial proposal. The proposed 120 page book eventually became the two volumed, 888 paged classical work on *The Mystical Element of Religion*.

On the evening of 27 January 1899 von Hügel attended a meeting of the Synthetic Society[69] and read a short reply to Wilfrid Ward's paper "Authority a Reasonable Ground for Religious Belief". The baron spent that night at the Westminster Palace Hotel and at 9.15 the next morning he set off for Paris. He visited Loisy on 31 January and on 8 February made his first acquaintance with Henri Bremond. Bremond called on von Hügel the next day and they spent three hours together. The following day the baron's new friend saw him off on his journey to Aix where Maurice Blondel met him and took him to stay at his house. For the next week both men were engaged in constant philosophical discussions before the baron set off to join his family on vacation at Grasse in the south of France.

During March von Hügel read Andrew Seth's *Man's Place in the Cosmos*, Richard Falckenberg's *Geschichte der neueren Philosophie*, Ehrhard's *Stellung und Aufgabe der Kirchengeschichte* and on 17 March Loisy's "La théorie du développement de la doctrine du C. Newman". On the 21st he went to Fréjus and after lunch he had a long talk with Bishop Mignot. He returned again on 13 April with his wife and Thekla and after a "long talk with Bp. Mignot" the diary records that "He [Mignot] made us hear his graphaphone". On 1 May von Hügel set out for Paris, stopping on the way at Lyon for four days with Henri Bremond. The day after his arrival in Paris he called

68. Diary, 14 November 1898. On 21 November the baron related the details to Tyrrell: "The publisher of the *Hampstead Annual* has proposed to me to publish, at his own risk and expense, a little book on St. Catherine of Genoa, and the questions suggested by her life, — something six times the length of the article as finally accepted. It has 3000 words, 16 large print 8 vo pp.; I would now be given 24,000 words, and 120 pp. large print 12 mo. I have accepted, since ... it would, I think, be an actual relief and bracing, to be able to unfold at a reasonable length what I have vainly tried to pack into those short pages; and indeed, even now, I have MS ready to fill, I think, quite 60 of these 120 mo pages. I want to try and carefully abstain from introducing any new points, and simply to attempt working out, as soberly and clearly as possible, the points I have, or had, indicated. I would make five chapters of it: (1) Introductory; (2) The Life; (3) Sanity and Sanctity; (4) Exterior Work and Interior Recollection; (5) Pantheism and Personality, — and each chapter could be a little longer than my present whole article". S.L., p. 74.

69. The Synthetic Society (1896-1908) was founded to consider the agnostic tendencies of the day and to help contribute to the upbuilding of a philosophy of religion. According to von Hügel the Society was not to be a continuation of the defunct *Metaphysical Society*, but, as he wrote: "we were to be all Theists of some kind, and were not to debate points not held by us in common, but simply on the best reasons and modes of presentation of the convictions we already had in common". S.L., p. 117.

on Huvelin and two days later, on 8 May, he received a visit from
Laberthonnière and later had a long talk with George Fonsegrive, the
editor of *La Quinzaine*. The baron journeyed to Neuilly to visit Loisy
on the 9th and after seeing Huvelin and Laberthonnière once more
he left Paris for London on 15 May.

17 May found von Hügel completing John Caird's *University
Sermons* and the following day he read Zeller's essay "Ueber Ursprung
und Wesen der Religion". Just over a month later he began his first
"Writing at the St. Catherine book"[70]. This work was to blossom
into his famous *Mystical Element*, but between its origin and the
book's final publication in November 1908 the baron had a long and
difficult road to travel. During July he began the section on Hellenism
for the first chapter of his book and he was greatly aided here by
Zeller's *Die Philosophie der Griechen* which he continually consulted on
Parmenides, Heraclitus, Socrates and Plato. He finished this preliminary
work on 11 August and during the second half of the month he
started *Vier Schriften von J. Ruysbroeck* and Joseph Surin's *Dialogues
spirituels* as spiritual reading.

After a short break von Hügel resumed his book-writing with Aristotle
on 11 September. At the end of the month he moved on to Plotinus
and in October to Philo. On 3 October he received a note from
Loisy's "announcing his retirement from Neuilly"[71] and in a reply nine
days later von Hügel "undertook to pay him 200 fr. a quarter
for 3 years beginning this (last) Michaelmasday"[72]. On 21 November
von Hügel left Hampstead for Paris where he met Bremond the
following day. He then went on to Bellevue to see Loisy and that
evening Laberthonnière called on him. The next day he visited the
Abbé Huvelin. After Paris the baron journeyed to Genoa where he
met Semeria who introduced him to two new friends, Guiseppe
Gallavresi and Tomassino Gallarati Scotti, both of whom were to play
important roles with him in the centre Catholic modernist periodical,
Il Rinnovamento[73]. In Rome, on 5 December, the baron resumed his
book-writing. Along with meeting all his old friends during the remainder
of the month, he managed to study Holtzmann's *Lehrbuch der neutestamentlichen Theologie*, Schmidt's *Leben Jesu* and Inge's *Christian
Mysticism*.

---

70. Diary, 19 June 1899.
71. Diary, 3 October 1899.
72. Diary, 12 October 1899.
73. *Il Rinnovamento*: a centre Catholic modernist periodical launched in Milan
in January 1907 and edited by A. A. Alfieri, Alessandro Casati, T. Gallarati-Scotti.
The periodical was strongly supported by von Hügel, cf. S.L., p. 172. In May 1907
Cardinal Steinhuber censured the Review naming von Hügel among others, cf. no. 127
below. The Review was forced to cease publication in December 1909.

During January 1900 von Hügel continued reading Inge and Holtzmann and at the end of the month he began William James' "The Will
to Believe". On 17 February he studied Ueberweg on "Gnosticismus"
and then on "Augustinus". He then broke off his study until April the
4th when he read Volkelt's *Kant's Erkenntnistheorie* and on the 18th
he returned to James' "Will to Believe". This latter work was especially
useful in helping him appreciate the experiential basis for the notion of
three elements in religion.

Throughout May von Hügel worked hard on his book. During the
first week he began Bergson's *Essai sur les données immédiates de la
conscience*. This work made a deep impression on him and along
with helping him articulate his views on time and eternity, it was
instrumental in him adopting a new more radically empirical conception
of experience. During this month also von Hügel began correcting the
proofs of Rudolf Eucken's *Der Wahrheitsgehalt der Religion*. The
distinction between universal religion and characteristic (particular)
religion proposed in this work was, as we shall see, accepted by
the baron.

Von Hügel left Rome for Genoa on 2 May and the following day he
was at the State archives examining "St. Catherine's first two vistas, with
the codicile to the first"[74]. Three days later he was back in the
archives making "extracts from volume of pamphlets etc., on St.
Catherine"[75]. Much of his free time in Genoa was spent in the
company of Semeria and before leaving for Paris on the 28th he had
a meeting with Gallarati Scotti and Guiseppe Gallavresi. In Paris
von Hügel saw Augustin Leger and Laberthonnière on the 29th, he visited
Loisy at Bellevue the next afternoon and the following day he went
to see the Abbé Huvelin. He returned to Huvelin on 1 June and the
next day he set out for home.

Back in London the baron renewed his book-work on 11 June,
beginning the section on St. Catherine's life. He continued reading and
working on this section until 26 July when he commenced a study
of the relationship between St. Catherine's *Vita* and her *Dialogo*.
August found the baron researching the sources of St. Catherine's
Trattato and while still working on this he received word that the St.
Catherine manuscripts had arrived at the British Museum from Genoa.
The next day, 20 November, he went to the museum and began his
"first work at Manuscript of St. Catherine"[76]. He visited the museum
consistently for three to four hours a day over the next week
and from then until the end of the year he worked on the manuscripts
approximately three times a week.

74. Diary, 3 May 1900.
75. Diary, 6 May 1900.
76. Diary, 20 November 1900.

After completing a précis of Fr. Sticker's *Life of St. Catherine* on the morning of 24 December the baron and his family went to spend Christmas at Herbert House with his mother-in-law, Lady Herbert of Lea. However, by 28 December he was back working on the St. Catherine manuscripts at the British Museum and the following day we find him reading "Dr. Max Scheler's thesis on Philosophical method"[77], sent to him by Rudolf Eucken, Scheler's professor.

Von Hügel's diary for 1901 is missing and so a detailed examination of his activities during this year is not possible. In January his wife and daughter, Hildegard, set off for Cannes while the baron remained at home with his youngest daughter, Thekla. Much of his time was in fact spent in attending to his sick sister, Pauline, who died after a long suffering illness on 29 March. It was during this period that von Hügel wrote his first letter to Ernst Troeltsch, a man who was to have a considerable influence on him[78]. Towards the end of April the baron travelled to Paris to see Loisy[79] and some of his French friends and then journeyed on the Switzerland. In order to ward off the criticism which was now beginning to mount against Loisy, von Hügel wrote to Cardinal Rampolla suggesting that a condemnation of Loisy would discredit the Roman Church among intellectual and university circles in England. He also wrote a letter to the review *Studi Religiosi* pleading Loisy's case as the most prominent Catholic scholar in historical criticism.

In October the baron and his family moved from Switzerland to Rome and in an interview with Cardinal Rampolla a few days after his arrival he warned the Cardinal of the detrimental effects any condemnation of Loisy would have on English public opinion. Through his friend, Giovanni Genocchi, he had a paper of his presented to Alberto

77. Diary, 29 December 1900.

78. Von Hügel gives us further details of this letter when he writes : "I wrote and told him all I had found in his writings, and received his first letter in April, 1901. 'It is an extraordinary joy to me to meet in you a man who, by his thinking and seeking, has been led along ways similar to my own.' And he then 'entirely assents' to my adverse judgment on the Ritchlian theologians, Kaftan and, especially Wilhelm Herrmann, as to their hostility to all philosophy in religion, their (violently Pauline) concentration upon only the Passion in the life of Jesus Christ, and their (more than Pauline) refusal to find God in any degree outside of His revelation in the historic Jesus". F. VON HÜGEL, *Ernst Troeltsch*, in *T.L.S.*, 1106, 1923, p. 216.

79. He wrote later to Tyrrell about this visit : "I also saw Loisy, twice; in better physical health than I have known him for some years, and as witty and astonishingly master of his great subjects as ever. Certainly, his writings, remarkable as they are, give but a very incomplete picture of his astonishing deep and delicate, wide and detailed outlook and perception. Generations will pass, before we are likely to again have anything like as complete a combination of as thoroughly worked out and mature qualities and competences. Meanwhile, his opponents are busier and more determined than ever". *Von Hügel and Tyrrell*, p. 77.

Lepidi (Master of the Sacred Palace). In his paper von Hügel "distinguished between questions of *orthodoxy*, which were his [Lepidi's], and of *policy* which were Cardinal Rampolla's ... and the question of *science* : that on this latter ... we were face to face, not with a question of individuals and their possible or real eccentricities; or of specific theological doctrines, true or false; but with that of a new science with its own immanent method, laws, and practically irresistible force"[80]. After Lepidi read the baron's paper he informed Genocchi that von Hügel could visit him. At the subsequent meeting Lepidi examined the baron on his conception of "Inspiration, Inerrancy, Development, Relativity, Scandal, Pious Ears, German Rationalism, French *fougue*"[81]. And when he seemed satisfied he asked von Hügel to help him "reconstitute the poor little defunct Biblical Society"[82]. The baron refused since he felt, at this stage, that his place lay on the side of the scholars seeking more autonomy and freedom for the critical method rather than with the authorities. Lepidi urged von Hügel to reconsider his decision. However, on 7 December the baron sent him a firm refusal. As he wrote to Loisy on 1 January 1902, he told Lepidi that : "I would have to wait and see what would happen me and my friends before we ourselves could act with the authorities"[83].

By this time plans for the organisation of the Biblical Commission were already at an advanced stage and on 4 January 1902 *The Tablet* was the first paper to announce its creation. Von Hügel's diary for 3 January reads : "News of Biblical Commission first published (in Tablet)". Father David Fleming, the Irish born Vicar-General of the Franciscans, who was the Secretary of the Commission leaked the news to *The Tablet* before it was officially announced in Rome. On 9 January von Hügel paid a visit to Louis Duchesne and while there he met Amelli, the Abbot of Monte Cassino, a member of the Commission, who showed him the Biblical Commission papers with names and guests. The baron was quite happy with the composition of the Commission[84].

80. Ibid.
81. Ibid, pp. 94-5.
82. Ibid, p. 98.
83. A. LOISY, *Mémoires pour servir à l'histoire religieuse de notre temps*, Paris, 1931, vol. II, p. 79.
84. As the baron wrote to Fleming on 14 January : "From what Monseigneur Mignot and I have been able to gather, I hope and trust so much, ... that this Commission. being practically permanent, will be able to take its time over its practically inexhaustible subject, — a subject which is still so much *in fieri*, in process of becoming a special science; that complainants and denouncers will have henceforth, on this subject, to address themselves to the Commission; and that this Commission, though practically a substitute, on this matter, for the Roman Congregations, will not, either in intention or in fact, suppress or limit, or attempt to do so, the work of Catholic scholars not upon it. It is because we take it as certain that the intention, and as probable that the actual effect of this Commission will be to gain time, both for corporate authority

On 22 January von Hügel resumed working on his book and by 8 March he had finished the "Life and Works" part and began planning for the chapter on the psycho-physical and temperamental questions involved in the life of St. Catherine. The baron read Houtin's *La question biblique* on 28 March. The book was attacked by members of the French hierarchy and Loisy believed that its publication was instrumental in bringing fresh pressure from Paris for his own condemnation. In the meanwhile Rome had still refrained from officially announcing the members of the Biblical Commission. Von Hügel took the initiative and prepared another paper for Cardinal Rampolla and when he saw the Cardinal on 5 April he urged the publication of the names of the Commission, as he believed this would act as a moderating influence for the attacks on Loisy. The baron left Rome for Genoa on 23 April. While there he saw Semeria a number of times and received a visit from Salvatore Minocchi. He also spent some time in the *Biblioteca Urbana* studying and copying the manuscript of St. Catherine's life. On 27 April, the Feast of St. Catherine of Genoa, von Hügel attended two masses at her *Deposito* and received communion. Later in the day he went with Semeria to Pra and "saw site and grounds of St. Catherine's old villa there, and site of stables (the chapel of her time), ... Taken to Misericordia Sodality Chapel close by, where we saw 'Christ appearing to St. Catherine (XVIIIth century) picture' from that old Church"[85]. The following day von Hügel returned to the University library where he worked on the St. Catherine manuscripts and discovered the dates of the death of both Don Jacobo Carenzio and Don Cattaneo Marabotto. That evening he left Genoa for Milan where he joined his wife and visited his friends, Gallarati Scotti and Padre Pietro Gazzola. Both he and his wife left Milan for Heidelberg on 2 May and the next morning Ernst Troeltsch called on him for the first time[86].

and for private work; to suspend the exercise and perhaps finish by weakening the habit of the denunciatory instinct so rife elsewhere; and to furnish more security of toleration for Catholic pioneer's work, — which would thus most rightly and indeed necessarily pursue its course neither approved in its particulars nor condemned, but tolerated, and would be then utilized later on, in what ever had proved itself and would be approved as true: it is because of these three closely related expectations that we are hopeful and glad as to this commission, and congratulatory to yourself". Von Hügel to D. Fleming, 14 January 1902, Franciscan archives London.

    85. Diary, 27 April 1902.

    86. Diary, 3 May 1902. Von Hügel is mistaken when he wrote later: "It was there [in Baden] that, after studying his writings for five years, I first communicated with him and visited him in April 1902". F. VON HÜGEL (ed.), *Christian Thought, Its History and Application*, London, 1923, p. XII. And again when he wrote: "I spent a week with him at Heidelberg at the end of that April 1901 — my first and last sight of him". F. VON HÜGEL, *Ernst Troeltsch*, in *T.L.S.*, 1106, 1923, p. 216. Troeltsch's considerable influence on the baron has not been sufficiently acknowledged.

Von Hügel left Heidelberg on 5 May to visit Rudolf Eucken at Jena. In the train he finished Troeltsch's two papers on Wilhelm Herrmann's *Ethik* entitled "Grundprobleme der Ethik". The following day Eucken called on him and in the afternoon they visited the "Schelers, tea there and talk and walk with him [Max Scheler]"[87]. The baron stayed in Jena for a week during which time he had a number of philosophical talks with Eucken and Scheler and attended a meeting of their Historical and Philosophical Society. Eucken and Scheler saw the baron off from the station in Jena on 12 May and while Lady Mary remained with some friends near Neuss, her husband returned to England. As the diary for 15 May 1902 reads: "Arrived at Liverpool St. (London) at 8. By outer Circle Railway to Hampstead Heath. Walked up to Holford Road, — home again, after 18 months". However, within a week the baron was off again, this time for a week at Cambridge where he completed the second volume of James Ward's *Naturalism and Agnosticism* and met and dined with Ward for the first time on the 27th. Three days later he received a number of off-prints from Ward. These, along with some later articles of Ward, were to be the decisive factors in von Hügel's acceptance and articulation of a broader more radically empirical conception of experience.

Back in London on 5 June the baron returned to his study of St. Catherine and mysticism reading William James' *The Varieties of Religious Experience* on 17 July and finding its first chapter "simply admirable"[88]. During August the baron visited his mother and brother in Cambridge and later went to Hickleton Hall where he spent three days with Lord Halifax. On 18 August he travelled on to Richmond, Yorkshire, for a holiday with his good friend, George Tyrrell. He remained with Tyrrell until 6 September during which time he read and discussed the letter's *Religion as a Factor of Life* and *Oil and Wine*.

After returning home the baron resumed his own book-work on 11 September but on the 25th he paid another visit to Cambridge and called on James Ward. Three days later he began Ward's "Psychological Principles" and on 8 October Ward's famous articles on "Psychology" in the ninth and tenth editions of the *Encyclopaedia Britannica*. These articles were of immense importance in laying the basis for von Hügel's later development of a radical empiral conception of experience. While still studying these articles he returned to Cambridge and on 12 October had, what he termed, a "most instructive talk"[89] with Ward, most probably about the latter's notion of experience.

87. Diary, 6 May 1902.
88. W. JAMES, *The Varieties of Religious Experience*, London, 1902, Hüg. B945.J2, SAUL, inside front cover.
89. Diary, 12 October 1902.

Back in Hampstead on 13 October the baron continued his work on St. Catherine but, soon overworked, he was compelled on medical advice to take a break from study. However, he was not allowed much respite, for on 6 November the first four copies of Loisy's *Etudes Evangéliques* arrived and four days later his ill-fated *L'Evangile et l'Eglise*. From now until the end of December von Hügel busied himself reading and propagating Loisy's book and it was only on the last day of the year that he was able to return to Ward's "Psychology" articles.

January the 13th, 1903, saw the completion of the "whole of Vol. I of St. Catherine"[90] and on the same day the baron "resumed writing at ch. XI", the first chapter of his second volume. He received a note from Loisy on the 21st telling him of Cardinal Richard's pastoral condemning *L'Evangile et L'Eglise* as seriously disturbing the faith of the laity in the fundamental dogmas of Catholic teaching. Over the next two and a half years von Hügel's defence of Loisy consumed a great deal of his time and energy and postponed the eventual completion of his *Mystical Element* for a number of years.

While on a visit to the Duke of Norfolk at Arundel Castle on 8 February the baron happened to see the previous day's *Tablet* and to his surprise he discovered the "names of the 40 consultors of the new Biblical Commission"[91]. The original twelve members of the commission were now swamped by twenty-eight men who, in von Hügel's opinion, were either scholastically trained scholars or non-scriptural men at all. His diary entry for the day remarks that the commission had "all the old party on it" and in a letter to Loisy the following day he admitted that the new list meant a "victory for the other side"[92].

Throughout February and March the reactions arising from Loisy's *L'Evangile et l'Eglise* preoccupied von Hügel and on 8 April these prompted him to initiate a correspondence with A.L. Lilley[93]. Twelve days later he walked to St. Mary's Terrace where, as the diary relates, he visited "the Rev. A.L. Liley [sic]: my 1st sight of him. Two hours talk. Lent him art. of Laberthonnière's, 3 arts. of Fr. T[yrrell]; and addits to Loisy's (abandoned) 2nd ed. of his l'Ev. et Egl.". Lilley would soon become one of the baron's closest friends

90. Diary, 13 January 1903.
91. Diary, 8 February 1903.
92. See n. 83, p. 217.
93. As the baron wrote to Tyrrell in an unpublished letter: "Revd. A.L. Lilley, the (Anglican) vicar of St. Mary Magdalen's Paddington, whose two papers on Loisy, one in the *Guardian*, Febr. 25, and the other in *The Commonwealth* March, have much pleased and interested me. I am going to try and know him: must be a powerful, masculine mind: an Irishman; and seems to personally know so many of our workers abroad". Von Hügel to Tyrrell, 3 April 1903, BM.

and he assisted von Hügel immensely during the terrible years of the modernist crisis.

Loisy's problems now began to take up an inordinate amount of the baron's time for, as the diary shows, he was continually breaking off his book-work to go to Loisy's defence and aid in various correspondences and public letters. On 2 May he began preparing a paper which he had been invited to read before the Synthetic Society. The paper entitled "Experience and Transcendence" was presented before the Society on 28 May. Although in his paper von Hügel concentrated on the experiential approach to God his method was to examine the manifestations of religious experience historically rather than philosophically. In other words, he attempted to uncover and expose this experience through a variety of testimonies offered to it by a number of Jewish and Christian representatives over the centuries. A little over two years later when asked by Wilfrid Ward to publish this paper in the *Dublin Review* the baron was forced to concede that his thought had undergone such a fundamental change in the interval that he would have to rewrite the paper. While the new paper bore the same title its approach was philosophical rather than historical and unveiled for the first time the baron's novel, wider, more empirical notion of experience as the basis and framework for his analysis of religious experience. As we shall see, by 1906 the influence of James Ward, Henri Bergson and William James has taken root and von Hügel has made the breakthrough to a full articulation of his radically empirical conception of experience.

While still labouring on his book on 20 July, the baron received word of the death of Pope Leo XIII and on 3 August his diary notes : "Cardinal Guiseppe Sarto, Patriarch of Venice, elected Pope (Pius X), at 11 a.m."[94]. Von Hügel spent his annual holiday with Tyrrell at Richmond in mid-August, after which he stayed at Cambridge and on 12 September he left Cambridge and "Drove in cab to 13 Vicarage Gate, Kensington, to begin residence there"[95].

The baron resumed his book-work at the start of October and on the 23rd of the month he visited the new Archbishop of Westminster, Francis Bourne, for the first time. As the diary relates they "talked about Hogan, Mignot, Touzard; Semeria, Duchesne, Biblical Commission — Tyrrell's *Oil and Wine*". On 9 November Joseph Wicksteed and Wilfrid Ward called on von Hügel and the three men discussed the "possible foundation of a London Theological Society"[96]. This initiative

94. Years later referring to this date he wrote : "August 3 1903 — Mid February 1906 — The accession of Pius X. rapidly brought on the bursting of the storm [the modernist crisis], although the tempest's full height was not reached till 1907". See n. 65, p. 240.

95. Diary, 12 September 1903.

96. Diary, 9 November 1903.

would eventually result in the formation of the London Society for the Study of Religion. On his appointment as Pius X's Secretary of State the baron sent an "important letter of congratulation and in favour of Loisy to Cardinal Merry del Val"[97] on 11 November, but as his diary notes the reply was "short, entirely evasive, possibly snobby". A little over a month later, on 17 December, in a decree of the Inquisition *L'Evangile et L'Eglise* along with four other books of Loisy was put on the Index[98].

During January 1904 almost all of the baron's time was taken up correcting the proofs of the "Lettres Romaines"[99] and in defending Loisy. On the 22nd he began a rough draft of an address entitled "Official Authority and Living Religion" which he read before the Rota Society on 28 January. The address was to be the baron's most sustained and severe criticism of the church authorities and it was only published posthumously. During the following weeks and months the baron was continually busy correcting the proofs of the "Lettres Romaines", defending Loisy and the relative autonomy of the historical critical method, especially in his correspondence with Blondel and again in public debate with Blondel in *La Quinzaine*[100].

In response to an inquiry from Dr. James Hastings von Hügel wrote to him on 23 March "with 10 suggestions for writers of articles in his *Dictionary of Religions*"[101]. He himself proposed to take four: Eternal Life, Intermediate State, Christian Mysticism and Quietism. On 11 April he journeyed to Cambridge and the next day he visited James Ward and received a copy of his article on "The Definition of Psychology". Von Hügel completed a careful reading of this on the 14th and at 2.30 p.m. he went to see Ward and both men had a "good talk about Loisy; his [Ward's] paper; Hastings' Dictionary of Religion; his [Ward's] coming American tour; and recent psychological and religious philosophy work"[102]. The baron left Cambridge on the 16th and two days later he resumed work on an article "Du Christ éternel" which he was preparing for *La Quinzaine* in defence of

97. Diary, 11 November 1903.

98. The other four books were: *La Religion d'Israel, Etudes Evangéliques, Autour d'un petit livre* and *Le Quatrième Evangile*.

99. The baron acted as the intermediary for these "Lettres Romaines" which were published in *Annales de philosophie chrétienne*, 3rd series, Vol. 3:4-6, January-March 1904, pp. 349-59; 473-88; 601-20. Although he was suspected of being the author himself, von Hügel never divulged the name to anyone. The actual author is now said to have been Giovanni Genocchi (1860-1926).

100. R. MARLÉ, *Au cœur de la crise moderniste. Le dossier inédit d'une controverse*, Lettres de Maurice Blondel, H. Bremond, Fr. von Hügel, Alfred Loisy..., Paris, 1960, and J.J. KELLY, The *Modernist Controversy: von Hügel and Blondel*, in *Ephemerides Theologicae Lovanienses*, 55, December 1979, pp. 279-330.

101. Diary, 23 March 1904.

102. Diary, 14 April 1904.

Loisy and the relative autonomy of the historical critical method against Blondel. On completion he sent the manuscript to Henri Bremond for translation into French while he himself "wrote communi- cation for *Times*, to precede the Saunders-Loisy letters and sent them, with a letter of conditions to Bailey Saunders"[103]. The following day, 27 April, Joseph Wicksteed called again to discuss what was now termed "The London Historical Theology Society" and on the 16th of the following month von Hügel went to Caxton Hall, Westminster, where the programme and rules of the new society now definitively called "The London Society for the Study of Religion" were laid down. The next day the baron completed the first three parts of a five part paper on "Biblical Criticism and the Life of Faith" and presented it at a *Rota* meeting that evening. This diary reference is, unfortunately, the only one we found to the existence of such a paper.

During the first half of June von Hügel read C. P. Tiele's *Elements of the Science of Religion* and F. C. S. Schiller's "Activity and Substance", two works which were to feature in his *Mystical Element*. Thereafter he revised the chapter on "Catherine's Life from 1473 to 1506, and its Main Changes and Growth", and then commenced studying for the section on "The Main Literary Sources of Catherine's Conceptions". The baron went to Caxton Hall on 8 July for the second informal gathering of "The London Society for the Study of Religion", more generally known as the L.S.S.R. Along with von Hügel the meeting was attended by George Ernest Newsom, Claude Montefiore, Estlin Carpenter, Henry Corrance (his first attendance) and Joseph Wicksteed. The meeting decided to bring the membership of the Society up to 30: "7 Anglicans, 6 Catholics, 3 Jews, 3 Unitarians, 2 Congrega- tionalists, 2 Presbyterians, 2 Quakers, 1 Wesleyan, 1 Baptist and 3 Nondescripts"[104], truly an ecumenical group.

Archbishop Eudoxe-Irénée Mignot arrived on 16 July and stayed with von Hügel at Vicarage Gate until the 20th when the baron accompanied him to Oxford and Cambridge to meet some of his friends there. After Mignot returned to France on the 27th von Hügel resumed work on

103. Diary, 26 April 1904.
104. Diary, 8 July 1904. In 1922 Nathan Söderblom wrote of von Hügel and his Society: "this old, fine nobleman [von Hügel], now in London, ... forms a pilgrim's resort for seeking and religiously thinking personalities from various countries and communions and where his Society for Research in Religion gathers Anglicans, Nonconformists, Jews, Roman Catholics, Agnostics and even one Lutheran in a small selected circle to confidential and clever discourses about religious problems". N. Söderblom to von Hügel, 26 April 1922, SAUL. In a jocund reply the baron wrote: "But, my dear Archbishop, just think, you have given me credit for large-heartedness only up to fifty per cent of the reality, for our Religion Society now holds, not one Lutheran but two Lutherans; and very useful, pleasant members they are". Von Hügel to Nathan Söderblom, N.S. Stiftelsen Uppsala Universiteitsbiblioteket, Uppsala, 1 June 1922.

the "Literary Sources" section of his *Mystical Element* and put the final touches to a "rough draft of St. Catherine's utilization of St. Paul"[105] on 9 August. The next morning Lady Mary left for a holiday at Fort Augustus (Scotland) and in the afternoon the baron set off for a vacation with George Tyrrell at Richmond where he remained until 5 September. He then proceeded on to Glencoe, finishing the sixth of Troeltsch's articles "Was heisst 'Wesen des Christenthums'?" during the train journey. The baron returned home from Scotland on 17 September and two days later he was reading up on the Johannine Writings in Holtzmann's *Lehrbuch der Neutestamentlichen Theologie* for his chapter on the "Literary Sources of St. Catherine's Teachings". When he completed this Johannine section on 6 October he immediately began examining the influence of Pseudo-Dionysius on St. Catherine. Von Hügel continued working on Dionysius over the next two weeks. However, on 12 October he received definitive news that Gertrude, his eldest and favourite daughter, had tuberculosis and must enter a sanatorium at Davos. The illness would eventually lead to her early death, in 1915, at the age of thirty-eight. After arranging matters for Gertrude he continued his book-work, finishing a rough draft of his "Literary Influences" chapter on 7 November and the next day he "began first sketch of last 4 cc. of book"[106]. December the 6th saw the "First Paper-meeting of the L.S.S.R."[107] with A. L. Lilley in the Chair and a paper read by a Dr. Hunter from Glasgow entitled "The Tendencies to Religion in the Nature and Life of Man". Von Hügel was the first to speak, making three points "as to certain cautions to be observed in seeking God within ourselves"[108]. The baron continued working on his book during the rest of the month copying out passages from Spinoza and Kant and on the 24th he and his family left home to spend Christmas with his mother-in-law at Herbert House.

Von Hügel resumed working on *The Mystical Element* on 2 January 1905, completing the section on Hell on 21 February and beginning his treatment of Purgatory two days later. On 4 March he read the last chapter of the first volume of Edward Caird's *The Evolution of Theology in the Greek Philosophers*. On the 27th he broke off his book-work to visit his mother and brother in Cambridge where he also called on James Ward and received two new important articles from him. Two days later he read the first of these entitled "Philosophical Orientations and Scientific Standpoints" and the following day he finished the second, "The Present Problems of General Psychology"[109].

105. Diary, 9 August 1904.
106. Diary, 8 November 1904.
107. Diary, 6 December 1904.
108. Ibid.
109. James WARD, Philosophical Orientation and Scientific Standpoints, *University*

This latter most significant article of Ward's was to be decisive in von Hügel finally adopting and articulating a new position in epistemology which can be termed a radical empiricism of the metaphysical type.

The baron returned home from Cambridge on 1 April and on the 10th he started writing a paper on "The Place and Function of the Historical Element in Religion". After completing the final draft a week later he sent it to Joseph Wicksteed and on 2 May he read his paper before a meeting of the L.S.S.R. From the latter half of April onwards von Hügel worked continuously on his book until 28 July when his diary proudly announced "Finished 1st draft of whole book". He then began revising and expanding his final chapter and on 4 August he "began Preface to book".

In need of a holiday the baron left home for Hickleton Hall (Yorkshire), the family seat of Lord Halifax, on 7 August. The following day he "had a long talk with Halifax about Scripture Criticism" and the next day he "left Hickleton at 1.30 for Richmond ... arrived 5.47"[110]. George Tyrrell, von Hügel's closest friend, was at the station to greet him. The baron stayed with him until 29 August. During this period he finished studying Boutroux's *Pascal* (14th) and Höffding's *Kierkegaard* (22nd), and resumed reading Edward Caird's *The Evolution of Theology in the Greek Philosophers*. On the 17th he agreed to a proposal from Wilfrid Ward to contribute his 1903 "Experience and Transcendence" paper to the January issue of the *Dublin Review* of which Ward was the editor. Von Hügel then left Richmond and journeyed on to Inverness for a holiday with his wife.

After returning to London on 7 September he continued studying Caird's *Evolution of Theology* which he finished on the 28th. On the last day of the month Semeria payed the baron a visit. An extraordinary meeting of the L.S.S.R. was held on 10 October and Semeria delivered a paper in French on the "Present State of Religion and Religious Studies in Italy". However, the cumulative influence of his summer reading began to make itself apparent now as we learn from a highly important hitherto unpublished letter of von Hügel to Wilfrid Ward on 24 October 1905 regarding the proposed publication of his 1903 Synthetic paper "Experience and Transcendence". The baron wrote : "the article that I undertook to give you for your January no. I am in serious perplexity about it, for the following reasons. When I accepted, I did so, as you will remember because I then sincerely believed that I could let you have "Experience and Transcen-

Chronicle (California) September 1904, pp. 1-24. Offprint among von Hügel's miscellaneous papers, SAUL. James WARD, *The Present Problems of General Psychology*, in *Philosophical Review* (American) 13, 1904, pp. 603-21.

   110. Diary, 8 August 1905.

dence", substantially as I printed it for the "synthetic", i.e. with only such changes as the difference of audience and an attempt at more ready understandableness might require. But, on carefully studying it these last days, I have come to feel, *quite clearly and finally*, that I have, — evidently gradually and, up to now, all but unconsciously, — *seriously changed my own views* on the important matter in question. Just exactly the most emphatic passages, and indeed the general drift and emotional tone of the whole, no more represent what I believe to be true. So that I could not let you have it without, practically, producing a new paper, of a different tone and drift, in which I could incorporate parts of *this* article, — but these parts would perform different functions from those allotted to them in their present positions. — I find that it has been James Ward's criticism and the study of Höffding's *Kierkegaard* and Caird's *Theology in the Greek Philosophers* (these books were only finished by me with the end of my holiday, 4 weeks ago) which, have produced this change in me"[111]. This decisive but nowhere adverted to admission by von Hügel marks the turning-point in his search for a wider and more truly empirical notion of experience. On the basis of this breakthrough we shall propose a reinterpretation of von Hügel's religious philosophy in Part II.

Another article of James Ward entitled "Mechanism and Morals" which emphasised the importance of the subjective pole within experience and the difference between the historical and the natural sciences was also to exert an influence on von Hügel. But now, at the end of October, the baron was once again drawn away from his studies for over the next month he was busily engaged in attempting to secure a bishop for George Tyrrell who was seeking release from the Society of Jesus. On 27 November von Hügel set off for Cambridge to visit his mother. While there he re-read Ward's "Mechanism and Morals" and on 1 December he spent an hour and a half in deep discussion with Ward. During the remainder of the month the baron attended the monthly meeting of the L.S.S.R. and read Raoul Gout's *John Henry Newman* and Antonio Fogazzaro's *Il Santo* before resuming his own book-work on 30 December.

On 3 January 1906 von Hügel began revising the final draft of chapter XIX of his *Mystical Element*. On 15 February Wilfrid Ward wrote urging the baron to prepare his "Experience and Transcendence" article for the April issue of the *Dublin Review*. Consequently von Hügel decided to postpone the conclusion of *The Mystical Element* and began immediately on a scheme for the article. In the afternoon of the same day he sent a telegram to Stauffer's bookshop for Harald Höffding's *Religionsphilosophie* which arrived three days later. On the

111. Von Hügel to W. Ward, 24 October 1905, SAUL.

16th he spent two hours on his article, however, in the evening he received a letter from Tyrrell saying that "the general gives him notice to quit S.J.'s"[112]. The baron called to see Tyrrell on the 18th and two days later he returned for a long talk. The diary for this date notes "The Provincial came yesterday and handed him [Tyrrell] his expulsion from the Society, — on grounds of his non-repudiation of the *Corriere della Sera's* account of the 'Letter to a Professor'". On the 22nd von Hügel returned to his article and four days later he finished his "16 pp. ms and sent it off to typist"[113]. The diary for the 28th notes "Finished copying out fair of my 'Experience and Transcendence' 9900 words long". The following day he reduced this to 8500 words and sent it to Wilfrid Ward.

On 7 March the baron resumed the conclusion of his book. Eight days later he wrote to Tyrrell : "Wilfrid Ward has taken my Paper, — it appears in the April *Dublin Review* — with only the opening modified into something a good bit Wardian. But all the rest remains untouched"[114]. In his introduction von Hügel called for a shift away from the current abstract discursive and deductive method in theology and a return to a more concrete experiential and inductive approach. He then proceeded to develop and articulate consistently for the first time a wider more radically empirical notion of experience and to demonstrate that a faithful analysis of the data of experience delivers an increasing and cumulative variety of evidence for holding some "direct and deep, though dim and only indirectly ascertainable, experience by the human soul of the Infinite and God"[115].

On 25 April von Hügel took up his book-work once more and in the afternoon set out to look for some rooms nearby for his friend, George Tyrrell, who had promised to correct the manuscript of *The Mystical Element* when it was completed. In fact, von Hügel finished the revision of the first volume of his book on 12 July and eight days later the diary notes "Finished writing clear of ch. XII, — leaving thus no part of body of book not finished". On 10 August the baron began a rough draft of the Table of Contents and the following day he forwarded his manuscript to Tyrrell for correction. Four days later the index to volume one was also sent. On 3 September Tyrrell wrote to von Hügel from Boutre where he had gone holidaying with Bremond : "S. Catherine has been getting her six solid hours a day for nine days, and I hope she will be able to start home by the time you mention. The Index is a great help, and so I want to be ready to start Vol. II with that help"[116].

112. Diary, 16 February 1906.
113. Diary, 26 February 1906.
114. Von Hügel to Tyrrell, 15 March 1906, BM.
115. E.T.II, p. 358.
116. *Von Hügel and Tyrrell*, pp. 190-1. And after receiving the index to the second

While all this was in progress von Hügel was also engaged on another front. On 27 June 1906 the Pontifical Biblical Commission had declared Moses to be the author of the Pentateuch though they allowed that he might have employed a number of secretaries for this purpose. On 23 August the baron began a letter to Charles Augustus Briggs in which he asked him to publicly criticise the Biblical Commission's decision and for this purpose sent him a number of cuttings from *The Tablet* and the Decree of the Biblical Commission. Von Hügel received a reply on 9 September and five days later he wrote to Briggs asking for permission to alter his reply into the form of a query which he would then attempt to answer publicly. Having revised Briggs' letter and completed his own response the baron sent the correspondence to Sir James Knowles, the Editor of the *Nineteenth Century*. However, since the manuscript could not appear in the following November issue of the periodical von Hügel requested its return and on 1 November he called on Charles Longman, the publisher, who "readily accepted Publication of the Correspondence: to be a pamphlet pf 60 pp. cloth bound, for 2/6 net. 1000 copies to be printed at once"[117]. With the addition of a short prefatory note the 64 pp. booklet appeared as *The Papal Commission and the Pentateuch*[118]. On 3 December the baron began an article on the Fourth Gospel for *The Encyclopaedia Britannica* which was only completed in February 1907. From 27 February until 21 March von Hügel inserted a précis on the margin of the two volumes of *The Mystical Element* and then commenced the Preface which he completed on 1 April.

The baron set out for France on 5 April. Two days later Edouard Le Roy called on him at 3 p.m. and they went for a walk together. Later, at 8.30 that evening, von Hügel received his first visit from Albert Houtin. Shortly afterwards he went to see Loisy and left him his "Fourth Gospel article and Dr. Briggs answer to Dom Janssens"[119]. That evening he began Le Roy's articles on the "Notion du miracle" and after finishing these the next day, the 12th, he visited Abbé Huvelin and "found him very gouty, but as movingly spiritual

---

volume Tyrrell wrote to the baron on 20 September: "I trust soon, before we leave this (October) to return the MSS. with my poor attempts at comment and suggestion. I know you will not take them too seriously — *discipulus non est super magistrum suum*. I feel it would take me a year of study to form a really competent judgment on a work of such depth and subtlety". Ibid, p. 192.

117. Diary, 1 November 1906.

118. On 5 December the baron sent a copy of the booklet along with a note to Albin van Hoonacker of Louvain and four days later he received a postcard reply from van Hoonacker which the diary notes was "appreciative of and quite frankly at one with the Briggs-Hügel booklet".

119. Diary, 11 April 1907.

and great as ever : remarks of his on SS. Cathr. of Genoa, Teresa"[120].
At 3.30 von Hügel visited Jacques Chevalier at the *Fondation Thiers*
and while there Chevalier introduced him to the director, Emile
Boutroux, "who was most affable and talked of various points of
mysticism"[121]. The baron then called on George Fonsegrive who
showed him the many sympathetic letters he had received on the
cessation of *La Quinzaine*. After dining with Fonsegrive and Chevalier,
von Hügel went to Le Roy and found the "Abbé Laberthonnière
there, — worried, angry look and tone not him"[122]. On Sunday,
14 April, Jacques Chevalier, called and both men attended a meeting
arranged by Abbé Fernand Portal at 10 a.m. As von Hügel's diary
recounts it : "About 40 young men (30 clerics) there. I spoke on
The New Theology and religion in England". After the meeting the
baron visited Laberthonnière and after lunch with Le Roy, both men
called on Henri Bergson. As von Hügel notes : "very friendly; long
talk : my 1st sight of him [Bergson]"[123].

The baron left France for home on 15 April. A week later he
had finished reading Reginald Campbell's *New Theology* which he had
been asked to review. He journeyed to Cambridge on 1 May where
he learnt of Cardinal Steinhuber's letter in the *Osservatore Romano*
of 4 May condemning the Milanese Review *Il Rinnovamento* and
naming Fogazzaro, Tyrrell, Murri and von Hügel as men who wished
"to arrogate to themselves a magisterium in the Church and to
teach the Pope himself"[124]. On the 6th Anatole (Friedrich's younger
more conservative brother), spoke to him about his "views and
ways in theological matters"[125]. The baron returned home the next
day and found a copy of the *Osservatore Romano* with the censure
awaiting him. Four days later he began a "Draft of a rectification
about Fr. Tyrrell and myself to be sent by Alfieri for publication
in the 'Giornale d'Italia'"[126].

On 13 May von Hügel corrected the typed copy of his article on
the "Fourth Gospel" for the *Encyclopaedia Britannica* and sent it
off to the editor the next day. On the 17th he received a "long important
letter from Alfieri (with their answer to Archbishop of Milan's
communication of Cardinal Steinhuber's letter). They are respectful
and Catholic, do not abandon review"[127]. Directed by a postcard

---

120. Diary, 12 April 1907.
121. Ibid.
122. Ibid.
123. Diary, 14 April 1907.
124. *Acta Sanctae Sedis*, 40, Rome, 1907, pp. 272-3.
125. Diary, 6 May 1907.
126. Ibid. This appeared in the *Giornale d'Italia* on 17 May 1907.
127. Diary, 17 May 1907. The previous day von Hügel wrote to W. Ward : "You
will, of course, have seen Cardinal Steinhuber's extraordinary vivacious censure of

from Tyrrell, von Hügel went to the public library on 9 June to examine the previous day's *Times*. There he found "a declaration of the Biblical Commission affirming emphatically apostolicity and full historicity of the Fourth Gospel (Document signed by Pope)"[128]. The baron's *Encyclopaedia Britannica* article which had been sent to the Editor on 14 May questioned both these assertions. With problems looming on the ecclesiastical horizons von Hügel wrote the following significant paragraph on the notion of the church in a letter to Wilfrid Ward : "I feel sure that we ought never to use the term "Church" pure and simple, for "Official Church", "Teaching Church". It is simply un-Catholic to restrict "Church" in such manner. Though the *Eccl. Discens* is not, and should not aspire to be, the official tester, formulizer, and proclaimer of the collective Church's experience, tradition, analysis, etc., that *Eccl. Discens* is an integral part of the material and means on which and by means of which the *Eccl. Doc.* thus acts. But let us frankly admit : we have a Pope who will have none of this. *Hinc illae lacrymae*"[129].

Events in the Church now moved fast. On 18 July the baron's diary relates : "The 'Standard' announced this morning that the "Syllabus" (65 condemned propositions) was to appear last night". On the 22nd the *Osservatore Romano* arrived with the Syllabus (Lamentabili), and the next day von Hügel read it through carefully for the first time[130]. At 5 p.m. he visited A. L. Lilley and both men went through the Syllabus again together. Later in the evening he received some notes from Tyrrell on the Syllabus. The following day he re-read *Lamentabili* with Tyrrell's notes and at 3 p.m. van den Biesen joined him and both men again studied the Syllabus with Tyrrell's notes[131].

'Rinnovamento', and the blame attached to Fogazzaro, Tyrrell, Murri and myself. I have little doubt that it was not, at least primarily, the Briggs-Hügel correspondence, but our appearance in the Milanese Review that got me included in this reprimand". Von Hügel to W. Ward, 16 May 1907, SAUL.

128. Diary, 9 June 1907.

129. Von Hügel to W. Ward, 4 June 1907, SAUL.

130. Concerning *Lamentabili* von Hügel was to write later : "The Inquisition, by its decree *Lamentabili sane* (2nd of July 1907), condemned sixty-five propositions concerning the Church's *magisterium*; biblical inspiration and interpretation; the synoptic and fourth Gospels; revelation and dogma; Christ's divinity, human knowledge and resurrection; and the historical origin and growth of the Sacraments, the Church and the Creed. And some forty of these propositions represent, more or less acurately, certain sentences or ideas of Loisy, when torn from their context and their reasons". F. VON HÜGEL, *Alfred Firmin Loisy*, in *The Encyclopaedia Britannica*, 11th edition, Vol. 16, Cambridge, 1911, p. 927.

131. Shortly afterwards, the 27th, the baron sent a long hitherto unpublished letter to Tyrrell concerning *Lamentabili* : "The document contains, if we ignore a certain number of less salient propositions, two sets of sentences, proceeding, qua extracts here, from at least two excerptors and from two diametrically opposite motives. (a) The coarse

Later in explaining the root-causes of Tyrrell's irritation regarding *Lamentabili* von Hügel in fact reveals his own reaction to the encyclical : "These were, as to *Lamentabili*, its continuous assumption, indeed insistence, that official theologians have, as such, a direct *magisterium* over historical science, and the manner in which absolute interior assent was being expected of scholars concerning condemnations to which the condemning authorities did not bind themselves for good and all"[132].

On 1 August the baron set off for Levico in the Tyrol where his wife and eldest daughter were holidaying and arrived there the following day. Four days later Ajace Alfieri came from Milan and both men enjoyed a "long talk and short walk in the vineyards"[133] together. On the 7th the two men discussed the Syllabus before Alfieri left on the 6.30 train for Trent. Von Hügel began Schweitzer's *Von Reimarus zu Wrede* on the 18th and in the evening he started reading Tyrrell's *Through Scylla and Charybdis* aloud to his eldest daughter, Gertrude. On 24 August he received a letter headed "Velo d'Astico, August 22" from Fogazzaro "offering to wait (with Scotti) at Caldonazzo Station at 13 hr 38 (without specifying day) if I [von Hügel] cared to come there"[134]. The baron sent a telegram to Fogazzaro suggesting, because of the late arrival of his letter, that Fogazzaro come to Levico or that they meet somewhere else. However, on Monday 26 August, he proceeded to Caldonazzo Station and so began the famous modernist meeting at Molveno. After leaving Molveno on 29 August the baron returned to his holiday at Levico and on 10 September he travelled to Baden-Baden to meet J.H. Holtzmann. Although he had been corresponding with Holtzmann for many years, their meeting on 13 September was the first personal encounter between both men. Von Hügel left Baden-Baden on the 14th and the next day he took the noon express from Paris to Calais and then to Dover.

caricature propositions : these are, I am confident, the work, as they here stand, of D[avid] F[leming] or some other secret friend of ours; for they could readily be signed by us all, with but the humiliation of being supposed by any sane mortal to hold such stuff. E.g. propositions 4, 5, 6, 7, 8, 9, 10, 14, 15, 19, 20, 41, 65. (b) Then there is a set which has been pretty carefully extracted by some deliberately hostile theologian, (Billot?); and here subscription, even apart from the all-important implied principle so well unmasked by you, would be, I think, all but impossible for us, — at least I feel so at present as regards my own self. E.g. propositions 12; 13; 16-18; 27, 29, 30; 32-34, 36-38; 39, 40; 45, 52, 59-61. (c) no 45 has been formally passed by Lepidi in his approbation of Semeria's 'Dogma'. (d) no 28 is the contradictory of Loisy's persistent contention". Von Hügel to Tyrrell, 27 July 1907, BM.

132. See n. 65, p. 245.
133. Diary, 6 August 1907.
134. Diary, 24 August 1907. Cf. *infra*, p. 220.

On the day after his return to England the papal Encyclical *Pascendi dominici gregis*[135] was published in Rome or as the baron's diary entry for that day recounts: "Pius Xth's Encyclical against 'Modernism' published this evening". Von Hügel read *Pascendi* on 20 September and afterwards, in the company of George Tyrrell, he went to A. L. Lilley to discuss the Encyclical. Again, in describing Tyrrell's (also his own) reaction to the Encyclical some years later he wrote: "his [Tyrrell's] anger arose from its apparent contempt for mysticism and all the dim, inchoate gropings after God; its wholesale imputation of bad motives to respectable, hardworking scholars and thinkers; and its disciplinary enactments"[136]. In the meanwhile Tyrrell had published a rather extreme reaction to the encyclical and on 29 September the baron's diary notes: "read Fr. Tyrrell's very strong, indeed vehement but I expect useful letter (Sept. 26) to *Gior. d'It.* on Encyclical". On 2 October he received a "long, important letter from Alfieri, as to the hesitations that had to be overcome, for Tyrrell"[137]. Tyrrell's seemingly personal attack on Pius X in his letter to the *Giornale d'Italia* offended many Italians including Alfieri and some of the *Il Rinnovamento* group. Von Hügel decided to go to Storrington on 5 October and after a "$1^1/_2$ hr talk with Fr. Tyrrell, — as to general Church situation, his action and motives and his prospects" he was able to telegraph Alfieri "as to Fr. Tyrrell's deeply Catholic motives in writing *G. d'It.* art. on Enc."[138].

On 9 October the baron began collecting material for an article he had promised the editor of *The Encyclopaedia Britannica* on Loisy. Ten days later he wrote to Alfieri promising to "write for them [Il Rinnovamento] at least anonymously if they will keep loyal to Tyrrell and Loisy"[139]. Under the same date the diary relates that the publication of *The Mystical Element* had been "rejected by Murray, Longmans, Blackwood, William and Norgate" and on the 23rd it was refused by Methuen. The following day he received a letter from Tyrrell enclosing a note from Bishop Amigo announcing that the latter had received word from Cardinal Merry del Val that Tyrrell "was debarred from the sacraments and his case reserved to Rome"[140].

135. As the baron later wrote: "The encyclical *Pascendi Dominici Gregis* (Sept. 6th, 1907), probably the longest and most argumentative papal utterance extant, also aims primarily at Loisy, although here the vehemently scholastic redactor's determination to piece together a strictly coherent, complete a priori system of 'Modernism' and his self-imposed restriction to medieval categories of thought as the vehicles for describing essentially modern discoveries and requirements of mind, make the identification of precise authors and passages very difficult". F. VON HÜGEL. *Alfred Firmin Loisy*, in *The Encyclopaedia Britannica*, p. 927.

136. See n. 65, pp. 245-6.
137. Diary, 2 October 1907.
138. Diary, 5 October 1907.
139. Diary, 19 October 1907.
140. Diary, 24 October 1907.

A. L. Lilley called the same afternoon and, after discussing the situation, they agreed that von Hügel should send a letter to Tyrrell with "three points for his present action : silence as to fact, till authors publish it; communicate to Bishop expression of regret as to tone etc., expecially of *Gior. d'It.* article; not publish anything now till January 1st"[141]. As a later insertion in his diary the baron has written in brackets : "(I fear that this letter somehow changed his [Tyrrell's] tone towards me for time)". Von Hügel later decided to talk the matter over with Tyrrell and on the evening of 26 October he went and spent two full days ironing out the issue with him at Storrington. However, there was no warding off the official sanction and Tyrrell's excommunication was published in Rome on 28 October 1907.

The baron began preparing a rough draft of his Loisy article on 1 November. But on the 16th he received a severe blow when Guiseppe Gallavresi sent word of the "suspension from the Sacraments of all writers in *Rinnovamento* and pain of mortal sin of all sellers, buyers, readers of it in Diocese of Milan. With irregularity incurred if they are priests"[142]. In his reply to Gallavresi the baron declared that he could not "recommend *Rinnovamento* to abandon the conflict"[143] and on the same day he sent off the following telegram to Alfieri : "Profonde sympathie — vif désir — ne pas changer dispositions — Résolutions Huegel"[144]. He then wrote a card to Alfieri and Scotti "in same sense, quoting Bagehot to them; only if materially, finally impossible or if their own consciences, sincerely interrogated, make them feel obliged to take that course, would desistance be right"[145]. On 2 December he received a letter from Gallarati Scotti informing him that he had broken with *Rinnovamento* as he could not bear the idea of excommunication. Von Hügel left London the following day for Genoa where his eldest daughter, Gertrude, was to be married on 8 December. After the ceremony he went to Milan to see Alfieri. On the 12th Scotti escorted him to the Ambrosian Library where the baron met Don Achille Ratti (the future Pope Pius XI). As the diary notes "He [Ratti] talked to me about *Rinnovamento* in characteristically scholastic, traditional way, though with kindly feeling for the young men". Von Hügel left Milan for Genoa on the 13th and finally for home on 16 December. However, any hopes he retained for the continuation of *Il Rinnovamento* were crushed when on 28 December he received a note from Alfieri informing him, as the diary recounts, "excommunication published against *Rinnovamento* if it continues"[146].

141. Ibid.
142. Diary, 16 November 1907.
143. Ibid.
144. Ibid.
145. Ibid.
146. Diary, 28 December 1907.

George Tyrrell moved to London temporally on 20 December 1907. The baron had found lodgings for him near his own house in Kensington and Tyrrell lunched and dined with him almost every day. The close contact between both men continued all through January 1908. About this time Loisy also began to experience fresh difficulties and von Hügel was constantly writing advising him on various courses of action and organising an international response of scholars in the event of a condemnation. On 20 January the baron received word from Loisy that he had been summoned by Rome "to subscribe to *Lamentabili* and *Pascendi*"[147] and five days later he read in *The Daily Telegraph* of the "suspension *a Divinis* of Minocchi (for lecture on story of the Fall)"[148]. The same evening he received "a letter from Frederici [di Genoa] announcing that on 16th Jan. Semeria had read out from Pulpit of San Bartomacio dei Armeni, Genova, an acceptance of the Encyclical Pascendi"[149] and that, as a result, Frederici had decided to leave Genoa for either Fribourg or London.

In the afternoon of 29 January von Hügel visited Mr. Charles Longman, the publisher, to obtain an estimate for the printing of *The Mystical Element*. Longman had previously decided not to publish the book and he now told the baron that "His two readers (a Catholic and an Anglican) had criticised (1) length so great; (2) mixture of history and philosophy; (3) style (Germanisms)"[150]. However, on 10 February the baron received word from Edmund Gardner that Dent was prepared to publish *The Mystical Element* and although many difficulties had still to be surmounted, Dent finally brought the work before the public in November of this year.

On 2 March von Hügel read a notice in *The Tablet* about "The Church in France and M. Loisy". The article reproduced an interview of Loisy published in *Le Matin* in which he was portrayed as having admitted that his distinction between matters of history and matters of faith was a mere rhetorical precaution. The baron decided to answer this insinuation. In his reply he reported that in a letter to him of 19 February 1908 Loisy had written: "Certainly the distinction between the point of view of Faith and the point of view of Science is *essential*, *real*: I have ever thought so, and have ever said so"[151]. Nevertheless, on 9 March von Hügel read an "announcement in the *Daily Telegraph* of Holy Office inflicting, March 8, Major Excommunication upon (no Catholic to have relations with) Abbé Loisy"[152]. The baron immediately sent the following

147. Diary, 20 January 1908.
148. Diary, 25 January 1908.
149. Ibid.
150. Diary, 29 January 1908.
151. F. VON HÜGEL, *The Abbé Loisy*, in *The Tablet*, 3, 1908, pp. 378-9.
152. Diary, 9 March 1908.

telegram to Loisy: "Just read substance of new act. Seems relatively moderate. Accept expression continuous affection, respect, sympathy, and of conviction that we all will act with strength of chivalrous moderation. H. Kensington"[153].

Throughout this period von Hügel continued working on his review of Loisy's *Les Evangiles Synoptiques* and when he finished the draft of the first of his articles on 11 March he sent it to Angelo Crespi for translation into Italian. After Crespi returned this on the 14th the baron revised and forwarded it to Alfieri for publication in *Il Rinnovamento*. Three days later he addressed a meeting of the L.S.S.R. on the same subject, Loisy's *Les Evangiles Synoptiques*. The following day, the 18th, he received word from Dent that they were willing to publish his *Mystical Element* provided he shortened its 1300 pages by 300. Dent proposed then to publish the work in two volumes for 21/- net. The baron decided to visit Mr. Joseph Dent that afternoon and, after a lengthy discussion, Dent agreed to permit notes at the bottom of the pages and to publish 700-800 copies. Von Hügel returned home and immediately began revising and shortening his manuscript[154]. Over the next few weeks von Hügel ploughed on with his revision, however, on 13 April he sent a long letter to Loisy expressing certain reservations he was beginning to feel about some of the latter's positions. In the letter he "spoke out against his [Loisy's] occasional identification of religion with morals, and his apparently holding God in sense of an *anima mundi*, itself reabsorbing into it all individual consciousness, and material as truly as spiritual"[155]. On 1 May Dr. Briggs and his daughter dined with the baron. Briggs had just read Loisy's *Quelques Lettres* and was very hostile to it. As he said to von Hügel "he [Loisy] has made terrible mistakes; his friends have had too favourable a view of his opinions"[156].

Throughout June and July von Hügel continued revising his *Mystical Element* but the hard work and critical situation within the Church were instrumental in bringing about a return of the ill-health and nervous exhaustion which had plagued him during his early life. As the diary notes he had many "White [sleepless] nights — with over-active brain" during this period. On 1 August therefore he decided to take a holiday with Tyrrell at Storrington. Henri Bremond joined

153. Ibid. Translation by present writer.
154. Tyrrell helped the baron considerably with his revision though in the midst of it he wrote to Maude Petre: "The Baron has sent me his St. Catherine again for revision. A hopeless book; a battery of heavy artillery to bring down a flea. He never asks himself: will this interest people who have not spent 10 years on the subject, and to whom St. Catherine will seem a very mediocre personage?" Tyrrell to M.D. Petre, 1 April 1908, BM.
155. Diary, 13 April 1908.
156. Diary, 1 May 1908.

them there on the 4th but, as the baron's diary entry for the 6th shows, Bremond was "very depressed and sceptical over Church-prospects". Von Hügel quit Storrington on 10 August for a vacation with his wife at Briarcombe. While still there he received word from Christian van den Biesen that he was leaving Mill Hill and his professorship for good to take up a position in the Society's sanatorium in Devonshire. As his diary notes curtly: "evidently another 'Modernist' case".

Von Hügel went on revising his book until mid-November. Dent had been printing the sections as they were completed, so when the last section arrived the whole book went immediately to press and the first copy landed on the baron's desk on 25 November[157]. The diary notes his first reaction to the form of the book: "The colour good, but the lettering rather poor. The two volumes are very stout, — look like Royce's *World and Individual*". Thereafter the baron spent most of December sending copies of his *Mystical Element* to his friends and directing it to reviewers. He suffered recurrent sleepless nights during the month and in order to seek some relaxation and distraction during the day he began frequenting "living-photographs"[158] which became a real passion of his in the following years.

Von Hügel read the various reviews and received many congratulatory letters concerning his book during January 1909. On the 28th he went to Cambridge at F. C. Burkitt's request to address the Cambridge Theological Society on the "Three Laws and Forces operative in the growth of Religious Biography". Twenty-two professors attended the meeting but the baron "was tired and did not feel it a success"[159]. Nevertheless, three days later at the request of Professor John Skinner he delivered an informal lecture on modernism to some 23 Presbyterian students at Westminster College, Cambridge. As the diary relates he "spoke to them on 'Modernism' — as R[oman] C[atholic]; as a *horizontal* not *vertical* difference; as not organized or unified; as composed of 2 main convictions; as opposed by Protestantisers and Puritans; as going back to Erasmus (Savonarola) and

---

157. In a lengthy review of the book Tyrrell wrote: "That the mystical element is not the whole of religion; that the rational and historical-institutional are its indispensable co-factors; that any one of these three without the other two, or any two without the remaining one, yield a perverse and distorted religion is a leading thesis of Baron von Hügel's work. It is the work of one who has read widely and thought deeply about religion under almost every possible aspect — mystical, ascetical, philosophical, literary, and historical. Large as it is, it suffers from the attempt to compress so much into so little. There is a chapter in many a sentence, and a volume in many a chapter". G. TYRRELL, *The Mystical Element of Religion (Review)*, in *The Quarterly Review* 211, 1909, p. 105.

158. Diary, 1908 and thereafter.

159. Diary, 28 January 1909.

Synoptics, not Luther, Calvin, Augustine, St. Paul". Later on 29 May the baron journeyed to Oxford at the invitation of Albert Way, the Librarian of Pusey House, to address a group of Way's "students about Inge's article 'Modernism' in Quarterly Review [April 1909] on modernism in Italy (4 groups among catholics there); on the 2 stages of the relations between Church and Bible; on the Fourth Gospel; on Holy Eucharist and liberal views"[160].

While studying Bergson's *L'évolution créatrice* on 9 July von Hügel received a telegram from Maude Petre "asking", as his diary notes, "whether I could come down at any moment to Storrington to help decision about Fr. Tyrrell gravely ill — answered yes". The baron received a second telegram from Miss Petre at 4.00 p.m. and left immediately on the 5.10 train from Victoria. On his arrival he had a long discussion with Maude Petre about Tyrrell's situation regarding reception of the sacraments. Tyrrell was still deprived of the sacraments and Rome was demanding an unqualified submission, an acceptance of *Lamentabili* and *Pascendi* and the complete repudiation of all his modernist writings as a prerequisite for regularisation. Tyrrell remained in a stationary condition for the next forty-eight hours. However, he then began to deteriorate so quickly that Miss Petre and von Hügel were forced to call the somewhat hostile Prior of Storrington in to administer the last sacraments. As the baron relates: "The Prior, in the presence of 3 witnesses ... administered Extreme Unction to him [Tyrrell], without attempting to extract even a merely interpretative recantation from him — a proceeding which would, it is true, have been physically blocked or impossible"[161]. Tyrrell died at 9.15 a.m. on the 15th. The next day Bishop Amigo of Southwark sent a telegram to the Prior of Storrington demanding "Retraction in writing in Presence of Priest, or no religious funeral"[162]. The funeral took place with no religious ceremonial. At the graveside the Abbé Bremond simply recorded: "how institutional and sacramental had ever been the religion of the deceased, and addressed to his friend an adieu, full of tenderness but free from all protest, in the name of the many who had been helped by Father Tyrrell to love the Catholic Church and Christ the Everliving"[163].

Both Loisy and Maude Petre have insinuated that due to the fear of ecclesiastical censure von Hügel had been somewhat reluctant

160. Diary, 29 May 1909.
161. Von Hügel to A. L. Lilley, 13 July 1909, SAUL.
162. Diary, 16 July 1909.
163. F. VON HÜGEL, *Father Tyrrell's Death and Burial*, in *The Daily Graphic*, 79, 1909, p. 12. Because of his actions at Tyrrell's burial Bishop Amigo suspended Bremond from his priestly functions within the diocese of Southwark. And when he returned to France this local suspension was made universal. Bremond had to sign a statement adhering to *Lamentabili* and *Pascendi* before being rehabilitated.

to participate in Tyrrell's funeral. There is absolutely no evidence whatsoever for such a suggestion. On the contrary, the baron was to the fore in all the arrangements and publications about Tyrrell's death-bed situation and, at the funeral Bremond and himself took the two most prominent positions. As the diary indicates "Funeral Bremond with Tyrrell on his right and I on his left in front of coffin, rest of us behind coffin — G[ertrude] present". With these words from von Hügel's diary we come to the end of one of the saddest, most unchristian episodes of modern church history.

When Maude Petre and von Hügel examined Tyrrell's papers they discovered that the only private correspondence not destroyed were the baron's letters to the deceased. Von Hügel had also preserved all Tyrrell's letters to himself so it was decided to publish the complete correspondence. The baron approached Edmund Bishop to act as editor but the latter refused "on ground that only if duty required him to do so, should he act in this matter"[164]. As Bishop felt no such obligation von Hügel decided to edit the letters himself, but as time would show he never fulfilled this desire. Maude Petre prepared a manuscript *Christianity at the Cross-Roads* which Tyrrell had left behind for publication. As the baron had proof-read the manuscript and given some criticism, Miss Petre offered to insert a note of thanks to this effect in the Introduction. Von Hügel declined the offer and this, along with her interpretation of his attitude at Tyrrell's funeral, led Maude Petre to conclude that the baron wished to distantiate himself from Tyrrell[165].

Tyrrell's death did not pass without incident within the baron's own family. As we read in the diary, his brother "Anatole asked about Fr. Tyrrell's death and funeral and the controversy arising therefrom

---

164. Diary, 19 August 1909.
165. Von Hügel had a positive long-term reason for his actions as his reply to Miss Petre indicates: "One thing that E[dmund] Bishop made more plain to me at Downside than I had perhaps ever seen it, is the great duty we have, not because of our comforts or even of our individual spiritual safety, but because of the truths and the future we stand for, to avoid expulsion or even condemnation, as far as ever elementary honesty and loyalty permit, since, uncondemned, it is pretty well impossible to draw limits to all that we may be allowed and blessed by Providence to do for souls and for the Church; whereas, condemned, we are at once greatly hampered or neutralised, in our work amongst what are the majority of Christians and the kind of Christians we have been born of. It is then not necessarily cowardice or trimming, but may come from the deepest, wisest love of souls, if we look well around us before each step, if we plant our feet, very deliberately and slowly, alternately on the stepping-stones, between and around which roars a raging, deep, drowning stream. ... I now feel ... I had better not be mentioned ... After all, it will be a very great point gained if you and I remain uncensured, or without their attempting to get us to subscribe to *Lamentabili* and *Pascendi*, with the alternative of suspension from the Sacraments". Von Hügel to M. Petre, 14 September 1909, S.L., pp. 168-9.

managed to keep temper and yet firm". Although von Hügel's wife did not fully appreciate his theological positions and actions, she stood by her husband but, as the diary relates, she did worry "as to what the church authorities might do to me". On 19 October the baron "began arranging Tyrrell-Hügel letters in view of an article in Hibbert Journal"[166] about their twelve year relationship. And in order to obtain some relaxation from the ecclesiastical crisis, von Hügel returned to his earlier pursuit of geology. On 27 October he visited Dr. Sibley at the geological laboratory at King's College and arranged to have 2 hours of private lessons every Wednesday from November 17 to 21 December. On 30 December he received some little comfort when he read a press cutting from the Birmingham Post "putting Harnack's 2 volumes, my *Mystical Element* and Fr. Tyrrell's *Cross-Roads* as the chief theological works of the year"[167].

166. Diary, 19 October 1909.
167. Diary, 30 December 1909.

CHAPTER III

THE LATER PEACEFUL YEARS (1910-1925)

STEADFAST TO THE END

During January 1910 von Hügel read a number of reviews of Tyrrell's *Christianity at the Cross-Roads* but by now he was growing increasingly alarmed at what he felt to be an immanentist trend in some modernist publications and he feared that this group would claim Tyrrell as one of their adherents. On 17 February, therefore, he wrote to Ernesto Buonaiuti a "(detailed praise and criticism of 6 of his Eazzi di Teologia e storia del N.T.) and warning as to not claiming in print Fr. Tyrrell as member of the anti-transcendental group of *Nova et Vetera*"[168]. On 13 March he discussed a plan with Angelo Crespi "for resuscitating a believing, right wing modernist Review à la Rinnovamento"[169]. The following day he read Loisy's "Magie, science et religion" in the March-April number of *Revue d'histoire et de littérature religieuses*. Von Hügel was now becoming convinced that an immanentist trend had crept into the writings of many of his friends.

The baron wrote a long letter to Loisy criticising "his purely immanentist religious position"[170]. After reading Loisy's article on "Jesus or Christ" in *The Hibbert Journal* on 1 April the baron wrote to the editor offering a full article (12 pages) or a discussion paper (3 pages) on Loisy's paper. Nothing came of this proposal but on the same day, 2 April, he wrote to Bishop Edward Talbot concerning Loisy's article: "I only wish that a distinctly sceptical, purely immanentist current were not now painfully evident in *some parts* of L.'s own work, and that we had not a pretty strong specimen of this current in parts of his article in yesterday's new *Hibbert Journal*"[171]. Because of this desire to penetrate deeper into the problem

168. Diary, 17 February 1910. *Nova et Vetera*, a fortnightly organ of the International Scientific Society, appeared in Rome first in January 1908, but ceased publication in December 1908.

169. Diary, 13 March 1910.

170. Diary, 15 March 1910. In the letter von Hügel "predicted that either man would return to acceptance as true of universal affirmation, by religion, of its object being, ontological, transcendent or would have to abandon the ethical heroism, admitted by Loisy to have in part, been produced by this faith. That latter would turn out impossible, and impossible also their production without the old ontological fundamental conviction; hence this conviction would again be recognised as truly indicative of an ontological Reality". Ibid.

171. S.L., p. 177.

of immanentism von Hügel started studying Feuerbach's *Das Wesen des Christenthums* on 9 April. The next day he received an invitation from the Director of Coenobium to contribute an article on Loisy's "Jesus or Christ" as the periodical had decided to reprint Loisy's Hibbert article. The baron agreed in a letter the following day on condition that he be allotted twenty pages and that his article would appear immediately after Loisy's contribution. The persistent ecclesiastical crisis and the differences with some of his most intimate friends were now taking their toll on von Hügel's weak nervous condition. On 28 April he wrote to Maude Petre: "On Tuesday afternoon I had a bad nervous break-down, — the third now, alas, at distances of only 10-12 days between each"[172].

The baron's health showed no sign of improvement, so on 24 May he enrolled in Sandow's Curative Institute for a six month course of exercises. Initially the exercises failed to alleviate his condition, so on 17 June he approached Edmund Gardner requesting him to become his literary executor. The same day he had a heart examination and it was decided that he ought to discontinue his exercises for a short while. Edmund Gardner visited the baron on 20 June and agreed to act as his literary executor. Von Hügel then decided, as he tells us, "to leave my father's and other family papers not with him; he to have only my personal books, manuscripts, letters etc."[173]. On 11 July he destroyed many "early drafts of early manuscripts"[174] and thereafter began selecting the books he would use to prepare his *Coenobium* article. On the 14th he began copying out pieces from Feuerbach's *Wesen des Christenthums* and nine days later he sent a long letter to Loisy telling him about his failing health and his intention "to write against his [Loisy's], purely immanental religion"[175]. An angry and bitter reply in which Loisy spoke not only of answering the baron's article but of attacking the inconstancy and impossibility of his ecclesiastical position arrived on the 29th. Von Hügel continued preparing his article, however, he consulted his friend, Clement J. Webb, about the matter and on 22 August he received a letter from Webb advising him to publish "an examination of Illusionism but without even naming Loisy. To take instead Reinach, Frazer, Jane Harrison, with (or instead of) Natorp and Feuerbach"[176]. The baron finally decided to analyse Natorp and Feuerbach in his coming article and communicated his intentions to Loisy on 23 August. He began the

172. Von Hügel to M.D. Petre, 28 April 1910, BM.
173. Diary, 20 June 1910. It is these personal books, letters, etc., which were later deposited by Edmund Gardner in the University Library at St. Andrews.
174. Diary, 11 July 1910.
175. Diary, 23 July 1910.
176. Diary, 22 August 1910.

rough draft of his paper entitled "Religion and Illusion" on 12 September but we find no evidence of any further work on it until 19 October. On 10 November he addressed the Rev. Mr. Engelback's Religious Society on "Religion's Ontological Affirmation and Illusionism"[177]. Thereafter he continued working on his *Coenobium* article and after having it typed he sent it to Angelo Crespi for translation into Italian. Finally, after revising Crespi's translation on 18 January 1911, he sent it off to the editor of *Coenobium*.

On 5 February the baron attended a dinner at Bishop Edward Talbot's where he met Adolf Harnack for the first time. Both men had a twenty minute talk together but, as the diary records, von Hügel "soon felt a prick at having not sufficiently spoken up for the great sides of Loisy"[178]. Nine days later he tried to rectify this by writing to Harnack declaring his "non-acceptance of his Lukan positions"[179]. During this month also von Hügel dined at Liddon House and afterwards spoke informally to a group of about thirty on the Abbé Huvelin.

During March and April the baron took things rather easy, frequenting the cinema, reading the Bronte sisters and his favourite poet, Robert Browning and continuing with his Sandow treatment. On 8 May, however, he began preparing an address on Rudolf Eucken scheduled for the following month. Von Hügel now discovered that a translation W. Tudor Jones was preparing of Eucken's *Der Wahrheitsgehalt der Religion* was quite defective. He spoke to Tudor Jones about it and in the end promised to revise the entire work for him. On 17 May Jones informed him that Eucken would visit London with his wife and daughter between June 3-10 and it was arranged that the family should stay at von Hügel's home from 5 to 6 June. After his arrival on the 5th the baron took Eucken to both the Albert and British Museum and in the evening he held a dinner party in his honour. Eucken departed on the 6th and two days later the baron set out for Oxford, still working on his Eucken paper, and that evening at 8 p.m. he addressed a meeting at New College organised by Clement Webb on Eucken's religious philosophy.

On 4 July von Hügel looked up his old papers on Huvelin and copied out a number of the latter's sayings for an address he delivered the following day to a group of Anglicans at King's College. The baron began Evelyn Underhill's book on *Mysticism* on 13 July and three days later the author visited him for the first time and they discussed the work. At the beginning of August von Hügel commenced an article on "Eternal Life" for James Hastings' *Encyclo-*

177. Diary, 10 November 1910.
178. Diary, 5 February 1911.
179. Diary, 14 February 1911.

paedia of Religion and Ethics. In the meanwhile he read the Introduction to Wilfrid Ward's forthcoming Life of John Henry Newman[180]. The baron went to Cambridge on 9 October and the following afternoon while walking with James Ward he discussed "Eucken, Troeltsch, Bergson, Spiritualism and Theism, H. Holtzmann"[181]. On the 16th of the month he began writing his "Eternal Life" and continued almost every day until the end of the year writing out each of the sections, correcting them and then having them typed at an unprecedented rate.

During January and February 1912 von Hügel completed the sections on Kant, Fichte, Schleiermacher, Hegel, Feuerbach, Kierkegaard, Nietzsche and Darwin. However, on 26 February he took a break from this work to prepare a paper on Rudolf Eucken's religious philosophy for *The Hibbert Journal*. Thereafter he resumed his "Eternal Life", finishing the section on Bergson on 10 March and the next day he began reading for his treatment of Socialism. Within a fortnight however the diary notes: "Finished all 'Eternal Life' manuscript, and sent last three batches, Socialism, Institutional Religions and Conclusion, registered to Dr. Hastings (Aberdeen)". When Hastings received the work he realised it was much too long for insertion in his *Encyclopaedia*[182]. He proposed its publication as a book and von Hügel agreed. The baron therefore spent July, August and September revising his coming book and perfecting his style. In the meanwhile, on 17 September, he had a sad letter from Giovanni Semeria informing him that he had been "banished by his general from Genoa and Italy to Brussels"[183]. Von Hügel promised to visit him there and after he had corrected his proofs on 6 October he took ten days rest and then left for Brussels. Semeria visited the baron on the evening of his

---

180. When returning the Introduction to Ward the baron wrote: "I cannot but feel, more strongly than formerly and doubtless quite finally, one, to my mind now grave, peculiarity and defect of the Cardinal's temper of mind and position. His, apparently absolute, determination never to allow, — at least to allow others, — any public protestation, any act or declaration contrary to current central Roman policy, cannot, simply, be pressed, or imposed as normative upon us all. For, taken thus, it would stamp Our Lord Himself, as a deplorable rebel; would condemn St. Paul at Antioch as intolerable; and censure many a great saint of God since then. And certainly this way of taking things can hardly be said to have done much good or to have averted much harm". Von Hügel to W. Ward, 20 October 1911, SAUL.

181. Diary, 10 October 1911.

182. Hastings wrote to the baron on 12 April 1912; "I have now gone through your article Eternal Life and I am greatly impressed with its value. I believe that it is the most thorough investigation of the subject that has ever been made. You have also succeeded in presenting it very attractively. You will not be astonished to be told that it is too long for the Encyclopaedia. That was quite evident to me at once. It would never do. I see also on reading it that any attempt to reduce its size would be a mistake". J. Hastings to von Hügel, SAUL.

183. Diary, 17 September 1912.

arrival, the 16th. He returned the following day and the third day both men "talked of Delehaye, van Ortroy, Scotti, Casati, Soragna, and about religious authority"[184]. After Semeria's visit on 20 October von Hügel began his "answers to Semeria's written questions"[185] and he continued this the following day. At home on the 31st he "began writing out in rough in French the answers to Semeria's questions"[186]. The ultimate destination of this paper is now believed to have been the baron's son-in-law, Count Francesco Salimei.

Back in London on 22 November von Hügel attended a dinner for A. L. Lilley and in an intervention afterwards he "dwelt upon need in A. L. Lilley's teaching upon need of greater emphasis upon importance of historical happenings and upon Distinctness, Difference of God — the Otherness in our Experience"[187]. The baron addressed a gathering of George Newsom's students on "God, Christ, Church their abiding reality and need"[188] at King's College on 6 December. Three days later he spoke to a group of Unitarians at Essex Hall on "The Present Battle and Problem of Religious Faith Amongst the Cultivated Younger Men of the Roman Catholic Church"[189]. In his talk he "insisted on 5 prominent dangers: pure Immanentism; elimination of all *need* of *history*; denial of various *degrees* of truth and worth; the mantle of *magic*; loss of deep asceticism in matters of sex and in matters of intellectual submission"[190]. On 11 December the baron received a disciple of Huvelin, Adeline, Duchess of Bedford, to lunch. He continued a "longish talk with her afterwards alone — about Huvelin, Fr. Tyrrell and prevalent Immanentism, as the danger now"[191]. The Duchess asked von Hügel to write against this immanentism and promised to send him some typical books. The next day the baron left to visit his mother at Cambridge and after a walk with James Ward the following afternoon the diary notes: "Ward is evidently much impressed with what he has read of *Eternal Life* and feels much experience in it".

During the early part of 1913 von Hügel began reading Troeltsch for a lecture he had accepted to deliver in Oxford the following November. In the meanwhile, on 22 May, he spoke on "The Essentials of Catholicism" at Liddon House in the presence of Edwyn

184. Diary, 18 October 1912.
185. Diary, 20 October 1912.
186. Diary, 31 October 1912. This reply is now believed to be von Hügel's *Petite consultation sur les difficultés concernant Dieu*, in P. SCOPPOLA. *Crisi modernista e rinnovamento cattolico in Italia*, Bologna, 1961, pp. 367-92.
187. Diary, 22 November 1912.
188. Diary, 6 December 1912. This address has not survived.
189. Diary, 9 December 1912. This address has not survived.
190. Ibid.
191. Diary, 11 December 1912.

Bevan and Rabindranath Tagore. Both men visited him on 17 June
and an interesting discussion ensued. The baron gave an address "On
the Place and Function of Sense, History and Institution in Religion" to
the *Religious Thought Society* at Caxton Hall on 1 July. The meeting
was presided over by Dean Inge and during the proceedings von
Hügel became angry with the Dean because of the latter's hostility to
Tyrrell and Loisy. The Dean apologised saying "that he had evidently
forgotten, when criticizing ideas and tendencies that behind them were
living men like himself"[192].

On 8 September the baron resumed his study of Troeltsch's
Gesammelte Schriften for his Oxford address and on 22 November
he journeyed to Oxford and spoke on "Professor Troeltsch on
Christianity, its Nature, Finality and Prospects" before a distinguished
audience of University professors. Two days later he held an interesting
discussion in Clement Webb's study with Leslie Johnston and Edwyn
Bevan "about need and nature of historical element in Religion and
uniqueness and divinity of Christ"[193]. When the baron returned home
he completed his paper on Troeltsch and on 8 December he sent
off a typed copy to Silas Mc Bee for publication in the *Constructive
Quarterly.*

Von Hügel attended a luncheon of the *Hornsey Clerical Society* on
19 January 1914 after which he "spoke for 30 minutes on 'the
Christian conception of Liberty' — its exclusion of all atomistic,
interchangeable individuality, and its continuous sense of the prevenience
of God, the givenness of religion, of our very freedom. The 3 stages
of N.T. development in the matter, in their relation to the Kingdom
of God, as purely given, and to the Church, as partly preparing and
as partly identical with the Kingdom of God"[194]. Lady Miller, the
daughter of Sir Alfred Lyall and her first cousin, Bernard Holland,
called on the baron on 23 January and requested him "to write
about Sir A. Lyall's religious instincts and convictions ... during the last
6 or 7 years of his life"[195]. Von Hügel welcomed the idea, but before
he began working on the book he accepted an "invitation from the
Board of the Faculty of Theology of Oxford to become one of the
seven electors of the Wilde Lectureship in Natural and Comparative
Religion from April 1914 to April 1920"[196]. This honour, as de la
Bedoyère observes, put him "among the country's *short list* of out-
standing academic men in the subject"[197]. After some background

192. BEDOYÈRE, p. 270.
193. Diary, 24 November 1913.
194. Diary, 19 January 1914. The baron's notes have not survived.
195. Diary, 23 January 1914.
196. Diary, 10 March 1914.
197. BEDOYÈRE, p. 273.

reading the baron began a rough draft of his Lyall booklet during the second half of April and continued it throughout May and the early part of June. On 10 June he received word from A. E. Taylor that he was to receive an honorary degree from St. Andrews University (Scotland). The official communication came the following day and von Hügel accepted the honour[198].

The baron broke his journey to St. Andrews at Edinburgh and on 7 July he addressed a meeting in Dr. Alexander Whyte's library "On certain central requirements of Religion, and the difficulties of Liberal movement in face of the needs: as experienced within the Roman Catholic Church during the last fourty years". He then travelled on to St. Andrews for the conferring of the honorary LL.D. Degree[199]. After his return von Hügel completed a rough draft of a second Troeltsch article but on 24 July Austria declared war on Servia and within eleven days the whole of Europe was in arms. The baron was still an Austrian citizen, however, after a long process he was naturalised and on 26 November he "took the Oath of Allegiance to King George V and his lawful heirs"[200].

Von Hügel began a paper on "The War and Christianity" on 4 November and this appeared in *The Church Quarterly Review* for January 1915. On 6 January of the same year he started a paper on "The German and English souls and the present War" for *The Quest*. He finished the first part on 11 February but while working on the second part on 4 March a telegram arrived from his son-in-law, Count Salimei, informing him of his eldest daughter, Gertrude's, serious illness and asking him to come immediately. The baron set off on the dangerous journey to Rome with his second daughter, Hildegard, the following day, and on 8 March he saw Gertrude for the first time in three years. Gertrude had suffered from tuberculosis since before

198. On 17 June von Hügel wrote to Maude Petre : "I only want to tell you of a pleasant little event in my life — the conferring upon me by St. Andrews — the oldest of the four Scottish Universities — of the Honorary LL.D. Degree... This is the first Academic Degree or Honour I have ever received; yet, though it comes at 62, it comes not 6 years after my first book, and hitherto my only full performance — hence it has come quickly and handsomely". S.L., pp. 210-11.

199. The diary recounts the event as follows : "I went to the New Honorary Graduation Luncheon in St. Mary's Hall : sat at right of Sir James Donaldson. At end, he made a little opening speech — very warm and kind. Then I made the first of the little speeches of thanks — $7\frac{1}{2}$ minutes long, — thanking for those who came late thus to get their 1st university honour; for the natural aristocracy of Scotland (myself being $\frac{1}{2}$ Scotch); for those who would apply seriously scientific, i.e. intrinsically appropriate method also to the epistemology and psychology of religion; and for those who believe in the need of institutions and traditions for the full vitality of religion. I am convinced practising R C grateful for tolerance within that greatest of all the communions". Diary, 9 July 1914.

200. Diary, 26 November 1914.

her marriage and she was in a critical state when von Hügel arrived. The baron remained with her until her death on 12 August. Four days after her sister's death Hildegard went to the Vatican to obtain a Papal audience for her father and herself. However, on 19 August Francesco Salimei informed the baron as his diary notes "about objection at Vatican now raised to my reception. That 'there still remains something for me to do, in connection with Fr. Tyrrell affair'". Von Hügel "asked Francesco to hold his hand, and do nothing for present. Not even seeing P. Genocchi about it"[201]. A week later the baron left Rome for home and after a short time he resumed working on his *Quest* article. On 9 November we find him in Birmingham at the invitation of the Rev. J. M. Lloyd Thomas addressing a meeting of the *Religious Thought Circle* on "The Categories of Nature and Super-nature; and of Sin and Redemption"[202]. After returning from Birmingham the baron settled the final text of his article for *The Quest* and on the last day of October he began working on the Alfred Lyall book and continued this throughout December.

1916 turned out to be another active year for the baron. On 13 January he accepted an invitation to address a Summer School at Woodbroke near Birmingham the following August on "Progress in Religion". Exactly one month later he agreed to a request from Evelyn Underhill to speak to the *Religious Though Circle* on "What do we mean by Heaven and Hell"? And finally on 19 February he made an agreement with Dent to publish his *Quest* articles in the form of a book. When the day of his Birmingham address arrived on 8 August von Hügel was still writing his paper. Nevertheless, at 5.30 p.m. he delivered his "address on "Progress in Religion' in 3 parts of 15, 45 and 30 minutes"[203] and at 8.30 p.m. he answered written questions on it for an hour. Three days later we have a very touching description of the baron as the diary recounts: "on croquet lawn slope in the sun and I sitting on the chair in middle of and below them [a group of students], .spoke to them, for an hour, on 'The Four Last Popes' — entirely colloquially". After returning home von Hügel revised his paper which was later published by F. S. Marvin along with the other papers of the school.

On 2 November the baron gave a talk to the L.S.S.R. on his impressions in Rome during the previous summer[204] and then

201. Diary, 19 August 1915.
202. Diary, 19 November 1915. This address has not survived.
203. Diary, 8 Agust 1916.
204. As the minutes of the meeting relate: "He described the general attitude of educated Italians towards the war ... He also spoke of the work done by Pius X in raising the spiritual tone of Rome and of the Personality of the present Pope". L.S.S.R. minutes, 1904-25, 2 November 1916, p. 99, MS WL80 OD17, Dr. William's Library, London.

proceeded to prepare a paper for the *Religious Thought Circle*. Two days after completing the manuscript (12 December), von Hügel spoke on "What do we mean by Heaven and what do we mean by Hell?" in the presence of Evelyn Underhill and Dean Inge. After his fourty-five minutes speech the Dean responded with some kind remarks but refused to accept Hell.

On the first day of the New Year, 1917, the baron began an article on "The Convictions Common to Catholicism and Protestantism" for the *Homiletic Review*. After some background study in Thomas Lindsay's *History of the Reformation*, Heinrich Denifle's *Luther und Lutherthum* and the fourth volume of Albert Hauck's *Kirchengeschichte Deutschlands* he wrote his article and sent it off to the *Homiletic Review* on 20 April. On the 19th of the following month he journeyed to Oxford for a meeting of the Wilde Lectureship Electors. Three days later he addressed the Nicene and Origen Societies in the Old Senior Common Room at Balliol College on "The Teaching of Jesus, a Doctrine of Immense Alternative and Abiding Consequences"[205].

At the invitation of Bishop Edward Talbot the baron joined a committee which was investigating the attitude of the Army towards religion. On 10 August he sent the following two points for the committee's consideration: "(1) that military Chaplins *for the front* should all receive general orders to go under fire whenever their units do so; (2) that not the average soldier, but the future teachers of them should be instructed in Biblical criticism"[206]. Three days later the baron "resumed — after months of break — composition of Lyall-book"[207]. He took leave from this work in November to give a talk on "Religion and Illusion" to *The Quest Society*. There is no evidence to suggest that von Hügel ever returned to work on the Lyall book again.

Early in February 1918 the baron accepted an invitation from Tissington Tatlow to speak on "The Idea of God" that coming July to *The Anglican Fellowship* at Oxford. The unforeseen deaths of Julius Wellhausen and Archbishop Mignot in February and March respectively brought forth an obituary notice of von Hügel in *The Times Literary Supplement* on Wellhausen and a long article in *The Contemporary Review* on Mignot. During April the baron revised an earlier paper of his on "*Religion and Reality*" for publication in *The Quest*. On 8 May he sent a letter of thanks to Norman Kemp Smith for the presentation by the latter of his *Commentary to Kant's Critique of Pure Reason*. The baron began a systematic study of this work on 20 May

205. Diary, 22 May 1917. This address has not survived.
206. Diary, 10 August 1917.
207. Diary, 13 August 1917. His unfinished manuscript was published posthumously as *Religion and Agnosticism* in R.G., pp. 155-256.

and four days later N. K. Smith called on him for the first time. They discussed the *Commentary* and in the course of the conversation von Hügel discovered that Kemp Smith was very familiar with all his publications. An intimate friendship which lasted until the baron's death grew up between the two men. And during the last years of von Hügel's life Kemp Smith wrote to him constantly and kept him informed about all the new developments in philosophy and theology.

At the end of May the baron began preparing for his Oxford address. On 4 July he turned his attention to Pringle-Pattison's *The Idea of God*. His analysis of this work was to form the basis of the Oxford talk. The first draft of the paper was started on 15 July and the address entitled "The Idea of God" was delivered before the *Anglican Fellowship* at the Lady Margaret Hall on 30 July. Von Hügel took a holiday during August and on 14 September he started a paper on "Institutional Christianity" for the secretaries of the *Christian Students Movement* which he delivered on the 23rd of the month. The baron's health was now deteriorating and on 19 October, after a general confession and a "long letter of Instructions to Edmund Gardner"[208], his literary executor, he entered a nursing home to undergo surgery. He remained there for three weeks but after his discharge he was compelled to spend the remainder of the year convalescing.

1919 brought about a very gradual improvement in his condition and while confined to bed he was happy to have many of his friends call on him. His illness also prevented him from beginning his paper for the *Birmingham (Anglican) Clerical Society* until 13 October. This, as the diary relates, was the "first systematic work since [his] operation" almost a year earlier. The baron journeyed to Birmingham on 26 October and the following day he delivered his address on "The Apocalyptic Element in the Teaching of Jesus; its Ultimate Significance and its Abiding Function". November the 10th found him preparing for a new book to be entitled *The Reality of God*. But hampered by ill-health he could not muster the strength for concentrated study.

During January 1920 von Hügel received a copy of *Das Gebet* from the author, Friedrich Heiler, and immediately read the section on "Das Wesen des Gebets". On 7 February he resumed working on the introduction to *The Reality of God*. Early in March he became quite ill but on the afternoon of the 11th he was able to leave his bedroom to receive the Sadhu Sundar Singh in his study at 5 p.m. Two days later he made a pencil draft of a paper on "Responsibility in Religious Belief" which he delivered to the executive committee of the *Christian Students Movement* on 23 March. A. J. Appasamy called on him the next day and the baron read him a pencil draft he had made entitled "Notes on the scheme for a new book on Sadhu

208. Diary, 19 October 1918.

Sundar Singh"[209]. Von Hügel reworked these in ink over the next five days and sent them to Appasamy. The following day he wrote a nine page letter "chiefly criticism of his [Heiler's] Lutheran 'pure' spiritual prejudices"[210] in *Das Gebet* and sent it to the author.

On 5 May the baron began the first draft of a paper on "Christianity and the Supernatural" which he delivered to approximately a thousand undergraduates at Oxford on 16 May. Later in the month he was pleasantly surprised when he heard from Arthur Headlam of Christ Church, Oxford, that the University intended to award him an honorary Doctorate of Divinity. Before accepting von Hügel sent Headlam's letter to Fr. Charles Plater S.J. of Campion Hall asking him advice. As Fr. Plater saw no obstacles to his accepting the degree the baron duly wrote his acceptance to the Registrar at Oxford on 29 May. The honorary degree of Doctor of Divinity was conferred on him in the Senate House, Oxford, on 24 June. The baron thus became the first Catholic to be so honoured since the Reformation.

When he returned home von Hügel began a rough pencil draft of the section on Kant for *The Reality of God*. He also accepted an invitation by Wildon Carr to speak to the Oxford Philosophical Congress in September on the relations between "Morality and Religion". At the end of July the baron took a three week's holiday and, on his return, he immediately started on his Oxford paper. He continued this until 13 September when he decided to publish a collection of his *Essays and Addresses*. After selecting his material he forwarded it to Dent on 22 September and the following day returned to his Oxford paper. However, it was now decided that the baron should only make a short contribution to the general Symposium. So, on 26 September along with Jacques Chevalier, Edmond Vermeil, J. A. Smith and Wildon Carr, von Hügel addressed the Congress for fifteen minutes.

At the beginning of October the baron began writing the Preface to his *Essays and Addresses*. The decision to publish was made mainly on financial grounds for, after the war, his Austrian moneys were frozen. While correcting the manuscript of his *Essays and Addresses* von Hügel began preparing a review of Friedrich Heiler's *Das Gebet*, which he had promised for the *International Review of Missions*. However, since he was not satisfied with his paper on "Institutional Christianity" (for inclusion in his *Essays and Addresses*) he decided, on 15 November, to rewrite the address. The baron worked on this until the 27th but then his health broke down and he was forced to rest until 9 December.

209. Diary, 24 March 1920. The final book was actually written by B. H. STREETER and A. J. APPASAMY, *The Sadhu : a Study in Mysticism and Practical Religion*, London, 1921.
210. Diary, 30 March 1920.

He completed his "Institutional Christianity" essay on 22 December and the proofs of his other essays on 12 January 1921.

Von Hügel resumed working on *The Reality of God* on 5 February 1921 and continued this throughout the rest of the month. After reading a review of Shane Leslie's *Henry Edward Manning: His Life and Labours* on 10 March, he wrote a letter to *The Times Literary Supplement* on Manning's relationship with his late wife. The baron's book-work was interrupted when Bishop Nathan Söderblom came to London and addressed the L.S.S.R. on 12 April on "The Psychology of Luther as the root of his doctrine". After Söderblom's visit von Hügel returned to preparing an address on "Suffering and God" which he delivered to the L.S.S.R. on 3 May[211]. The baron returned to *The Reality of God* from 13 May until 20 June when he broke off to prepare a paper on "Christianity and the World Outlook — the Fellowship of Nations" for the *United Summer School* at Swanwick. He addressed the school on 3 July for "35-40 minutes ... about 4 special dangers of nationalism and 4 special counter helps of Christianity"[212]. Two days later, at the same venue, he gave a ten minute talk "on custody of eyes in Church, and praying about all we allow ourselves to wish and dream" at 9.30 a.m., and at 8.15 p.m. he spoke on "Four last Popes, with a little about Pope Benedict XIV till 9"[213]. When he returned from Swanwick he completed the Index to his *Essays and Addresses* and then recommenced working on *The Reality of God.*

After returning from his vacation at the end of August von Hügel began a paper for a conference on prayer at Beaconsfield. On 26 October he delivered his first address on "The Facts and doctrines concerning God which are of especial importance in the life of prayer" and the following day he spoke on "The Facts concerning the soul in Prayer"[214]. Home again from Beaconsfield he resumed working on a paper he had started on 19 September entitled "The Catholic contribu-

---

211. As von Hügel wrote to his niece on 5 May 1920: "The thing was, as it were, externally a success: twenty-six of us met together ... Some twelve of my listeners spoke through my machine after and on the paper; and only two agreed with my fundamental — to me such a clear, dear, and important point: that although, of course, God is full of sympathy and care for us; and though we cannot succeed vividly to represent His sympathy otherwise than as a kind of suffering, we must not press this to mean that suffering, what we experience in our own little lives as suffering, is as such and literally in God. God is overflowing Love, Joy, and Delectation. I showed, I think, many and grave reasons as warnings against importing, or admitting suffering in God". L.N., pp. 132-3. The address was later published in E.A.II, pp. 167-213.

212. Diary, 3 July 1921.

213. Diary, 5 July 1921.

214. Both addresses were later published in E.A.II, pp. 217-42 under the title "The Facts and Truths concerning God and the Soul which are of most importance in the Life of Prayer".

tion to Religion" which was published in the December issue of *The Student Movement*. Von Hügel now turned his attention to *The Reality of God* but he interrupted this to answer a review of his *Essays and Addresses* in *The Times Literary Supplement*. Under the title "Apologist of Religion" the baron thanked the reviewer for his "excessively handsome" remarks but refused this role saying that he would feel himself "fatally hampered and oppressed by such a *rôle* as that of apologist, even though it be the first of all living Roman Catholic apologists"[215].

Op 19 January 1922 he gave an address entitled "Priest and Prophet" at Liddon House which unfortunately has not survived. He then returned to work on *The Reality of God* until 11 March when Albert Schweitzer came and stayed with him for three days. Schweitzer addressed the L.S.S.R. for 75 minutes in French on "The Mysticism of St. Paul" on 2 March. Von Hügel also spoke but after ten minutes he became ill and had to be taken to another room to recuperate. He remained there until the end of the meeting and then accompanied Schweitzer home where he "sat by him as he [Schweitzer] ate some cold supper"[216]. Both men had a good talk the following morning before Schweitzer left at 10.30 a.m. A fortnight later von Hügel started writing the Reid section of his *Reality of God* and when he completed this on 20 March he began studying Kant's *Critique of Pure Reason* alongside Norman Kemp Smith's *Commentary*.

Mgr. Louis Duchesne died on 21 April and the baron decided to write an obituary notice on his old friend which appeared in *The Times Literary Supplement* on the 25th. Von Hügel's own health now began to deteriorate considerably and on 27 May he began his "first sour-milk at bed-time"[217]. He continued to battle on with his book-work and his life's efforts were crowned when on 2 June Norman Kemp Smith informed him that the Senatus Academicus of Edinburgh University had elected him Gifford Lecturer for 1924-25 and 1925-26. The official invitation came the following day and the baron accepted. As his biographer, Michael de la Bedoyère writes: "This invitation academically crowned a life which had started in so unacademic a way, for he rightly regarded the task as 'the finest lectureship on these great subjects in the world'"[218].

Von Hügel's health became appreciably worse during June and July and his condition became so serious that he considered resigning the Gifford Lectures, but was persuaded by his daughter, Hildegard,

215. See n. 20, p. 860.
216. Diary, 2 March 1922.
217. Diary, 27 May 1922.
218. BEDOYÈRE, p. 343. Von Hügel decided to work his book *The Reality of God* into the form of 20 lectures.

"to postpone any judgment as to the Giffords till after long 6 weeks holiday"[219]. Revived by his holiday he was able to travel to the *Anglican Ordination Test School* at Knutsford in Cheshire on 24 July and the following day he spoke on "Anglicanism from Without"[220]. After returning home he prepared a paper on "The Difficulties and Dangers of Nationality" for publication in the *Challenge* on 4 and 11 August. However, over the next three months his health continued to deteriorate and on 19 November he was compelled to resign his Gifford Lectureship[221].

The baron was capable of very little work during December, yet on the 19th he began Dom Butler's *Western Mysticism* and continued arranging venues for a lecture tour his old friend Ernst Troeltsch was to make in England between 7 and 21 March. But tragedy struck, for as the diary of 31 January 1923 notes: "Dearest Ernst Troeltsch dies in the night". Despite his own ill-health, von Hügel decided, as a tribute to his friend, to read Troeltsch's paper at Oxford and another to the L.S.S.R. and also to edit and publish the various addresses. The result was Troeltsch's posthumous *Christian Thought, Its History and Application* with a prefatory note and introduction by the baron. However, the poor state of his health did not permit von Hügel to give the Oxford address[222]. And on 15 May he broke down while attempting to deliver Troeltsch's lecture to the L.S.S.R.[223]. The effort involved in translating Troeltsch's lectures and preparing the papers for publication also meant that the baron's own work on *The Reality of God* had to be deferred.

Von Hügel and his wife celebrated their golden wedding aniversary on 27 November 1923. Their marriage had been a very happy one and his wife had remained steadfastly loyal to him throughout the trying years of the modernist crisis, although she herself had not

219. Diary, 12 July 1922.
220. Diary, 25 July 1922. This address has not survived.
221. On the same day the baron wrote to his friend Norman Kemp Smith of Edinburgh University: "I ... beg you to abstain from any step or question which would aim at any exception for myself. I have always shrunk from exception in all matters". Von Hügel to N. K. Smith, 19 November 1922, SAUL.
222. As von Hügel related it to Clement Webb: "I find that death [of Troeltsch] and all it has involved for me has been a very big thing even merely physically. The arterial pressure has been worse, and now asthma has come to drive me out of bed into an armchair at night. I have now the strongest instict that, if only I can drop any bigger undertakings outside of this house for awhile, I shall get very fairly fit again, but that otherwise I shall have a most grave breakdown". Von Hügel to C. Webb, 21 February 1923, S.L., p. 365.
223. As the diary relates it: "I began to read out Troeltsch's 'Patriotism, Politics, Religion' after telling a few things as to origin etc. of Popes; but broke down after 1/3 reading; Bevan finished reading it out. Came back to meeting for a minute and said a few words".

shared his views. The baron's health continued to disimprove although
he continued valiantly to work on his book and on 27 February
1924 he received news from Professor W. P. Paterson of Edinburgh
that he had been elected for an Honorary Doctorate in Divinity by
the University Senate. His health was now so poor that he had to
decline the honour, since the journey to Edinburgh would have been
too much for him.

Over the coming months von Hügel's health continued to
deteriorate[224]. During this period Norman Kemp Smith kept him
informed of new developments in philosophy and theology by sending
him from time to time an article on Alfred North Whitehead or
some books of Emil Brunner. On 10 June the baron resumed his
study, reading Part Four "How men Know God" of William Hocking's
book *The Meaning of God in Human Experience*. However, most of his
reading over the following months was much less strenuous. Typical
examples are Walpole's *The Old Ladies*, the *Bad Ballads* and the
Journal of Dorothy Wordsworth. The baron spent many happy hours in
constructing various jigsaw puzzles. After a summer holiday and some
rest at home, he returned to his book-work on 16 September. But
on 2 October Hildegard told her father of "a series of articles
hostile to my *Mystical Element* now appearing in *Tablet*"[225]. Von
Hügel was gravely distressed by the articles and spent several days

224. His secretary, Miss Adrienne Tuck, recounts this decline as follows : "Throughout
February and the first half of March he had somehow been losing ground and
getting weaker with his heart, nerves, and brain, and by March 18 he reached a state of
unconsciousness which greatly alarmed his wife and which the Doctor found to point in
every way to death within the next two or three hours. Father Benedict Zimmerman,
that fine scholarly Carmelite, gave him Extreme Unction and both he and the highly
skilled nurse who had been called in at once did not believe he would survive long;
but somehow within the next two or three hours all the symptoms had changed and a
fresh supply of strength was given although there had been nothing to indicate it would
come. Since then he has slowly been getting better but he is still in his bedroom,
arranged now downstairs, and his next door Study in his dressing gown, and remains
fit for very little. He has started to-day for the first time again his book dictation ...
His great hope is to be allowed to go on with and finish his book, but that is a large
order and will require the continuance of growing and settled health on a larger scale
than has been granted him so far". A. Tuck to C. Webb, 29 April 1924. *Bedoyère*,
p. 351.

225. Diary, 2 October 1924. The articles were : MONTGOMERY CARMICHAEL, *St. Catherine of Genoa*, in *The Tablet*, 144, September-October, 1924, pp. 332-3, 365-6, 396-7, 428-9,
461-3. Regarding these articles von Hügel wrote to Norman Kemp Smith : "There has
been a series of 5 arts in 'The Tablet' on St. Catherine of Genoa which have brought me
a good deal of distress of mind, because of their revealing some 3 very stupid ignorances
or slips of my own and because even so smart in some ways capable a writer so
completely refuses to accept the deep and I still think reasonable, irresistible conclusions
of those many years of hard work. I have now to take several days break in my book
work for getting ready for Dent's insertion in the M.E. edition 1923". Von Hügel to N. K.
Smith, 12 November 1924, SAUL.

preparing an additional note dealing with the matter for the second edition of *The Mystical Element*. In the end Dent decided not to insert the special note. Nevertheless, the articles caused the baron considerable irritation and meant a great deal of hard work at a time when he should have been experiencing a justly deserved rest.

On 28 November von Hügel visited his youngest daughter, Thekla, in her Carmelite convent. As the diary relates they "talked about Gwen, my book, the Cardinal [Bourne] and myself". And Thekla then told him of Cardinal Bourne's remarks to her when sending his blessing to the baron a few days before: "I have never got him [von Hügel] into trouble and I never will" [226]. But the time was drawing near when such petty ecclesiastical squabbles would no longer concern the baron. In December 1924 von Hügel had his letter to Friedrich Heiler published in *Das Hochland* under the title "Der Mystiker und die Kirche aus Anlass des Sâdhu". Although his health showed no improvement he continued to work on his book right into the new year and was dictating a section of it to his secretary, Miss Tuck, up until the last evening of his life.

When the nurse from the Sisters of the Little Company of Mary who was attending him left on the morning of 27 January 1925 for the 8 a.m. Mass at the nearby church at Campden Hill, the baron asked her to pray for him. On her return she found that von Hügel had passed away. The baron was buried, as he wished, beside his mother and sister, in the grounds of the Catholic Church close to Downside Abbey in Stratton-on-the-Fosse, Somerset. The inscription on his headstone is from Psalm 85:

> For what have I in heaven but Thee;
> and besides Thee what do I desire on earth?

226. Diary, 28 November 1924.

PART II

BARON FRIEDRICH VON HÜGEL'S RELIGIOUS PHILOSOPHY

CHAPTER I

REALITY

1. *Introduction*

Since von Hügel refused to simplify reality or reduce it to a self-contained system of conceptualisations for logicians commentators have tended to see very little coherence or interconnection within the baron's thought. The idea of evaluating his religious philosophy by its adequacy and applicability to the religious reality it attempts to elucidate, and of judging its inner coherence and consistency on this basis seems not to have been taken seriously by them. For example, Algar Thorold, the initiator of the traditional interpretation of the baron's thought writes : "Von Hügel's thought may perhaps be best conceived as a mine, access to which may be obtained by sinking at various points independent shafts. The stratification of these various sinkings will be found to be identical — the stuff is there alright, richly and widely distributed — but we must not be disappointed if we find it extraordinarily difficult — even impossible — to establish underground connections. Perhaps we cannot sink a shaft deep enough for that"[1].

Implicitly this principle, which has become almost an axiom in von Hügel research, contains a fundamental criticism of the baron's religious philosophy. It relegates von Hügel to the role of a well cultured old man expounding with words of wisdom on a number of separate religious issues and it results almost inevitably in the publication of the traditional generalised commentaries comprising of a variety of autonomous Hügelian topics. It would seem, however, that this traditional interpretation arises not so much from the baron's thought as from the fact that his interpreters have been unable to formulate questions incisive enough to penetrate to the motivating experiences and problems which his philosophy responded to. As a result they have not succeeded in discovering the first principles or central theme around which all his thought revolves and consequently failed to grasp the inner unity of the whole.

This failure continues to the present. For example, with a complete acceptance of Thorold's theory, J. William Beatie continues in a recent article : "However, if von Hügel attempted no systematic philosophy of religion as such, he did attempt systematic analyses within specific

---

1. A. THOROLD, *The Religious Philosophy of Friedrich von Hügel*, in *The Edinburgh Review*, 235, 1922, p. 342. Also Thorold's introduction to *Readings from Friedrich von Hügel*, London, 1928, p. XIII.

problem areas, and this is particularly true in the area of the human apprehension of the reality of God"[2]. But, we are bound to ask, if this area of the human apprehension of the reality of God is not an all-englobing area for the religious philosopher, what can be? It must also be remembered that no particular problem area is a self-enclosed entity looking for its own specific solution without any reference to the other fields of knowledge. For example, Beatie's own article on the specific problem of "Von Hügel's Sense of the Infinite", while legitimate as a scientific work, is simply an abstraction if seen in isolation. Von Hügel's "Sense of the Infinite" cannot be correctly understood without an analysis of his notion of experience, religious experience and mysticism, and these latter cannot be grasped without an appreciation of his ideas on the traditional, institutional and historical elements of religion.

So, while we agree that the baron was no system-builder, we believe that his thoughts revolve around certain fundamental all-encompassing human experiences and problems and that his answers have an intrinsic coherence and consistency and as much adequacy and applicability to reality as is possible for a philosopher in this mysterious area. And while admitting that von Hügel himself never synthesised his views into an organic whole and that this must be accounted a failing, we contend that this was not due to the impossibility of the task, as Thorold suggests, but follows initially from the very concrete, experiential and personalistic nature of the problems and approach of the baron and the *ad hoc* character of much of his writings. Ultimately, it was his untimely death, while preparing his Gifford Lectures (1924-25) in which as Lester-Garland tells he intended "to bind together into a reasoned whole the various strands of thought which are to be found scattered through his writings"[3], which ended all hopes of the baron himself completing such a synthesis. This being the case, it becomes incumbent on von Hügel's students to continue this task of reconstruction. The present work must be seen in this light. In it we attempt to construct a new synthesis of the baron's thought integrating the many and varied insights which remained scattered throughout his works within the framework of a radical empiricism which, as we discovered in Part I, became his mature philosophical position.

2. J. WILLIAM BEATIE, *Von Hügel's 'Sense of the Infinite'*, in *The Heythrop Journal*, 16, 1975, p. 152.

3. L. V. LESTER-GARLAND, *The Religious Philosophy of Baron F. von Hügel*, London, 1933, p. 15.

2. *The Problem*

It is probably safe to assume that his [von Hügel's] intention was to bind together into a reasoned whole the various strands of thought which are to be found scattered through his writings. However that may be, there can be no doubt that the idea of Reality, as he understood it, is the foundation upon which the whole of his religious philosophy is built[4].

With this statement Lester-Garland directs us to von Hügel's central philosophical and religious concern. The problem which confronted the baron was the loss of reality by philosophers who had come adrift from the concrete and whose ideas and abstractions had penetrated theology and were undermining its basis. The recovery of reality, more specifically the reality of God, and the exegesis and articulation of its experiential basis was the primary task von Hügel set himself[5].

Besides the separation from reality perpetrated by the dogmatic and neo-scholastic theology of the time which the Abbé Huvelin had not tired of stressing to him during his early development, von Hügel came to realise an even more pernicious danger to reality from the prevalent scepticism in philosophy. In the baron's view the sceptical and subjectivist philosophies had resulted in a pure immanentism which attacked and destroyed religion at the core. And if he began by combatting a neo-scholastic and purely dogmatic philosophy and theology and attempting to bring the current abstract theology back to the concrete and the real, von Hügel quickly realised that this was only the contemporary facet of a much deeper problem. Further back, in the sixteenth century, there had already been a radical reaction to this purely dogmatic theology. However, in revulsion to all dogmatism, this reaction had gradually slipped into pure scepticism and subjectivism. Because he believed that there was an intimate connection, even causal relation, between this sceptical and subjective philosophy and the current immanentism in religion, the baron felt, if the problem was to be tackled at its roots, he must involve himself in the philosophical and especially in the epistemological problematic, since positions adopted on this level are decisive for our endeavours in all other areas[6].

While von Hügel's ultimate goal was the recovery of the reality of God, because of the interrelation of the various levels of life, he felt

4. Ibid.

5. As the baron wrote to Henri Bremond: "The central problem and solution of philosophy, lies first in Reality and our direct experience of it, and only secondarily in truth and our clear analysis of the obscurely given". Von Hügel to Bremond, 20 July 1915, SAUL.

6. Von Hügel clearly acknowledges this when he writes: "The most profound life, religion, only manifests itself as the most radical and ultimate example, of that which is shown in lesser degrees, at each level and kind of our experience and knowledge". D.C.D., p. 380. Translation by present writer.

obliged to involve himself initially in the problem of the reality of finites. Having accepted this continuity in all our knowing, it becomes evident that a denial of access to reality on one level, i.e. in our ordinary epistemology, would also preclude access to supernatural reality[7]. This being so one must become involved in the epistemological problem as a prerequisite for religious reflection[8].

3. *Scepticism and Subjectivism*

Because of the continuity in all our knowing and because the prevalent atmosphere of the time was infected with subjectivistic, sceptical, agnostic or projectionist theories of knowledge, von Hügel felt compelled to become involved in the epistemological problematic. His entry into this field and his attempt at a solution must be seen from this perspective. He was not a professional philosopher, but became involved in this area because of the havoc confusion in this field was causing on the religious level. Scepticism, subjectivism on the epistemological level, undercut the very soul of religion which, according to the baron, lies in the "affirmation of the distinct, different though all penetrating reality of God"[9]. Because of the almost limitless sway of subjectivism, especially since the eighteenth century, von Hügel believed that people no longer considered reality as given or found, but rather as something projected or created. They no longer conceived reality as existing independently of, or of being prior to their affirmations of it, but rather as a product of it.

To redress this situation von Hügel returns to Kant and focuses his critique on him since he believes that in modern times it was Kant's epistemological scepticism which undermined the basis for our experience of God. The baron indictes Kant for opening up the way to Hegelian gnosticism, religious agnosticism and the immanentism which followed. As he writes: "For if Knowledge, even of the least thing, is ever, for us men, not knowledge of that thing's Reality, but only of its appearance to our senses and of the elaboration of this appearance by our minds; if of Reality we only know, some-

7. This interrelationship and continuity in all our knowledge is again attested to as a basic principle of the baron's epistemology when he writes: "I have the general principle in my head that we are influenced by realities of all kinds, however finite and fleeting, in all sorts of manners and ways, quite apart from our consciousness of these influences, and still more, far more, than our right articulation and interpretation of these our experiences: and this principle I apply also and in a sense above all other realities to God". S.L., p. 363.

8. To put it mildly von Hügel believes: "that it makes an enormous difference whether we come to religion with the habit of admitting and rejoicing in realities distinct from ourselves in all other subject-matters which we love, or if we come to the study of religion with subjectivist habits of mind". R.G., p. 6.

9. D.C.D., p..380.

how, that it exists distinct from our senses and minds, and, somehow, that it is radically different from these our apprehensions and elaborations; if hence everywhere our strongest impressions that we know Reality are but illusions: then the Existence of an Infinite, Necessary Reality will, in a supreme degree and in a normative manner, be absolutely unreachable from any amount or kind of impression or implications to that effect. For here we have the supreme application of, and trust in, that *minimum of a realistic conviction*, the denial of which lands Kant elsewhere in continuous difficulties of various kinds and, at this point, tears up the elementary experience and affirmation of religion by the roots"[10]. If von Hügel regards the Kantian epistemology as tearing up "the elementary experience and affirmation of religion by the roots" one begins to understand his almost excessive reaction to it[11]. There is no personal vendetta against Kant, the baron is simply reacting to the sceptical philosophy which Kant typifies and made respectable.

It was only years later that von Hügel began to appreciate the historical background which had led to this subjectivism. He came gradually to realise that the modern extreme subjectivism had been a reaction to "the *naif* Realism or Objectivism of classical and mediaeval times (so little conscious ... of the always present, and often large, contribution furnished by the apprehending human Subject to this subject's apprehension of the Object)"[12]. It was this former onesided view of the objectivity of truth, disregarding the subjective conditions for its emergence and existence, leaving the knowing subject and his needs out of account which had led, as is usual with any pure reaction, to an equally onesidedness: subjectivism. However, the baron did not remain blind to the positive contribution made by modern philosophy in recovering the subject's active contribution in the attainment of truth. He lamented only the extreme conclusions this movement had drawn. As he saw it: "when the Renaissance and the Protestant Reformation, and later the French Revolution came, they, in part, only articulated, but also they, in part, each differently, yet all greatly, fed and excited a reaction which had permeated the educated average man of Western Europe ever since, say, A.D. 1300. It was a reaction away from the (by then too exclusive) occupation with the Object — with *things*, taken as though apprehended by us without our minds, and especially with *supernatural things*, taken as so different in kind from our natural endowments, as to require a sheer imposing from without — a simple plastering on to the human soul and mind"[13].

10. E.L., pp. 150-1.
11. Von Hügel has been taken to task for example by Nédoncelle for being excessive in the concentration of his criticism on Kant. Cf. M. NÉDONCELLE, *La pensée religieuse de Friedrich. von Hügel*, p. 78. English Translation, p. 73.
12. E.A.I., p. 56.
13. L.N., p. 11.

The reaction therefore was not against the doctrines of the Golden Middle Ages but rather against the errors which had crept in at its demise. The increasing emphasis on the object, especially the supernatural object, and its separation from the subject led to the two level or two storey theory of natural and supernatural. With this development, men soon began to feel that since the supernatural was no longer intrinsic to, but extrinsic and additional to the natural, it became a luxury which they could dispense with at will. But this could only take place when the experiential basis alive at the height of the Middle Ages, (when the two terms were differentiated), had been lost. To treat nature as an independent essence is to hypostatise one of the constituent poles of our humanity. The notion of "nature" (as the structure of our humanity) is formed on the experiential occasion which historically brings the supernatural formation of the spiritual soul into view. Only when these two polar terms had become separated from their engendering experience and subsequently from each other, could the supernatural be seen as superfluous and disregarded. Thereafter we witness the rise of the many immanentist movements which come to fill the gap left by the receding supernatural at the waning of the Middle Ages. However, while the supernatural pole of our humanity can be ignored or even denied, its reality cannot be abolished and so we must be prepared for its re-emergence in the various ideological attempts at its immanent actualisation which have plagued us up to the present. We still witness these endeavours to erect what the baron called "a sort of Kingdom of God, but without a King and without a God"[14]. And we will remain at the mercy of these frustrating attempts to bring Heaven or the Utopia on earth by purely human means until the true order of man's humanity is recovered and becomes socially effective. Within this perspective von Hügel's recovery and analysis of the mystical element must be regarded also as a milestone in the restoration of the true experiential basis of the old christian anthropology and its theory of nature and supernature.

Be this as it may, it was only very gradually that the baron came to understand the full significance of the change which began to take place after 1300. And while he nowhere analyses this movement in his published works, he gives the best general appraisal of the historic roots of modern scepticism and subjectivism in an unpublished letter to Henri Bremond. Von Hügel here contends that the philosophical and devotional formation of Luther and a large part of Western Catholicism at the time was in fact Occamist. In Occam's thought he sees a philosophical scepticism and a contradiction between reason and faith, with reason confined to the production of abstractions of a purely

14. E.L., p. 311.

nominal value. Elsewhere he speaks of Occam's theory of knowledge as
being "profoundly agnostic"[15] since it assumes that man attains to faith
only by a leap of despair and not through any activity of his
intellect. It becomes evident from this that a line can be drawn
from the "sceptical philosophy" and the "profoundly agnostic theory of
knowledge" of Occam through Luther to Kant and modern philosophy[16].

However, in its development from Luther to Kant, von Hügel believes
that the subjectivist philosphy was first clearly formulated by the
father of modern philosophy, Descartes. By refusing to start from the
concrete fact of the trinity in unity, (the knower, known and knowing),
involved in all knowledge, von Hügel believes that Descartes led
modern epistemology into a blind-alley from which there is no avenue
of escape to that illusive thing, the object[17]. According to the baron, the
subject and object always arise together within concrete experience and
must simply be accepted as such. To deny this interconnection and
to separate them quite artificially at the very starting-point of one's
philosophy is to set oneself the unenviable task of bridging over and
trying to recover what lies beyond the confines of experience as
defined in one's starting-point, an impossible task. There is therefore
no way out of the impasse. We must simply accept and admit the
triadic structure of our knowing. This will be von Hügel's basic criticism
of Descartes, Kant and Hegel respectively. Each of them, he maintains,
has forgotten that "all experience is always threefold: it is always
simultaneously experience of the subject, of the object, and of the over-
bridging thought"[18]. Indeed, as the baron reminds us "clear
consciousness always first concerns the object, and only much later
on the subject"[19]. As a result of Descartes' artificial separation of the
data of experience there quickly arose what von Hügel calls: "such
sheer figments of the brain as knowledge, not of objects at all, but of
subjective states alone; and (stranger still) [and here he strikes at Kant]
knowledge that objects exist, and that they all have an inside, but an
inside which is never actually revealed to us by the qualities of those
objects; and (culminating miracle of strangeness) that this inside abides

15. E.A.I., p. 250.
16. E.A.I., p. 186.
17. According to the baron: "Descartes in his fundamental principle, was so eager
to make sure of this kind of interiority and sincerity, that it started, not from
the concrete fact, viz., a mind thinking *something*, and from the analysis of this
ultimate trinity in unity (the subject, the thinking, and the object), but from that pure
abstraction — thinking, or thought, or a thinking of a thought; and, from this
unreal starting-point, this philosophy strove to reach that now quite problematic
thing, the object". E.A.I., p. 186.
18. R.G., p. 188.
19. Ibid.

ever essentially unknowable by us, and yet, all the same, we absolutely know that it contradicts all these appearances"[20].

Within this scheme man, while living within the world and participating in its reality, deliberately isolates and imprisons himself within his own faculties and so inevitably cuts himself off from the real world. Because of his scepticism and minimum of realistic conviction the baron blames Kant for opening the door to the Hegelian gnosticism, the Feuerbachian types of illusionism and the religious immanentism of his own time. Not surprisingly, therefore, in his attempted recovery of reality he returns to Kant's epistemology and it is to this we must now give our attention.

20. Ibid.

CHAPTER II

EXPERIENCE

1. *Kantian Agnosticism*

According to von Hügel the fundamental question which Kant asked was: "What is meant by an Object corresponding to Knowledge and therefore distinct from it?"[21]. In his answer Kant contended that we must regard the object as an unknown, as an *X*, since "we have nothing outside our knowledge that we can place opposite to this our present knowledge, as corresponding to it"[22]. In other words, we can only know the *that* of things-in-themselves, never *what* they are. The conception of a thing-in-itself (noumenon) is simply a limiting conception (Grenzbegriff) for our senses. Here we come to the decisive weakness in Kant's epistemology for understanding cannot be used assertively of any object outside the field of sense. Our cognitional activities are related to objects immediately only through sensitive intuition. Understanding and reason relate to objects only mediately, only through this sensitive intuition and so their value is no more than that of the sensitive intuition which reveals not reality, but phenomena. We are confined then to the merely phenomenal world. We never reach reality, the thing-in-itself.

By some curious paradox, however, Kant knew with certainty what reality was not. He assumed that it was completely different to our conception of it. As early as 1772 Kant had already concluded that the notion "that God has implanted into the human mind categories and concepts of a kind spontaneously to harmonize with things" was "the most preposterous solution that we could possibly choose"[23]. Here we have the paradoxical situation of man knowing nothing really of the real nature of anything and, simultaneously knowing quite certainly that reality is always utterly different from its appearances. What should remain, until more data are available, as an epistemological difference between the presentation and the thing-in-itself, becomes with Kant prior to any evidence or inquiry, a metaphysical exclusion of one by the other. The baron sees a self-contradiction here. On the one hand, we know nothing about reality, yet at the same time we are told that we know quite categorically that it is completely different to what our deepest and most critically controlled experiences reveal it to be. Von

21. E.L., p. 139.
22. Ibid.
23. Ibid., p. 141.

Hügel reacts against such scepticism. For, if accepted it destroys not
only all incentive for advancement and discovery in science and under-
cuts the foundation of all authentic human relationships, but also
the very possibility of religious experience. It is ultimately because he sees
this danger lurking in the Kantian epistemology, because he sees in
its excessive scepticism and subjectivism an immanentism which confines
man entirely to the world of phenomena that the baron is so
categorically averse to it.

In his efforts to unearth some deep-seated prejudice motivating
Kant's bias here the baron contends that Kant's Calvinist upbringing
had made him so suspicious of his own nature that he felt obliged to
distrust the native spontaneity of his own mind and go against his first
impressions. "Things *must* be totally different from what they seemed
to him to be"[24]. In opposition to Kant, von Hügel believes that
man's deeper convictions and his most worthwhile achievements spring
from an elementary belief and trust in a more than merely subjective
world and reality[25]. And further that as man forms "part of a larger
whole, nothing would seem more natural than that there should be
some real relation and similarity between that whole and man's
apprehension of it"[26]. Kant's denial of such a pre-established harmony,
von Hügel feels, was a completely *a priori* assumption. This is not to
say that because of his participation in reality man understands or
comprehends everything fully. The fact that the knower forms part of
reality precludes a complete knowledge of the totality from the outset.
Similarly ignorance of the totality prevents exhaustive knowledge of
any part. Reason may go on indefinitely apprehending reality, but it
will never completely comprehend it. However, while recognising that
we do not know the whole of anything, the baron insists that we can
and do know something of it. This agnosticism (with a small "a"
as we might say) is but the sense of mystery, the consciousness of how
much greater even the smallest reality is to all our clear and definable
knowledge of it. Within knowledge man is confronted with mystery,
with a certain unknowableness lying at the heart of reality which
cannot be expelled or resolved by purely rational means. Nevertheless,
von Hügel believes that reality is manifested in its appearances and not
distorted by them[27]. Consequently while he acknowledges that Kant's

---

24. R.G., p. 102.
25. Writing to his niece he passes on Norman Kemp Smith's remarks to him : "More
and more I am coming to see that the chief source of errors is subjectivism, is
distrust of, disbelief in, the natural, normal intimations of our senses, of our reason, of our
conscience, of our religious sense". L.N., p. 101.
26. E.T.II, pp. 373-4.
27. Because Kant denies this, the baron identifies his position with Agnosticism in
the strict sense of the word. According to this type of Agnosticism : "Our whole

intention throughout was to ground Theism, he feels bound to conclude that his achievement was hardly less agnostic than that of Hume himself.

2. *Hegel's Gnosticism*

Instead of continuing Kant's futile attempt to reach beyond the mind and distinguish between the regulatively useful and objectively true categories, Hegel, according to the baron, simply undertakes a systematic study of the mind's categories from within the subject itself. The result is an identification of thinking with reality, and a transformation of pure logic into metaphysics. In his analysis of the immanent categories of the mind Hegel believes he discovers forces both productive and constitutive of the real universe. With Hegel we gradually realise that these purely speculative categories which are ever abstract, secondary and instrumental replace the reality of experience and through the author's imaginative reconstruction become the real world. Step by step the dialectic takes on a life of its own and itself produces truth and reality. What happens is that we jump from logic to reality, deduce reality from logic and produce concrete existence through sheer thought[28].

With thinking now not only apprehending but producing reality, the more general and shallower stages producing the higher and more perfect ones, we soon reach the stage where thinking in general is producing Absolute thinking, which in turn produces Absolute Reality. We now arrive at the presupposition and culminating point of the whole process where Absolute knowledge becomes "equivalent to Absolute Reality's Absolute Self-Consciousness"[29]. Hegel's system becomes the absolute system (really ending all philosophy) for we can only think absolutely because we are the Absolute. By transforming man's participation in reality, and above all in Divine reality, into a speculative possession of all reality including the Divine, Hegel destroys the whole Western tradition of philosophy and of Christian theology. For philosophy is structured as a *philo-sophia*, a love of

knowledge of mind and of matter ... is relative — conditioned — relatively conditioned. Of things absolutely or in themselves ... we know nothing, or know them only as incognizable; and we become aware of their incomprehensible existence, only as this is indirectly and accidently revealed to us through certain qualities related to our faculties of knowledge. All that we know is, therefore, phenomenal of the unknown". R.G., p. 185.

28. Faced with this amazing mythology von Hügel can only exclaim in the words of Pringle-Pattison: "No sophistry can permanently obscure our perception that the real must be *given*. Thought cannot make it; thought only describes what it finds". E.L., p. 211.

29. E.L., p. 215.

wisdom. To advance beyond this structure into a complete possession
of wisdom is for philosophy to destroy itself. The practice of philosophy
in the Socratic-Platonic sense and the Christian sanctification of man
through growth in the image of God go hand in hand, and von Hügel
was too steeped in both these traditions not to see this danger inherent
in Hegel's system.

The stress on the impossibility of man fully comprehending God, or
for that matter any reality, is echoed throughout all the baron's
writings[30]. However, while reality can never be completely comprehended, it is open to a process of indefinite apprehension procurable
more through a purification of the heart than through an exercise of
reason. Consequently man's response to the inexhaustibility of reality
should, according to the baron, be one of humility, of creatureliness
and not the self-inflation of a Hegel. The baron attributes the
prodigious success of Hegel's gnosticism to the fact that it offered an
escape and hope to many caught in the conventional agnosticism
of the time. For what greater help could a man who was questioning the
possibility of his knowing reality receive than a philosophy which showed
that he not only knows reality and the supreme reality, God,
but also in part becomes this divine reality. By conveying the
impression that his speculative philosophy could solve all problems,
and by abolishing all real distinction between subject and object, thinking
and being, finite and Infinite, Hegel simultaneously produced a disdain
and contempt for philosophy among many scholars in the latter
half of the nineteenth century[31].

This anti-philosophical and anti-metaphysical reaction to the Hegelian
system prevented many attaining in epistemology to what von Hügel
calls: "the rich middle position, of an admittedly ever unfinished movement, tension, twilight, and mixture of knowledge and ignorance — of
a knowledge truly of reality, yet ever inadequate to such reality — a
knowledge ever partial, yet increasable"[32]. Because man inhabits this

30. Von Hügel demonstrates this clearly when he writes to Clement Webb: "What
I cannot abide, is any view that would make man contain God, instead of God contain
man: we shall ever have to look *up to* God, to apprehend, *not comprehend* Him; and our
reason will never become the *Reason*. Yet our reason even here is exceeded only by
a higher Reason, — a Reason indefinitely nobler and greater, but not simply contradictory of our own. We are not, and never will be, God; but already here we can be,
and at our best we are, God-like". S.L., p. 138.

31. As the baron tells us: "There was Döllinger, who had this precise feeling towards all
philosophy; he handed on this feeling to Lord Acton, and Lord Acton handed it on to
spiritual sons of his well known to myself, and they again to their disciples. All these
men had, and have, nothing but an impatient, amused, superior smile for that frothy,
shifting, arrogant, over selfconfident, overweening thing men will call philosophy".
R.G., p. 52.

32. R.G., p. 195. Here we witness an authentic description of the human search for
reality and truth which reminds one of Socrates' reply to Diotima in the *Symposium*,

twilight zone between knowledge and ignorance, the simple alternative of man's reflexive conscious possession of reality and his non-possession of it falls away. Von Hügel therefore seeks to replace the notion of utter ignorance of reality by terms expressive of an experience which if not completely clear and analysable by our critical reason is nevertheless profoundly real and indefinitely operative in our lives. It is only in comparison with his reflective knowledge that man's original experience of reality seems to be no knowledge at all. Experience at all levels of life exceeds our full consciousness and clear analysis. Man's lived experience encompasses an indefinitely wider range and is in more direct contact with reality than his conceptual analysis. Von Hügel makes a fundamental distinction therefore between man's dim obscure experience which ever exceeds his concurrent attention and all his subsequent clear conceptual analysis and knowledge. This distinction lies at the very centre of his thought. From the beginning the whole is given in experience and it only gradually becomes differentiated and articulated. Yet these explications never comprehend totally the full wealth hidden within the original more dim obscure experience, though they can and do clarify it. The further development of these insights lead the baron to evolve a new position in epistemology remarkably close to a radical empiricism of the more metaphysical kind.

3. *Von Hügel's Middle Position*

In the modern period, between the years 1701 and 1709, it was Leibniz, according to von Hügel, who first demonstrated that man's obscure experience is much wider and forms the basis of his clear, distinct knowledge. In 1798 Kant took up a similar position, (though as the baron says he often forgot it), in his *Anthropologie* when he wrote: "To have Presentations and yet to be unconscious of them seems self-contradictory: for how can we know that we have them, if we are not conscious of them? Answer: we can be mediately conscious of having a presentation of which we have no immediate consciousness"[33]. As we shall see later, we can become aware indirectly

when she asked: "is that which is not wise, ignorant?" and Socrates replied: "do you not see that there is a *mean* between wisdom and ignorance?" This mean is, as with the baron, a conscious movement away from ignorance and towards knowledge.

33. E.T.II, p. 359. C.G. Jung also traces the origin of these ideas back through Kant to Leibniz. He writes: "It is regrettable that in this year of grace 1931 ... over a century since Kant spoke of the 'immeasurable ... field of obscure ideas' and nearly two hundred years since Leibniz postulated an unconscious psychic activity, not to mention the achievements of Janet, Flournoy and Freud — that after all this, the actuality of the unconscious should still be a matter for controversy". C.G. JUNG, *Modern Man in Search of a Soul*, London, 1970, pp. 1-2.

of the presence of some reality within our experience without having an explicit consciousness of it at the time of its apprehension. According to von Hügel, Kant is directly reproducing Leibniz when he writes in his *Anthropologie* that "the field of our dark presentations is immensely large, whilst our clear ones constitute but infinitely few points'"[34]. Man's dim, obscure experience is immeasurable. It is only when the light of full attention and reflection is turned on a particular aspect of it that it becomes luminous and capable of clear conceptual elaboration. Since our living experience is wider and more fundamental than our conceptual knowledge, the baron draws a distinction between man's "*aboriginal, dim but most real sense of realities of all kinds, especially of the Reality of God ... and the reflective, more or less systematically developed*"[35] articulation of this. For von Hügel experience is primary. The clarification, however necessary, is but secondary and derivative. Our clear conscious expressions are only explications from within the more dim but much richer complex of our total experience. It is this initial obscure experiential whole which forms the origin and ultimately the goal of all knowledge. It is that from which we start and to which we must return clarifying portions of it in the process through our discursive reason. Therefore, when we return, we no longer see it so indistinctly as before, but through our explication a fresh clarity is introduced which makes the experience less unintelligible, more understandable and more easily communicable. We have then a real experience of reality in our dim lived experience long before our articulation makes us clearly aware of it. However, this experiential knowledge only becomes explicit for us and communicable to others when discursive reason begins its clarifying task.

Von Hügel sees three phases in all our knowledge. First comes reality. From the very beginning man finds himself in the midst of realities which he experiences. Yet while experiencing himself in contact with reality, he always remains aware that these realities transcend his experience. And just as the realities surpass man's experience, so also does his experience refuse to be confined to his theorisation and formulation. As the baron himself says : "reality of all kinds here rightly appears as ever exceeding our intuition of it, and our intuition as ever exceeding our discursive reasonings and analyses"[36]. Thus while man's experiential knowledge falls short of reality as such, this experience transcends all attempts at its com-

34. E.T.II., p. 359.
35. BEDOYÈRE, p. 337. Elsewhere von Hügel describes this distinction as between *"What is clear in and to the consciousness of the individual mind, and what, over and above this, is more or less dimly, unrecognizably operating within and upon it — what is, in varying ways and degrees, an essential condition of that clear consciousness"*. BEDOYÈRE, p. 336.
36. E.L., p. 86.

prehensive analysis. It is impossible to fully differentiate and articulate the wealth implicit in the more compact lived experience and this disproportionality and inadequacy of exhaustive expression or conceptual elaboration means that the way is always open for continual clarification and development of the experience.

With his discovery of this dim, obscure but most rich experiential area von Hügel believed that he had recovered the central truth of Plato's anamnesis doctrine. With Plato he believes "that knowledge, however obscure, is present in the soul whensoever it seeks deeply and fruitfully"[37]. In other words, we must have some dim, experiential knowledge of the various realities we seek to know, since otherwise we could not even begin seeking them[38]. From the beginning man has a dim experiential knowledge of reality which demands clarification and explication. However, his various articulations only elucidate the original living experiential whole from a certain perspective, they illuminate some aspects while allowing others to fall back into the shadows. We cannot explicate all aspects simultaneously because we do not start from a full comprehension of the whole. We move rather from the parts to the whole. But during this process, the whole is somehow present as a dim background all the time. Knowledge then starts from a dim experience of the living whole which is continually present and operative throughout the process of clarification, guiding and reminding us that all our articulations are ever inadequate to the richness and complexity of the living reality before us.

At times we may have the presentment that we have at last reached an adequate exposition, but there is, as the baron reminds us: "even then and there a strongly operative sense that, after all, the reality aimed at remains indefinitely greater and nobler than this attempt, or then the sum-total of all human attempts, to adequate it or exhaust it; and then a more or less early discovery, on the part of this very labourer or of others, that his work was largely limited and permeated by ignorances as to its subject-matter and passing modes of thought and feeling as to its appropriate categories; and hence that, to remain operative at all, it has to be sifted out, re-interpreted, transformed and incorporated by other minds and generations, who in their turn again, on the eternal quest, are as certainly doomed to similar noble disappointment and unrest"[39]. This notion of the necessity of continual, though always somewhat inadequate, articulation and development of the experience

37. R.G., p. 35.
38. As the baron writes: "all the deeper strivings and attainments of man are ultimately explicable with any adequacy only by the dim but most real knowledge by our mind of the very realities which we seek to express with clear analysis and clear synthesis". R.G., p. 60.
39. E.T.II, p. 362.

has its origins in von Hügel's conception of reality. Experiential reality, according to him, cannot be seen "as a geometrical figure of luminous lines, within which is sheer truth, and outside of which is sheer error"[40]. On the contrary, it must be regarded as a light with a blindingly luminous centre encircled by rings of lesser and lesser light which gradually become dimmer and dimmer until they fade into utter darkness. And while as finite minds we cannot articulate reality exhaustively and although others will come and correct the weaknesses and even errors inherent in our articulations and so enlarge the areas of light, nevertheless: "its borders will continue fringed — they will never be clear-cut frontiers"[41]. Consequently von Hügel finds an immense joy in man's partial possession and more especially in his never ending quest of reality. Ultimately, of course, this joy arises from the fact and experience that "we are not seeking simply the sheer unknown" but rather "the deeper penetration and the clearer articulation, the theory and analysis of what we find ourselves to be holding and to have held from the first"[42] or more correctly, in relation to Divine reality, what really holds us.

We start then with a dim confused, but most real experiential knowledge of the very realities we are seeking to know clearly. It is this dim, obscure knowledge in fact which awakens in us the desire and the need to question and search, and it helps us persevere when the searching becomes difficult. Furthermore, because of the presence of this more dim but vivid experiential knowledge operative within our seeking, the search has a direction and luminosity which guides our inquiry and also provides the criteria which reveal whether we have made a real, true discovery or not. In other words, this experiential knowledge remains alive as an existential judgment over against our particular discursive judgments. And it also entails a strange power of highlighting the shortcomings of each and every articulation of discursive reason and of forcing us to realise that there is a certain distance and gap, unbridgeable by any purely rational means, between experiential reality and its most adequate exegesis and articulation.

To summarize briefly. Man lives in a rich middle position of an ever unfinished movement between knowledge and ignorance, however, due to the luminosity of the direction within this movement, he is drawn away from ignorance and towards knowledge. Because we possess the dim knowledge of what we seek, our seeking is a form of knowing. In our seeking we do not yet fully know the reality we seek, but we desire and move towards something which will be recognisable when found. So, the desire to know more explicitly what we but dimly

40. R.G., p. 33.
41. Ibid.
42. R.G., p. 96.

experience injects internal order into the movement: the seeking is directed towards the reality which is recognised as the object sought, once it is found[43].

4. *Reality Within Experience*

Von Hügel's early studies and practical experience in geology had made him conscious of the immense world of reality all round him answering indefinitely to man's desire to penetrate and know it. From an early age the baron developed a deep sense of how much there was to get, how rich and self-communicative all reality was and with this came the conviction that the notion of man or thought simply creating objective reality was quite preposterous. He realised full well our enjoyment in geology, astronomy, the natural sciences and ultimately in religion depends upon our belief in "the real distinction of the real objects from ourselves and yet our genuine apprehension of them!"[44]. Along with insisting on man's participation in reality and the dim confused knowledge which accrues to him from this and which can never be fully articulated the baron emphasises the givenness, the otherness, the priority, the distinctness and difference (within likeness) of all reality[45]. Realism, he contends, must insist "that thought, primarily and normally, never stands alone, and never is thought of thought, but always thought of a reality distinct from this thinking of it"[46]. And his realism is not a naively accepted belief that we immediately perceive reality as it is. It contends rather that in spite of the bias and error in all our perception we can and do have some real knowledge of reality and that when the prejudice and bias has been critically sifted out, some real knowledge remains.

The baron's epistemological position may be summarised briefly as

43. The baron sums all this up very succinctly in the following quotation from Nicholas of Cusa's *The Plain Man and Wisdom*: "As the fragrance which is multiplied from a great fragrant object, and which now adheres to other similar objects, draws us to run after it, so that, whilst pursuing the fragrance of the ointment, we may run to the One Ointment Itself, so does the Eternal and Infinite Wisdom by its refulgence in all things draw us on by certain foretastes of its effects, so that we are carried on to this Wisdom Itself by a marvellous desire. It is owing to this foretaste that the spirit seeks with so great an assiduity after the fountain of its life, a fountain which it would not seek without such a foretaste, and which, without such a foretaste, it would not know it had found when actually it has found this fountain". R.G., p. 34.

44. R.G., p. 5.

45. These same qualities are demanded by Alfred North Whitehead of any entity before it may function as an object in the process of experience. According to Whitehead, to function as an object: "(1) the entity must be *antecedent* and (2) the entity must be experienced in virtue of its antecedence; it must be *given*". A. N. WHITEHEAD, *Adventures of Ideas*, Middlesex, 1948, p. 208.

46. E.A.I., p. 189.

follows. It will insist that man has an obscure, confused but most real experience of realities and that this results from the actual presence and immediate operativeness within his experience of realities other than himself. Within this experiential level von Hügel will place the emphasis on the prevenience and givenness of all reality. On this level of reality it is experience which is primary. The task of discursive reason is to move within the area of the obscurely given inchoate whole illuminating and clarifying it. With the delineation of the centrality of this experiential level for the baron we can now proceed to a detailed analysis of his notion of experience.

5. *A Radical Empirical View of Experience*

In developing his new notion of experience Kant again plays a decisive role in von Hügel's thought. According to the baron Kant arrived at his theory of knowledge by granting classical British empiricism two out of three of its basic assumptions. First, he took for granted that the only element to be given in experience was sensation, and secondly, that this sensation was "a mere contingent manifold, and furnished no necessity"[47]. By confining the given to the data of the senses and regarding these "as sheer contingency and wild flux"[48] Kant really remained within the sensualist tradition. Yet, if man's sensations are purely atomistic, if what he experiences are so many unconnected sounds, sights, etc. devoid of connections, then this inter-connectedness has to be introduced somehow, and Kant allots this task to the constructive activity of the mind. For Kant it is the mind alone which produces order, harmony and unity within the disordered manifold of sense[49]. Cognition is here assimilated to manufacture and the synthetic result is limited by the nature of the materials on which it works, namely sensa.

The decisive point as we said already is that we remain confined to the purely sensual, phenomenal world. According to von Hügel it was Kant's mistaken formulation of the problematic and the method implicit therein which led to this impasse. The question Kant set out to answer entailed an inherent bias. Instead of asking "How *do* I know?" or "What are the ever-present constituents in all my knowledge?", Kant asked "How can I introduce an Object into my knowledge?"[50]. As we shall see, the substitution of *can* for *do* presupposes a complete

47. R.G., p. 168.
48. Ibid.
49. Quoting Kant in this connection the baron tells us : "The order and conformity to law in the phenomena which we call *Nature*, we introduce ourselves; — and we could not find them there, had not we, or the nature of our mind (Gemüth), originally placed it there". E.L., pp. 141-2.
50. E.L., p. 140.

change in method. We are no longer examining the actual knowledge which we in fact *do* have, but only what *can* be given from outside and we are left with sensa alone. What is given in experience then is sense data and this accords with the classical British empiricism of Locke and Hume. Kant simply accepts this while adding that the patterns in these sensa are but forms introduced by the constructing mind.

According to the baron, Thomas Reid [51] was more radical than Kant in his criticism of the basic presuppositions of the sensationalist doctrine. Unlike Kant, Reid unfolded the facts of experience as he saw them and so knew that what is given in experience is never pure sensation alone, but that our perception is always "composed of certain practically irresistible mental suggestions of extension, duration, existence, etc." [52]. Von Hügel does not attempt to develop Reid's insights directly, he simply alludes to him as a contemporary of Kant who offered an alternative to the pure sensationalism and scepticism of Hume. As we shall see, the baron will turn to his own contemporaries, to Henry Jones and especially to James Ward for a complete refutation of the Kantian view of knowledge and for help in articulating his own more comprehensive and more radically empirical notion of experience.

Reacting against the Kantian view that the simply given element in experience is unconnected sensations, which need to be connected, ordered and given a meaningful pattern by the mind, von Hügel joins Henry Jones [53] in maintaining that: " 'The hypothesis that knowledge

51. Thomas Reid (1710-1796) was the founder of the Scottish school of common sense philosophy. His chief importance lies in his attempt to rehabilitate the common sense view of the world especially against Hume. Before publishing his alternative to Hume's scepticism in his *Inquiry into the Human Mind*, (1764), he sent Hume a copy of the manuscript. After reading it Hume wrote to Reid commending his work as a real challenge to his ideas. With the rise of absolute idealism and pragmatism in the latter half of the nineteenth century, Reid's ideas were ignored and continued to decline. However, when these two philosophical movements went into decline there was a return to realism and some of Reid's ideas were again taken up, especially by G. E. Moore. Von Hügel's belief that the object of knowledge is independent of our knowing of it is also maintained by Reid in his *Inquiry*. Cf. Baruch Brody's introduction to Reid's *Essays on the Intellectual Powers of Man*, Massachusetts, 1969, pp. VII-XXVI.

52. R.G., pp. 168; 170-1.

53. Like F. H. Bradley and Bernard Bosanquet, Henry Jones was, in his early years, influenced by Rudolf Hermann Lotze (1817-1887). The baron's quotation is but a summary of pp. 102-118 of Jones' book entitled *A Critical Account of the Philosophy of Lotze*, Glasgow, 1895. Referring to this work in an unpublished letter to G. Tyrrell, von Hügel writes: "Jones is making me reconsider, and, I hope, deepen my thinking on important points, more than anything I have read, on those matters since Bergson and Volkelt: it strikes me as a truly fine book and not requiring any previous knowledge of L. [otze], — it puts one right in the midst of all dianoetic". Von Hügel to G. Tyrrell, 10-12 November, 1903, BM.

consists of two elements which are so radically different as to be capable of description only by defining each negatively in terms of the other, the pure manifold or differences of sense, and a purely universal or relative thought,' breaks down under the fact that 'pure thought and the manifold of sense pass into each other, the one proving meaningless and the other helpless in its isolation.' These elements 'are only aspects of one fact, co-relates mutually penetrating each other, distinguishable in thought, but not separable as existences.' Hence we must not 'make logical remnants do the work of an intelligence which is never purely formal, upon a material which is nowhere a pure manifold': for 'the difference between the primary data of thought on the one hand, and the highest kinds of systematised knowledge on the other, is no difference ... between a mere particular and a mere universal, or a mere content and a mere form; but it is a difference in comprehensiveness of articulation' " [54]. What is given then in experience is the synthetic whole. Purely formal thought and an unconnected flux of sensa exist nowhere in isolation. They are co-relative aspects given together in our lived experience and the task of the philosopher is simply to explicate and clarify the more obscurely given original experience. All our systematic formulations are but simple differentiations from within the original more compact experiential whole. It is this insight which allows the baron break with the classical empirical and Kantian epistemologies and approach a radical empirical conception of experience.

Because of this breakthrough we are no longer caught in the vicious circle of trying to derive either the subject from the object or vice versa. Within this new conception both are given together within experience from the very start [55]. It hardly seems necessary to point out that the baron is here emphasising the intentionality of consciousness. The radical principle of givenness at work in radical empirical philosophy and in Husserl remains also at the centre of von Hügel's epistemology. Maurice Nédoncelle has gone so far as to maintain that the praise which Sartre has given to Husserl's theory of consciousness for delivering us from the "soft philosophy of

---

54. M.E.II, pp. 278-9; E.A.I, pp. 68-9.

55. Von Hügel only very gradually became convinced of this position. For instance, as late as July 1907 we find him writing to A. L. Lilley: "Such entirely non-Roman, non scholastic thinkers as the Broad Lutheran philosopher Volkelt and the Broad Presbyterian (?) Henry Jones have finally satisfied me that the human mind really does have from the first, a certain immediate contact with the objective. The mind has the objective and subjective, (an immediate touch of the former as well as its repercussions in the latter) from the first, and goes explicitating, both factors, on and on, up to the last. And if it were really shut up within itself, even at the first, it could not affirm anything but its own existence even at the last". Von Hügel to A. L. Lilley, 5 July 1907, SAUL.

immanence"[56] and bringing us back to the concrete, belongs in the first place to von Hügel. According to Nédoncelle, the baron in opposition to the majority of his friends and almost alone against the fashion of his day "taught, without naming it, the intentionality of consciousness"[57].

Within experience then man is in immediate spontaneous relation with a myriad of realities which surround him before any formal inquiry on his part. From the very beginning the subject is related not to an idea or a representation of its own but to various concrete realities distinct from, though not unlike itself. Indeed, as von Hügel maintains we have a clear awareness of these realities first and only later attain a clear and adequate consciousness of ourselves. Nevertheless, from the very start, alongside our consciousness of other realities, we are also dimly aware of ourselves, but this may be in so inattentive a fashion as not to be consciously noticed. However, this self which we gradually become aware of is not a purely thinking self, a simple *cogito*. It is rather "a thinking and striving, a feeling and willing, a peaceful or tempestuous, satisfied or dissatisfied, a happy or painful, self"[58]. And the baron envisages no "difference in originality, between the several activities, aims, and achievements of this self, as it thinks, feels, wills, and the rest"[59]. The human subject's reaction to objective reality then is not only sensual but emotional, cognitional and volitional as well. It is a response of the whole man, of the full personality[60]. In other words, it is to the person and not to any one or any number of faculties distinct from the self that we must attribute the apprehension and affirmation of any reality whatsoever. All knowledge arises from "the mutually necessary, mutually stimulating presence and interaction, within our own mental and spiritual life, of sense-impressions, imaginative picturings, rational categories, emotional activities, and volitional acts"[61] and these elements overlap, interpenetrate, mutually stimulate and complement each other so that each element and every stage of our apprehension is affected and in turn affects all the others. It is this complex organic conception of man and of all reality that von Hügel insists on. Man cannot

56. M. NÉDONCELLE, *A Recently Discovered Study of von Hügel on God*, p. 18.
57. Ibid., p. 19.
58. R.G., p. 85.
59. Ibid.
60. As von Hügel tells us : "man never was and never will be any more a merely feeling or merely volitive creature than he ever was an exclusively intellectual one, and all insistence upon the former views is but a ... reaction against the latter extreme; ... the preference is to be given not to one function or element of the living man, but to the sum-total, or rather the underlying unique root and centre of these functions and elements, against any one of them". S.L., p. 112.
61. M.E.II, p. 281.

be seen as "a mere sum-total of so many separable water-tight compartments"[62]. He cannot designate his brains to do one thing, his feelings another and let someone else do his willing for him.

Man's response to reality is an organic action, composed of sensible, cognitional, affective and volitional elements. He must not mutilate himself by attempting to separate or isolate these various functions from one another. Instead, he must allow them to continually supplement, correct and purify each other so that they all work together within his personality contributing to his ever fuller and deeper apprehension of reality. The human subject is not just a passive receptacle for sense data. To the objective revelation of reality there is always a subjective elaboration, a mental, emotional and volitional reaction, an interpretation by the head and heart. And if the experience is considered as positive by the subject, we obtain an incorporation and integration of it "by, and into, the living tissue and organism"[63] of the self. It is all this activity harmonised into a living organic unity which constitutes the essentially unpicturable experience and reality of the living person.

Man's receptivity, as we see, entails a complete personal involvement. Yet this complex subjective activity is usually the last element in the knowing process to be perceived by the subject himself. It is so much a part of the knower that even when he is aware of its existence he is often so preoccupied in penetrating and interpreting the data that his own contribution towards its affirmation continually escapes him. For example, when man's full attention is so absorbed in the objective pole in knowledge, there is no part of his consciousness sufficiently disengaged to be aware, for at least a considerable time, of his own subjective involvement in the knowing process. However, once the subject discovers his constant contribution, he immediately begins to feel that all he knows is a creation of his own mind. And after having held, as the naive realists, that all was objective, he is now tempted to fly to the other extreme and believe that everything he knows is purely subjective. This is quite natural, for with the discovery of our subjective contribution comes the possibility of separating the subject and its mode of apprehension from the object which can then be taken as

62. M.E.I, p. XXVII. Von Hügel says it was Rudolf Eucken (1846-1926), the philosopher of spiritual life, who : "Weaned me from giving any absolute preference to any one faculty of man, — the preference is to be given *not to one faculty above another, but to their totality and cooperation, or rather to the one soul deep down within and under them, as contradistinguished from any one* [of] *them singly*. And this, and only this, can save us from oscillating between an unwholesome sentimentalism or fanaticism and an intolerable rationalism and abstract-demonstration pedantry". Von Hügel to G. Tyrrell, 4 June 1902, BM.
63. M.E.II, p. 112.

the real world out-there. Furthermore, since our subjective activities, our senses, reflections, emotions, desires and interests etc. do in fact colour our perception of the object, they can be seen by the sceptical mind as sources of bias, prejudice and error. And although our uncritical subjectivity is indeed biased this can not be said immediately of that critical reflective subject who sets out to be impartial, truthful, conscientious and authentic and so transcend any inherent prejudice in his outlook.

The basic fact remains that we do not begin with a dichotomy between the subject and object. These result only from a later differentiation within the compact original experience. To believe that we begin with a full consciousness of the self, and that lying opposite us we have a separate independent world "out there", is to box ourselves up in a dualism with no avenue of escape to reality. It is a travesty of experience to think that we can explain or reduce our knowledge to the purely subjective or to the purely objective. Both factors always co-exist. They are mutually interpenetrating co-relates, which though distinguishable in thought, may not and are not separable in existence. They form together such an indissoluble organism, (such a unity in multiplicity) that neither can subsist without the other. To attempt to exalt one above the other as though life, reality or truth consisted in this one rather than that, is to completely misunderstand the new notion of experience von Hügel is advancing. As he continually stresses: "the true priority and superiority lies, not with one of these constituents against the other, but with the total subjective-objective interaction and resultant, which is superior, and indeed gives their place and worth to, those ever interdependent parts"[64]. Both the subjective and objective poles are given together within experience from the very beginning. The subject is not required to fight his way out of his own subjectivity or to ignore his own contribution to reality to reach the object. Unless we accept the fact that the objective pole is simply there, given immediately within experience, we will end up in the vicious circle of subjectivism from which there is no exit.

Von Hügel therefore develops a new conception of experience which he succinctly formulates and summarises with the assistance of his friend James Ward[65]. According to both men, we must not identify knowledge with experience. Experience is far wider and broader than

---

64. M.E.II, p. 114.
65. James Ward (1843-1925). The baron was greatly assisted in articulating his view here by an off-print he received from James Ward on 27 March 1905: *The Present Problems of General Psychology*, in *The Philosophical Review*, 13, 1904, pp. 603-21. The article itself was reprinted from a lecture Ward gave before the section of General Psychology of the Congress of Arts and Sciences at St. Louis, September 19-26, 1904.

knowledge. Knowledge, in fact, must be seen as falling within experience. It is a differentiation from within the more obscurely lived concrete whole. We cannot therefore infer our being purely from our knowing as in Descartes' famous *Cogito ergo sum*. Objective reality is not obtained by inference as appears to be the case with Descartes. It is "'immediately *given*, or immediately *there*, not inferred'"[66]. And as we shall see, this appears especially true of the Divine reality who is "our origin and foundation, our closest, all-penetrating environment, and our all-englobing end"[67]. However, we cannot say the same of subjective reality. This is not immediately given or immediately there. Such a parallellism does not exist between the two terms. "The subjective factor in experience is not *datum*, but *recipiens*: it is not *there* but *here*: a *here* relative to that *there*"[68]. They are co-relatives. Furthermore, this recipiens is no mere passivity. For within concrete experience even our receptivity is an activity and though it is often non-voluntary, it is never simply indifferent. Therefore not pure passive receptivity or inertia but conative and selective activity is the essence of subjective reality[69]. This will also be especially true of the Divine reality Whom we have ever required, desired and willed as much as we have known. Experience then is constituted by the interaction of these two co-relative, polar factors forming a real organic union which precedes and can never be exhaustively covered by our subsequent reflective, discursive knowledge.

In April 1906 we find von Hügel explicitly formulating this new notion of experience which was being developed in the U.S.A. by William James[70], in France by Henri Bergson[71] and in Germany by

66. M.E.II, p. 279.
67. E.T.II, p. 379.
68. M.E.II, p. 279.
69. Ibid., p. 277. It is interesting to note how close, even in terminology, all this is to A. N. Whitehead's analysis of experience in Chapter XI of his *Adventures of Ideas*, esp. pp. 204-210.
70. William James (1842-1910). For von Hügel's only letter to James cf. J. A. ADAMS, *Letter from Friedrich von Hügel to William James*, in *The Downside Review*, 98, July 1980, pp. 214-36.
71. Henri Bergson's (1859-1941) influence on the baron was considerable, especially through his *Essai sur les données immédiates de la conscience*, Paris, 1898, Hüg.B2430. B4D7, SAUL. Von Hügel's copy of this work contains the following remarks on the inside cover: "Un livre vraiment exquis et admirable: son point principal me semble absolument établi. Dommage que, comme toujours, celà nous laisse alors dans un dualisme, pénible, d'un monde intérieur sui-generis, flottant dans un monde extérieur radicalement différent". Von Hügel very carefully marked and underlined the book and shortly afterwards he wrote to Tyrrell: "I want to try hard to make you read the 180 pp. of Bergson's *Essai*. What analysis and heart-knowledge! He shows, in an utterly unforgettable way, how all will-affecting feeling and interior states necessarily change, in proportion as they are profound; and how in them each idea tinges and permeates every other idea: it is

Edmund Husserl. Within this conception experience always consists of connected sense-data with emotional, cognitional and volitional over-tones. These form a living pattern and an organic unity within whose growing process discursive reason simply has the task of exposing the connections and clarifying the more obscure process of the lived whole. And while the active involvement of the subject in the knowing process is acknowledged, the baron also stresses the priority, distinctness yet givenness of the objective pole of reality. As Husserl demonstrated consciousness is intentional. To be aware is to be aware "of something" and that of which we are aware retains a status irreducible to awareness and is as indubitably real as this awareness. In this way von Hügel escapes the subjectivist and immanentist impass. Experience is conceived as having a polar structure, within which subject and object are co-relative terms. And this subject-object relation cannot be reduced to, or identified with a pure knower-known relationship. Experience is far wider than knowledge and the subject far more than a pure cogito. However, we must now proceed to examine in more detail the role of reason within this new radically empirical notion of experience.

only in the dead cold analysis, that one constituent gets juxtaposed alongside of the other. His distinction between the soul's direct experience of duration, with its mutually inter-penetrative moments, and that artificial, bastard compromise between duration within us, and extension, space outside us, which we call clock-time, with its minutes each outside of, and simply alongside of the other, — has now got bodily into my head and heart, and into my attempted presentation of St. Catherine". Von Hügel to G. Tyrrell, 7 July 1900, S.L., p. 87.

CHAPTER III

REASON

1. *Intuitive and Discursive Reason*

Reality, as we have seen, is given to man in his more dim but vivid experience, (always with sensational, emotional, cognitional and volitional overtones), and must then be differentiated and clarified by discursive reason. This further stage in the process of knowledge is absolutely necessary, not only for the consolidation and development of the preceding experience, but also for its clear communication. Although man's intellectual activity is always secondary, it nevertheless, in von Hügel's view, furnishes the experiencing and ever changing subject with three indispensible necessities, namely, rest, expression and as we shall see later purification.

With regard to "rest" the baron believes that because man's intellectual activities essentially neglect emotion and are in a sense directly dealing with the abstract, the static and the impersonal, they can form a sort of refuge and retreat from the bustling process of reality. They offer something steady and stable for man to cling to in an ever changing and uncertain world. The intellectual activities are also important because they allow man to express and communicate the results of his deepest experiences which, if they are to remain alive and fructifying the world, need "to be constantly stated and restated by the intellect in terms fairly understandable by the civilization and culture of the successive ages of the world"[72]. The great formative generalities of mankind demand continual discursive formulation, for this increases their clarity, allows for vividness of apprehension and permits their essential meaning to be understood, kept alive and handed on to future generations. This necessary reformulation does not mean that a particular formula, or in theology an individual doctrine is wrong. It simply acknowledges the fact that each formula is limited to its own specific epoch and must be understood from within its own system of thought. When the thought-pattern changes, the individual idea defined in terms of that system must also seek a new mode of expression.

The danger nevertheless remains that the intellectual faculty detaches itself from its proper function within the total organism of the person and that its abstract logical formulae come to replace existential

---

72. M.E.I, p. 77.

reality. When this occurs the primary notion of reason as a cognitive element within experience is reduced to the speculative, abstractive aspect of reasoning, to a single intellectual logical faculty which gives a purely rational and impersonal account of reality. But within the broader conception of experience, intuitive reason or man's existential consciousness cannot be confined to a purely rational faculty. Reason is not a faculty outside the process of reality, but a cognitive, illuminative factor within experience spreading its luminous rays over the whole. The notion that we can stop the experiential process in which we participate and get off to articulate its meaning clearly, logically and comprehensively from outside is an illusion. Man is not an all-knowing spectator-intellect outside the movement sitting in judgment on the process as it passes by. He is himself an actor within the drama of existence, cognitively trying to explicate his existential lived experience and to express it reasonably. Two aspects of reason must be distinguished. On one side lies our deeper, intuitive reason, (the spontaneous cognitive and illuminative element within experience), which is always tinged with deep emotion and purpose and as such an activity of the whole man and not directly communicable or repeatable. On the other side we have the narrower more superficial discursive reason, (the fully conscious reflective intellect), which is the technical, logical action of but one faculty whose results are readily communicable since they contain little or no emotion. In von Hügel's time this secondary discursive aspect of reason had so usurped the primary notion of reason that it became the great enigma of life which he set out to resolve at the beginning of *The Mystical Element*.

2. *L'esprit de géométrie and l'esprit de finesse*

Following his distinction between intuitive and discursive reason the baron divides men's minds into two classes: into what he terms the scholastic or theoretical and the mystical or positive[73]. The former

---

73. According to von Hügel: "The first of these would see all truth as a centre of intense light losing itself gradually in utter darkness; this centre would gradually extend, but the borders would ever remain fringe, they could never become clear-cut lines. Such a mind, when weary of border-work would sink back upon its centre, its home of peace and light, and thence it would gain fresh conviction and courage to again face the twilight and the dark. Force it to commit itself absolutely to any border distinction, or force it to shift its home or to restrain its roamings and you have done your best to endanger its faith and ruin its happiness'. Wilfrid WARD, *William George Ward and the Catholic Revival*, pp. 371-2. Elsewhere the baron says: "There are such differences of souls! Some people are like geometrical patterns. They worship in wide geometrical lines. Others worship a light that fringes off into darkness". L.N., pp. XXIX-XXX.

group is *l'esprit de géométrie*. People in this group are not happy until they have narrowed the mystery of existence into a problem calling for a specific definite solution. They identify truth and orthodoxy with their system within which everything is true and safe and outside of which lies falsehood and error. For people with this mentality the dimness and complexity of experience must be reduced to clear, distinct and simple ideas from which a whole secure system can be deduced. Such a system affords us a safe abode against the questioning world. It contains all the solutions to our problems and should we feel obliged to go outside it for some answer, then we are made realise that we should not be asking such questions.

This was the mentality of "Ideal" Ward and the narrow absolutist neo-ultramontanism which he typified. This ghetto mentality had sprung up in the Catholic Church after the Reformation but more especially since the seventeenth century and had led to a complete gulf between Catholicism and civilisation. Von Hügel's generation was the first to emerge from this isolation fully conscious of the roots of the problem and eminently capable of rehabilitating the authentic tradition. Since tradition itself is a living developmental reality it could not be preserved by simply repeating the commonly accepted orthodox formulae from one age to another. As with all true developments and advances in personal and social existence such discoveries and insights are not secure possessions and legacies to be wrapped up safely and handed on unquestioned from one generation to the next. Along with Blondel, von Hügel realised full well that each achievement and discovery of the past was but a paradigmatic action to be explored in order to be continued anew by each generation under the special conditions of its own time. The baron's saintly director, Abbé Huvelin, seeing this, had counselled him to seek first experiential truth, for as he said: "Orthodoxy must come to terms with truth, that is its affair"[74].

It was Huvelin also who continually warned von Hügel against *l'esprit de géométrie* of scholastic philosophy[75]. In Huvelin's view

74. Some of the counsels of Huvelin to von Hügel run as follows: "Oui, vous avez horreur de '*bonne* philosophie', '*bien* pensant', parceque vous cherchez la vérité, non l'orthodoxie. Il faut que l'orthodoxie s'arrange avec la vérité, c'est son affaire à elle". And again Huvelin advised the baron: "Il vous faut une *très*-grande liberté d'esprit, avec une *très*-grande pureté de cœur: vous pourriez être très-orthodoxe aux yeux des hommes, et très-mauvais aux yeux de Dieu. Jamais l'on ne parviendra à limiter, à restreindre vôtre esprit. Soyez *très*-conscientieux: l'orthodoxie suivra la conscience. Et pour vous-même — je dis pour vous en particulier — ne blessez *jamais* la charité: la charité et la foi, chez vous, c'est la même chose: elles s'abaisseront, et elles monteront, *ensemble*". J. Kelly, "The Abbé Huvelin's Counsel to Baron Friedrich von Hügel", pp. 65-64.

75. "Pour vous, vous prenez l'apologétique, telle qu'elle se trouve dans la vie, telle qu'elle se présente à l'esprit candide et seul en face de la réalité. L'apologétique ordinaire

the scholastics had substituted formulae for the realities. Unable to understand that life escapes exhaustive analysis and cannot be reduced to definitions, they continued, according to him, to "believe they can put the moon in a bottle but this could be done only if it was cheese"[76]. Huvelin's criticism of the scholastics is very severe. In his view they failed to realise that their clarifications while illuminating certain areas of reality left other aspects in the shadow and even somewhat distorted. He saw the whole scholastic edifice as housing one in a purely abstract, conceptual world which had little relation or relevance to real life.

Against this logical conception of truth Huvelin had advised von Hügel to "see truths, realities, as *intensely luminous centres*, with a semi-illuminated outer margin, and then another and another, till all shades off into utter darkness"[77]. So while we can gradually extend a certain clarity to these various outer areas, a certain dimness always remains. This however should not lead to doubt or scepticism, for, as the baron tells us, it is from the luminous core of our real experience of reality that we live. No matter what the doubts or difficulties, we can always fall back on this central experiential truth and from this "gain fresh conviction and courage to again face the twilight and the dark"[78]. The problem begins when minds of the geometrical type try to force *l'esprit de finesse* to move away from the fringiness and compel it to accept clarity and distinctness as the only valid test of reality. Such tests were a feature of a debased scholasticism which regarded all personal involvement in knowing as subjective (biased), confined truth to the purely logical and conceptual and then set out to judge experiential truth and its personal appropriation from within this sub-area of experience.

We witness here an attempt at what Whitehead has called the "fallacy of misplaced concreteness"[79], which has not only occasioned great confusion in philosophy but has also caused great personal suffering especially in religion. When the sub-field of doctrinaire knowledge becomes the conventional wisdom, then reality and the realist suffer. For everything and everyone is judged in terms and within the confines of the acceptable system, the current orthodoxy, and if they do not fit or conform, then so much the worst for them.

---

ne vaut rien; elle est souvent ingénieuse mais toute fausse. Ce sont des figures géométriques : elles ont une grande régularité ; elle n'ont nulle réalité". Ibid, p. 63.

76. "La scholastique ... n'explique pas tout : la vérité vivante échappe aux définitions de tous cotés. Ils croient pouvoir mettre la lune en une bouteille : celà pourrait se faire, si elle était un fromage". Ibid, p. 65.

77. BEDOYÈRE, p. 330.

78. W. WARD, *William George Ward and the Catholic Revival*, p. 372. As von Hügel paraphrases Newman : "not one hundred difficulties make one doubt". R.G., p. 64.

79. A. N. WHITEHEAD, *Science and the Modern World*, London, 1975, p. 68.

Within this frame of reference it was almost natural for "Ideal"
Ward to suspect a mind such as the baron's of Liberalism. However, von Hügel believed that people like himself were "more in danger
of personal conceit than of objective Liberalism"[80]. The baron here
moves away from a purely objective conceptual notion of truth and
emphasises the necessary subjective dispositions for its emergence. This
shift towards interiority cannot be labelled mere subjectivism, for
truthfulness, reasonableness and conscientiousness are not simply
capricious whims, but embody demands which oblige us to follow the
right direction experienced within our search for truth. This obligation
also entails a personal sensitivity, humility and submissiveness to the
data, through continual openness, the constant purification of the
heart and will and the sacrifice of all a priori and convenient ideas,
schemes and systems. By transcending the selfishness and bias inherent
in his individual subjectivity, man attains to his authentic self and with
it the possibility of real objectivity in knowledge.

This more personalistic view of knowledge, in which moral effort and
personal dispositions enter into and are constitutive of our knowing
was lost early in the history of philosophy. In von Hügel's view
the general trend in Greek philosophy moved in the direction of a
static essentialism and an almost pure intellectualism. As he characterises
it : "things here are *known*, and adequately known, by the intellect, the
abstractive process, and by that alone; actions and character here can
be taught, for the will is not a power really distinct from the reason,
but follows the latter automatically, as the shadow follows the
light; and *perfection of all kinds is here strictly limited, is found in
limitation*, because all things are made to move, begin and end within
the scheme of reasoning, ever clear and definite, and under the image
of concrete, especially sculptural forms, which are ever beautiful in
proportion to their clearly defined proportions and outlines"[81]. Here
the baron is also attacking the abstractness and essentialism of the
deformed scholasticism of his own day, whose system left almost no
room for the subject's role in knowing, for the dynamic conception
of personality or for a real becoming and change in man through
the self-constitutive effect of human activity. Characterising the
differences between this Greek and scholastic essentialism and his own
more existential personalism von Hügel writes : "the former is previous
to and independent of Action, the latter is posterior to it and its
fruit; the former is fixed and stable, the latter is ever growing and
shrinking; the former is adequately cognisable in its true concept, the
latter is but partially apprehensible, from an analysis of the results
of the experience of the reality itself, gained in and through action;

80. W. WARD, *William George Ward and the Catholic Revival*, p. 374.
81. S.L., p. 92.

the former can be as fully known by the bad as by the good, even though it be but the latter who utilise and build upon such knowledge, the latter can be really known only in and through moral devotedness, since it is the latter that alone supplies adequate material and sufficient earnestness, and the humility and livingness which will ever begin again and again the happy, enriching round of action and analysis, love and light"[82].

Within this existential conception, thinking must be seen within being and knowing within living. Logic, no matter how clear and systematic, cannot be the measure of reality. As the baron, quoting Schopenhauer, tells us: "General concepts are the material of philosophy, but only as marble is the material of the sculptor; it ought to work not *from* them, but *into* them"[83]. The concrete has always to come first and be reached last; the analysis, the criticism, the conceptualisation is always a means, not an end. So the richer the reality, the higher in the scale of being, the more obscure and inexhaustible, the less definable and immediately transferable is our knowledge of it. On the other hand, we shall find more clearness and facility of definition the closer we come to simple abstractions and creations of our own mind. In fact, the only thing that we are really capable of completely defining is what we construct ourselves.

3. *Verification*

With the advancement and success of science and mathematics many philosophers took their methods and tests as the only valid criterion for the whole of reality. The methods of the physical sciences, of "subjecting all phenomena to rigourous quantitative and mathematical analysis" and of insisting "upon clearness, direct comparableness, ready transferableness of ideas and their formulae, as the sole test of truth"[84], were accepted by the philosophers as the only true methods and tests for the qualitative, personal and existential aspect of life also. This restriction of truth to what conforms to the methods and tests of the natural sciences is a perversion of reality. For the assimilation of all experience to clear and distinct ideas is only obtained by the exclusion of all that is specifically human in it[85]. Clarity and distinctness, strict proof and logical certainty are applicable only to the very surface of reality. Ultimately, it is only abstract

---

82. Ibid.
83. E.L., p. 248.
84. M.E.I, p. 7.
85. E.T.II, p. 377. As von Hügel reminds us in quoting Aliotta: "Reality generally eludes our thought, when thought is reduced to mathematical formulas". E.A.I, p. 70.

ideas, numerical and spacial relations which can be quite clear, utterly
certain and directly transferable. This is because we there prescind
completely from specific cases or particular individuals and the question
of *existence* or *reality* never arises. When we speak of largeness,
smallness, fullness, etc. or when we number things and add, divide
or multiply with these numbers, we are entirely abstracting from the
quality or the entity's reality or existence. We are only affirming
that *if* there exist so many realities, then such and such clear and
logical conclusions can be drawn. But as to whether one single instance of these exists, this is completely irrelevant as far as the whole
mathematical process is concerned.

It is another matter when we come to reality. The existence and
reality, for example, of the external world can be denied by philosophers
and no amount of clear argumentation will convince them of their
mistake or compel them to accept its existence. Our knowledge of
reality therefore is never simple, clear, purely rational and directly
transferable. On the contrary, the process is very complex, vague,
obscure, most personal and never immediately communicable and
acceptable to others. According to the baron this view is also exemplified
in the work of Charles Darwin. Darwin did not begin his work as a
purely dispassionate, merely rational, objective observer, but engaged
himself completely and personally in it. And Darwin's conclusions
were acceptable, the baron observes, because the evidence from so
many various areas accumulated and converged to verify his positions.
And these conclusions became even more probable when it was seen
that, once accepted, they led to the discovery and illumination of
many other areas and facts. Nevertheless, as von Hügel admits, no
one specific fact or proof renders any of Darwin's convictions strictly
compelling. Even today the most reasonably assured of his conclusions
are still open to certain objections which cannot be completely
denied or resolved. This is always the case with our knowledge of
real existences and real qualities. We come to know these realities
only gradually and partially, not apart from our dispositions but only
if we are sufficiently open, humble and willing to purify all our
selfish dispositions and prejudices and allow reality to manifest itself
to us. In other words, we get to know reality only in proportion as
we become worthy of knowing it. And we can be reasonably sure
that we are truly in touch with reality when we find our knowledge,
(obscure and non-communicable though it be), being fruitful and
illuminating in other areas of life. As the baron writes articulating
this principle of verification : "We could and would consider ourselves
in touch with reality and truth whenever our conclusion, however
indirectly, continued or resumed the most pertinacious (even if now
forgotten or unpopular) work and results of the past ages; when
the same conclusion turned out, unforcedly again, more or less

unexpectedly to meet and to explain difficulties and obscurities as these obtruded themselves upon us in the course of our own work and fortunes; and when, finally, the same conclusion also elucidated the precise root, range and reason of the error thus rejected in the opposite view, and when it did so leaving such a view in possession of much truth in other, often closely-connected, points"[86].

In a sense then, one of the tests of truth will be the lack of originality in our conclusion and of course, its fruitfulness in other areas[87]. And in connection with the test of fruitfulness von Hügel reminds us that besides the literal meaning of Newman's text "By their fruits you shall know them"[88] there is a deeper sense implicit in this saying which Newman himself insisted on. According to this interpretation: "the inconsistency or other error of some moral or metaphysical position does not show itself at once, but has to be found, if found at all, in the process of true thought or system as it passes on from mind to mind"[89]. Von Hügel also admits the value of the literal sense of Newman's priciple, i.e. "that you need but look at a man's behaviour to be able to judge thence as to the good or evil of his moral theory"[90]. This in fact becomes the supreme test in the mystical and religious domain. Against the psychological arguments of visions, levitations, the gift of tongues or other miraculous effects as the tests for the supernaturalness of the religious or mystical experience the baron stresses the mystics' own supreme test, namely "the spiritual content and effect of such experience"[91]. The authenticity and supernaturalness of the mystic's experience therefore is not dependent on the degree of the mystic's withdrawal from the contingent, but on his or her freedom from selfishness, the consequent deepening and fruitfulness of their spiritual and ethical life and on the degree of harmonisation and subordination of everything "under the supreme motive of the Pure Love and service of God in man and of man in God"[92].

So while the proper proof for the adequacy of abstractions and of spacial, numerical, mechanical relations may indeed be clearness, distinctness and ready transferableness, the appropriate test for

---

86. E.A.II, pp. 137-8.
87. E.L., p. 134; E.A.I, p. 52. Fruitfulness does not mean simply the pragmatic test of practical utility. As von Hügel himself says: "I mean quite as much that the wise acceptance and practice of these things is rich in suggestion, explanation, completion of the theory of religion, indeed of the analysis and system of our life generally, and of its apprehension of realities in proportion to their depth". E.A.II, p. 102.
88. R.G., p. 120.
89. Ibid., p. 121.
90. R.G., pp. 120-1.
91. M.E.II, p. 48.
92. Ibid., p. 170.

experiential, real truth "is vividness (richness) and fruitfulness"[93]. Abstract and rational truth may be ever so empty and merely conditional, if it is clear and readily transferable it is appropriate and adequate. Existential, experiential truth on the other hand may be ever so dim, obscure and difficult to transmit directly, it will be appropriate and true when it is rich, vivid and fruitful. In neither set of affirmations do we assent without evidence and proof. But in each area we only require that kind of evidence and proof natural to that particular group. In the mathematical, abstract realm we will require more clearness and direct transferableness the wider and the more universal is the claim of a particular proposition, while in the existential concrete sphere we require, in proportion to their importance, more richness and fruitfulness in its own but also in other fields and areas. For von Hügel then, it is not clearness, distinctness or ready transferableness, but efficacious power (fruitfulness) and vividness (richness) which are the really true and valid tests in the existential domain.

4. *Personalistic View of Knowledge*

This movement towards a more comprehensive existential view of reality and its verification forms part of an attempt to redress an inbalance which had been growing for three centuries and which had narrowed reality to within the confines of the purely scientific and mathematical method. This simplification led to the great success of the method. But once confronted with the more radical notion of experience, the adequacy of the method and the comprehensiveness of its criteria collapses. The scientists and mathematicians were satisfied because within their limited world it brought about the required results. But in our own century especially, scientists have at last begun to see that the purely scientific method is too narrow for the concrete data with which it has to deal. Henri Bergson in his *Essai sur les données immédiates de la conscience* was one of the first to protest against this scientific view with specific reference to the notion of time. He recalled science from the notion of "clock-time, with its minutes each outside of, and simply alongside of the other"[94] to the more concrete notion of duration, *durée*. Von Hügel continued this return to the existential and concrete by emphasising that our experience is not only sensational but also emotional, cognitional and volitional and that reason must be conceived not merely as a discursive faculty, but more primarily as the cognitive factor within experience illuminating and articulating the more obscure whole. On this

93. E.A.I, p. 105.
94. S.L., p. 87.

experiential level reason cannot be separated from the person, his emotions or his will. It is the whole man with all his faculties working "successively and simultaneously under the domination of the good will"[95] who is involved in the search, discovery and articulation of truth.

Thus existential truth is not something out-there which can be known by simply taking a look. It cannot be passively received or inadvertently appropriated. We cannot know or really assimilate it apart from moral effort and action, moral devotedness and fidelity. Real knowledge is not simply given to us from the start but is the result of personal effort and action. It grows with the growth of our personality. So it must be continually conquered, reinforced, often lost and regained by us with and through the growth and conquest of our personality. The emphasis here is no longer on the purely intellectual but shifts rather to the level of conscious decision and moral activity. As the baron stresses: "The goodwill here first precedes, and then outstrips, and determines the information supplied by the intellect"[96]. Similarly, the evil will closes certain aspects and levels of reality to man. And while von Hügel admits that "true and perfect knowledge is a source of love"[97], he constantly reminds us that we only truly know reality when we love it. Therefore we must continually try to make up by our loving for what is lacking in our knowledge. It is through such creative love that we really grow in knowledge. Ultimately real knowledge is more the effect than the cause of our ethical activities. Our apprehension of reality becomes, in von Hügel's own words, "an actual ever-increasing apprehension, more through the purification of the heart than through the exercise of the reason"[98]. And since man's heart is capable of indefinite purification, reality (and ultimately the Divine reality) is indefinitely apprehensible.

In agreement with the close alliance of man's knowledge and his moral activity, the baron maintains that our obscure impressions and experiences are given primarily for action and that it is only by our acting on them that they yield their light and reveal themselves fully. In this way, life stimulates theory and theory in its turn envigorates life. And though theory must never take the place of life, it can as we saw help elucidate and explicate our more obscure, lived experience. So while reflection contributes to the articulation of the life of action, action itself will "help to give experimental fulness and precision to what otherwise remains a more or less vague and empty scheme"[99].

95. Von Hügel to G. Tyrrell, 4 June 1902, BM.
96. M.E.I, p. 49.
97. C.B., p. 317; E.A.II, p. 14.
98. S.L., pp. 71-2.
99. M.E.I, p. 50.

Von Hügel is here emphasising the illuminative character of action which opens up new ways for the intellect to chart. As he reminds us : "He that doeth the truth, cometh to the light"[100].

Throughout the baron's thought therefore we witness a shift away from the excessive objectivism of classical times and from the passive notion of the subject in early British empirical philosophy and a recovery of interiority through the involvement of the whole person in the knowing-process. The stress now falls on the subject's sensitivity, truthfulness, reasonableness, conscientiousness, on his humbly, faithfully, lovingly seeking objective reality by a continual purification of his dispositions and an ever-increasing attempt to become and to be all he knows. Because the movement towards truth is sensed as an impulsion within experience, we feel an obligation to follow this direction if we are to be true to ourselves. Certainly, a life of untruth and deceit can be very convenient and may afford a so-called easy existence. By ignoring or consciously opposing the movement towards truth and the luminous direction this gives to existence, we do not turn our existence into a question-free fact, but rather into a recognisably questionable course of life. By taking the wrong direction we do not make it right, but slide into existence in untruth, and suffer the loss of our true self. To borrow a phrase from Michael Polanyi : "The freedom of the subjective person to do as he pleases is overruled by the freedom of the responsible person to act as he must"[101].

The baron nevertheless cautions against overstressing this more formal, subjective side of life, for as he explains the dispositions necessary for our apprehension of reality cannot of themselves create reality. They simply afford the possibility of discovering what is already there. As the baron writes : "not truthfulness, simply as a formal virtue, but valuable realities reached and served by our veracity — this is what we seek"[102]. This, as we have seen, has been von Hügel's position all along. Reality comes first, then its active reception and perception and finally its clarification and articulation.

5. *Personal Communication*

Because of the obscure and more personal aspect in all our experiential knowledge, its clear and direct communication becomes almost impossible. The problem of how to communicate this dim experiential knowledge is introduced by von Hügel on the very first page of his *Mystical Element*, though his solution is offered, and then in a very nuanced way, only 364 pages later.

100. Ibid., p. 37.
101. M. POLANYI, *Personal Knowledge*, New York, 1964, p. 309.
102. E.A.II, p. 161.

For the baron the enigma of life, as he calls it, lies in the fact that while on the one hand our experiential knowledge and its first-hand expression is persuasive and can move others to action, it is so tied to our individual personality that it cannot be adequately communicated. When, however, these experiential truths have been formulated discursively, they become increasingly clear and easy to transmit, but lose their persuasive power. As the baron, accentuating the difference, writes at the beginning of the *Mystical Element*: "more and more we seem to see that mere Reasoning, Logic, Abstraction, — all that appears as the necessary instrument and expression of the Universal and Abiding — does not move or win the will, either in ourselves or in others; and that what does thus move and win it, is Instinct, Intuition, Feeling, the Concrete and Contingent, all that seems to be of its very nature individual and evanescent. ... the Reasoning would appear to be the transferable part in the process, but not to move us; and the experience alone, to have the moving power, but not to be transmissible"[103]. Although we shall only later fully appreciate the richness of von Hügel's solution, suffice it to say that the dichotomy can not be resolved on the level of the pure logic but only by recourse to a deeper notion of reason and a more comprehensive and organic notion of experience and personality within which general ideas and concepts obtain concrete embodiment and become incarnated. Personality as the concrete universal can be both really communicative and persuasive simultaneously.

The initial enigma arises however because every individual's experience is so personal and his perceptions so coloured by "circumstances of time and place, of race and age and sex, of education and temperament, of antecedent and environment"[104] that it is almost impossible to accept or change himself because of another's experience. If we attempt to communicate some of our particular emotions or convictions to another, it becomes apparent that the particular unique organic unity which cost us so much to appropriate and which means so much to us has to be completely disorganised and broken up. Only some of these elements will be accepted by the other into his personal synthesis or, if he accepts them all, he will quite naturally rearrange them in a new and different combination within himself. As the baron writes: "And yet the second soul ... will at once, quite spontaneously, most rightly, clothe and colour these its new convictions with its own special qualities and habits and experiences of thought, feeling, imagination, memory, volition"[105]. There is, as we stressed, no such thing as a passive acceptance or reception of data, but always an interior

103. M.E.I, p. 3.
104. Ibid., p. 4.
105. L.N., p. 27.

elaboration, interpretation, incorporation and integration of some or all of the data into the living organism of the subject. If we try to compel the other to accept our impressions exactly as they are in us, we will most probably arouse a spontaneous reaction against everything we wish to impart. On the other hand, the baron continually warns against "all straining and all strainedness"[106] on the part of the recipient. As recipients, we must not strain ourselves in thinking that we must receive and appropriate everything that is offered. We should accept and try to assimilate data only to the extent that they answer to our appeals or evoke a comparable need within us. We must never force ourselves to accept what we feel to be against our best needs.

If he wishes to help another therefore the giver must be prepared for a real death to himself. First, from within the totality of his experience the giver must isolate the essential substance of his message from its accidental particularities and offer only this essence to the recipient. Furthermore, he must be prepared if he finds that even this essence might in some way be detrimental for the recipient to withdraw it or induce the other to reject it. However, even if the essence is acceptable to the other, the giver must be always ready to see this appropriated and integrated in its own unique fashion by the other personality. After the communication he can only try to sustain and encourage the other in times of darkness and doubt to be faithful and persevere in his new ways. In this manner the giver recognises and respects the otherness of the other and does not try to make him into another self. There always remains the danger of the do-gooder going around with a plastercast of himself into which he wishes to fit everyone. As the baron says: "The golden rule is, to help those we love escape from us; and never try to begin to help people, or influence them till they ask, but wait for them. Souls are never dittos. The souls thus to be helped are mostly at quite different stages from our own, or they have quite a different *attrait*"[107]. The disclosures then of one person of good will to another is especially difficult for the appealer, since his offer must be revealed in the specific concrete incarnational character which means so much to him and yet he knows that even if accepted, his entreaty must be reconstituted and appropriated according to the subjective needs of the recipient. The giver

106. M.E.I., p. XII.

107. L.N., p. XXIX. Von Hügel continues here: "One should wait silent for those who do not open out to us, who are not intended, perhaps, ever to be helped by us — except by our prayers (the best of all helps)". And on the following page he writes: "I love Browning's poem *Muléykeh*. It is the story of a man who gives up his mare, his Pearl (because) if he kept her she would become less than her best. How beautiful that is, and how touching! I will read it to you. He teaches her himself how to escape from him, though it breaks his own heart". L.N., p. XXX.

therefore must find his joy through the death to self in the new life which springs up through the encounter.

Finally, there remains the possibility that the message will be rejected, not because it is not good for the other, but because the recipient consciously refuses it. The very concreteness, particularity and individual expression of even the most universal and general appeal gives the will that is not-good or not-yet-good an added opportunity for rejecting the total offer. The recipient can always blame the necessary difference within the other's appeal as sufficient reason for rejecting it totally. There is thus in every real encounter, in every offer and reception "an element of noblest generosity and death"[108] on both sides which cannot be evoked, elicited or responded to by abstract formulae, but only by concrete living persons.

6. *Social Experience and Tradition*

Von Hügel's approach to the question of social experience and tradition is quite personal. From his own experience he realised that he had been awoken to the full depth of reality by other, especially by one other human being. As he tells his niece : "I never learnt anything myself by my own old nose"[109]; "I learnt all that I know from Huvelin"[110]. Experiential truth is not learnt through abstract formulae or general laws but concretely as qualities in persons. These concrete personalities constitute the great tradition in which one mature personality teaches another, "One torch lights another torch"[111]. The persons who can teach us most, in the baron's view, always belong to some great social or institutional complex and have themselves come to maturity with the aid of others from within such a body. So although artistic genius is something more than all education and training, yet von Hügel maintains that "even genius cannot dispense with at least the more indirect forms and effects of such training"[112] if it is to achieve its full development.

In a similar fashion, though the great scientists or philosophers do not grow solely by means of schools and tradition, nevertheless they seldom grow without such an environment and discipline. The historical process and accumulation of experience then takes on objective form as tradition, custom, social fact, etc. and is channelled best and most concretely to us by members of the great institutions which spring up to embody, preserve and protect the great treasure of insights

108. E.A.II, p. 88.
109. L.N., p. IX.
110. Ibid, p. XV.
111. Ibid.
112. E.A.I, p. 259.

which have been discovered throughout the ages. Thus the family, the nation and the various social, political and religious institutions become the major bodies into which the largely potential individual is simply born, and if he is to grow and develop he must at first simply trust, accept and endorse their values as though they were his own. Social tradition with its preexisting value system environs us all from the start. Throughout life this objective social system remains necessary because our individual capacity and range for creativity and novelty is really very limited. Here the great unbroken traditions and training schools come to our aid. They extend our limits and bridge the gaps in our individual experience. It is only by a preliminary trust in tradition and in those wiser than ourselves that we have any chance of developing. As the baron writes: "It is by my not denying as false what I do not yet see to be true, that I give myself the chance of growing in insight"[113].

Moreover, the individual himself cannot perceive anything really new without his past (which constitutes his present) influencing his reception and interpretation of it. This is a universal fact and law of apperception. As von Hügel tells us: "it is as it were with the tentacles, the mouth, the digestive apparatus of what I already know, hold, and am, that I can and do seize, swallow, and assimilate what I do not yet know and have, and what as yet I am not"[114]. Our newest insight, our most recent discovery therefore require and depend upon our previous insights, our past, our personal tradition, which is itself encompassed by the larger and greater social traditions. Even our most individual experience always embodies some traditional elements. And although each novel experience never entails a simply passive acceptance of some traditional and conventional truth, it is nevertheless, even when in conflict with this tradition, never completely independent of it. From the beginning man possesses, no matter how obscurely, the sense of both individuality and community. No matter how much these may become differentiated and distinguished later, man's life is always both individual and social from the start. There exists nowhere a self-sufficient, pure individual completely separated and isolated from society and tradition. Not even the greatest individual genius or prophet in the world can escape or replace this social or traditional element[115]. Thus in the constant struggle and tension between the

113. Ibid., p. 14.
114. E.A.II, p. 75. And von Hügel continues: "Professor William James's small boy who, under the great Horseshoe Fall of Niagara, stood dazed with the thought, with the appearance, of such thundering masses of the stuff which his mother, a week before, had blown up his nose, as a cure for some little trouble: there you have the mighty new thing offered, and the tiny sole means of incorporation in the preceiving mind".
115. As the baron writes: "it [tradition] was there, surrounding and moulding the very prenatal existence of each one of us; it will be there, long after we have left the

individual and the tradition no matter what the errors and abuses of the latter, some tradition is not only necessary but operates positively within the most independent and even the most anti-traditional attacks of the individual.

On the other hand, von Hügel is convinced that our social and traditional environment can make no real impression on us unless it answers to and is met by certain subjective needs and desires within us. For no amount of simple exterior attestation or appeal could occcasion an answering perception, interpretation or assent within us, unless we already possessed some sense or dim experience which this appeal evoked within us and which provided us with the possibility to respond to it. Accordingly, though the contribution of tradition is quantitatively or materially the most important, the contribution of the individual is qualitatively or formally for that individual more important still. Both, of course, like matter and form, vocabulary and grammar are always jointly present. But if the authority of tradition expands and deepens individual reason, it is the latter which embraces, restructures and renews or at the very least reinterprets and assimilates the former in a new and unique manner within its own organism. Thus, while tradition's authority cannot simply substitute or supplant our personal experience and activity, it can and ought to supplement and complement it. The difference between these two elements, according to von Hügel, is one only of degree, not of kind. They are not really separate genera but rather two poles within an original experience whose interaction and continual development bring forth something ever new but always old simultaneously. Ultimately the achievements and insights of tradition must be regarded as paradigmatic activities which we accept, explore, renew and hand on as our personal contribution to the perennial problems which face mankind anew in every age. To think that tradition holds a mumified solution to all questions which we must blindly and passively accept and pass on effortlessly to future generations is in fact to destroy tradition as a living reality.

7. *Personality: A Dynamic Conception of the Person*

Experience is a living organic growing process within which the human subject, the articulator, is also a participant, an actor fully involved in the drama. He cannot abstract himself from the process of reality and, as an observer, give a so-called objective picture from outside, nor can he withdraw to some sheltered spot within the flow of

scene. We live and die its wise servants and stewards, or its blind slaves, or in futile, impoverishing revolt against it : we never, for good or evil, really get beyond its reach". M.E.I, p. 59.

existence to recover its meaning or his own selfhood. He must simply explicate the various phases of the movement as they become luminous to the clarifying power of reason from within the ever-growing living process. Von Hügel recognises that man is often tempted to stop this movement and extradite himself from the process. But in a real sense man is condemned to action.

Because he is part of the process of reality man cannot simply remain the same or come to a stand-still when he reaches a special stage or level of existence. The only alternative is "between shrinkage and expansion; between the deteriorating ultimate pain of self-seeking and self-contraction, and the ennobling immediate pangs of self-conquest and self-expansion"[116]. There is a constant conflict and friction between the self as self-seeking, self-attached, self-interested and the same self as it exhibits the opposite attributes of self-transcendence, detachment and disinterestedness. This tension constitutes the fundamental law of our being, since there is an essential and constant conflict and opposition on all levels of our lives between self-attachment and self-detachment. For the present we shall confine our remarks to the more dynamic and formal aspects of this tension. In our final chapter we shall concretise and personalise this.

According to the baron man is essentially a creature of action. Through the action of some parts of himself against others or of his complete self against the exterior would, man gradually grows and becomes his real self. In other words, through his concrete action man not only changes the external world, but more inportantly, he changes and makes his own self. Action is always from, by, of and ultimately on the person himself. And this reflex effect of its own actions upon the central self is the most important result of all our activities for it "culminates in a modification of the personality"[117].

As we have already seen man's personality is a dynamic organism, a multiplicity in unity. This unity is actually constituted, and its perfection is measured by the degree to which it is able to harmonise the multiplicity of elements which go to make it up. However, it is not simply the multiplicity of elements which is important, but also the tension and friction created by their differences. Only through a certain conflict can these supplement, stimulate and purify each other and so propagate further process and growth through their continual attempted higher integration within the organism. So the organic unity by which the person is constituted is only obtained through the slow harmonisation of a variety of conflicting functions and activities. Within the living organism of the person each element is then "an energy and a quality

116. S.L., p. 89.
117. M.E.I, p. 58.

which at each moment modifies and is modified by all the other elements"[118]. No one element can be isolated, separated or allowed to dominate the others without a distortion and a sterilisation of the dynamic whole. Our ideal must be the greatest possible development and interstimulation between the various elements so that the greatest possible unity and harmonisation within the resulting organism is obtained.

But such a complete unification of all the various elements always lies before man. It is a *terminus ad quem*, not a *terminus a quo*[119]. This inner integration and harmonisation, which is ever more required than realised, must be continually reinforced by ever fresh acts. As von Hügel writes: "Strengthen it, and you have interior expansion and life; weaken it, and you bring on shrinkage and death"[120]. Man must leave himself and become involved in the multiplicity of the world, but only to return and through the inner unification of his worldly achievements to construct his own personality. And this double movement of man is not content to remain on the same level, for the ever moving and changing person is "according to the faithful thoroughness or cowardly slackness of these its movements"[121] able either to become more his true self, what he is to be, or fall away from this and deform himself.

Against what he considered to be the Greek, static, quantitative, thingified view of man, von Hügel advances his own dynamic, qualitative, personalistic conception. He contends that from the beginning the Greek or scholastic essence is fixed and stable because it is previous to and independent of action. Personality on the other hand is initially more a possibility than a reality. It is the result and product of action and as such is ever growing or shrinking[122]. Von Hügel is here attempting to weane us away from the then prevalent notion that man was born with a materially fixed essence. Instead he insists that man is always becoming and must from his earliest days set about "*making for*

118. Ibid., p. 106.
119. As the baron writes: "the harmony between the different aspects and levels of life is not, ... the static starting-point or automatically persisting fact in man's life; but it is, on the contrary, his ever difficult, never completely realized goal, — a goal which can be reached only by an ever greater transformation within the worker than within the materials worked upon by him". M.E.II, p. 381.
120. M.E.I, p. 15.
121. Ibid.u pp. 18-19.
122. According to the baron within Greek and scholastic philosophy: "there is no room for the conception of a slow, indefinite acquisition of spiritual substance, of a gradual change, through successive will-acts, in the quality and value of the spiritual entity in man, nor any tolerance for any real becoming, for any measuring of reality by the depth and significance of its growings and its changes, for any apprehension of perfection as necessarily infinite and eternal (not simply very great and immortal), above all for any at all adequate conception of Personality, its passion and its pathos". S.L., p. 92.

himself a character and personality"[123]. Man's personality has to be slowly built up amidst all the various and conflicting cirsumstances of life. His possibilities can be made into actualities and integrated within himself only by a constant struggle with his selfish self, and by a continual emission of fresh individual acts. In this constant struggle to overcome and surmount our various lower selves as they thus appear to us at the various stages of our development, we grow and gradually become our true selves. But on attaining each higher level of selfhood we realise that there must be a renewed movement and conflict, for spontaneously we become aware that our particular achievement and new integration is itself only partial and somewhat imperfect in comparison with our true end. It too must now be relinquished and transcended by ever new and painful acts which will never be completed within this life.

Besides the various relative selves which are constituted and then transcended at the different stages of our life, there are the more fundamental changes. We thus regard conversion as a basic development in man which takes place in the basic self and which makes all further developments possible. These fundamental changes cannot occur, as the baron reminds us, "without a break-up, not only of the soul's habits but even of its standards"[124]. These standards or basic principles of our being lie below our surface activity and our particular actualisations in our various relative selves. They remain deep in our basic self and motivate and ground all our actions. Change here is not from one particular determinate actualisation of our particular capacities at a given time to another, but rather demands a turning of the whole man in his fundamental orientation. Through these changes the person is not simply at a different stage or an a higher level than before, with his inclinations towards good and away from evil materially strengthened, but he is now endeavouring to live a completely different kind of life. Nevertheless, even in this new life man remains man and must continue to make himself through various successive acts. No one specific act, no matter how fundamental, all-englobing or perfect it be, can ever abolish the basic tension and movement of existence and so remove the need for ever fresh and continuous action throughout life. Every new way of life or personal achievement requires to be continually defended and reinforced. We must accept this as a fundamental law of our being. Try what we may, the basic tension of existence between the true and false self can never be surmounted or abolished.

This continuing movement, this never fully accomplished aspiration in man demonstrates, as von Hügel tells us : "that the most fundamental

123. S.L., pp. 88-9.
124. E.L., p. 148.

and irreducible human characteristic lies more in an indefinite capacity for reception and development than in any definite achievement and perfection... for we cannot rid ourselves of the basic desire which lies at the greatest depth of our soul and which in our good moments is transformed into effort or at least into an inclination to effort; though none of these efforts can ever exhaust the exigencies of our being or stop the movement by achieving our perfection. It is this *basic desire* and effort which tends to unify our interior life, to enrich it, to purify it, to determine it and to render it fertile. But with each progress we discover new perspectives and higher summits to be conquered"[125]. Thus after each change in the schemata of our personality a new set is constituted. Yet, as soon as this latest scheme is achieved, we again feel the need to go beyond this new integration to form further and further, deeper and higher integrations. As we continually stressed, the tension between each limited development and achievement and our unrestricted desire, which is the dynamic unifying principle formally structuring our personality, cannot be abolished. This tension and its continual realisation constitutes the dynamism of our personality. And the more truly we become ourselves, the more conscious we become not only of our inability to satisfy our basic desire, but also of the fact that the exigencies which ultimately constitute our being come from beyond ourselves. As the baron expresses it: "One feels very distinctly that it is not in oneself that one should search for the source of one's inquietudes and desires ... for the more one advances the more distinctly one acknowledges that one has a need of grace and that that need would be inexplicable if grace was not already there provoking it. It is the same with the spiritual thrist as with other things. Without the presence of a certain salt in the mouth, one would not feel the need to drink"[126]. Von Hügel likens the salt here which creates the thirst to prevenient grace, and actual grace is seen as the water which quenches this thirst. And while admitting that it is possible for example to proceed like Maréchal and speak of the dynamism of man's intellect or his whole being for transcendence; or again to speak with St. Thomas of man's "natural exigency of the face-to-face Vision of God"[127], von Hügel will not do so. Instead of stressing the dynamism and analysing it as such the baron will insist more on the reason and ground, the cause of this movement, namely the actual presence and givenness within concrete human existence of God's gift of love to each man. In this manner von Hügel believes himself to be following in the footsteps of all the great mystics and saints. These, he maintains: "have, in the very forefront of their consciousness and assumptions,

125. C.E., p. 286. Translated by present writer.
126. Ibid., p. 288.
127. M.E.II, p. 337.

not a simply moral and aspirational, but an Ontological and Pre-established relation between the soul and God; and not a simply discursive apprehension, but a direct though dim Experience of the Infinite and of God"[128].

So as we stressed in our earlier analysis of experience, reality and here the Divine reality, is immediately given, immediately there within the specifically religious experience which is continuous with, but arises as a contrast to and so colours all the rest of our lived experience. And while agreeing with the transcendental thomists that "all our intellectual faculties have a mystical tendency"[129], the baron insists more on the reason for this fact, namely that the mystical or religious sense is primarily an experience of presence. It affirms quite simply what is there, i.e. the real presence yet distinctness of the Divine reality which arises within man's conscious experience on occasion of and as a contrast to his experience of contingent realities.

This will be von Hügel's fundamental position on religious experience. But since he believes in a real continuity between experience as a whole and its religious dimension and since we experience divine reality only on occasion of and as a contrast to our ordinary experience, it has been necessary to articulate a notion of experience wide enough to ground and sufficiently rich enough to reveal in its deepest dimensions the specifically religious experience of the reality of God.

128. Ibid., p. 338.
129. Von Hügel to Bremond, 20 July 1915, SAUL.

CHAPTER IV

THE MYSTICAL ELEMENT OF RELIGION

1. *Finite and Infinite*

The most universal and most specific characteristic of all human life resides, according to von Hügel, in man's total incapacity to fulfill, exhaust or abolish his basic desire to transcend all limitations, finitude and contingency. This fundamental dissatisfaction with his existential situation cannot, in the baron's opinion, be attributed simply to the present limited state of man's knowledge. It springs rather from an ineradicable sense and longing in all men for something more, other and beyond all their present or future achievements. For von Hügel all true human life and all really creative activity always reveal these characteristics. There is a tremendous aspiration and effort after some ideal or perfection, and as von Hügel tells us: "a pathetic half-belief of having at last fully reached it, with, however, even then and there a strongly operative sense that, after all, the reality aimed at remains indefinitely greater and nobler than this attempt, or than the sum-total of all human attempts, to adequate it or exhaust it"[130]. In all our endeavours we quickly realise that even our best achievements are limited, permeated by temporary ignorances and curtailed by present modes and categories of thought. If they are to remain alive fructifying the world, they must be re-fashioned and transformed by other minds and generations who in their turn carry on the eternal quest, equally conscious that their efforts will only partially succeed and so leave them also continually disappointed and restless. Nevertheless, as the baron observes, this lack of finality, this relativity inherent in all man's action and knowledge in no way lessens his desire, even at the cost of great personal suffering and sacrifice to attain ultimate reality and truth. Man simply refuses to remain content with his past achievements or to be confined within his own subjectivity. As von Hügel writes: "the more man feels, and suffers from feeling himself purely subjective, the more is it clear that he is not merely subjective: he could never be conscious of the fact, if he were"[131]. According to the baron, even the most ardent sceptic must admit that if man did not have some real experience of objective reality and ultimately of the supreme

130. E.T.II, p. 361.
131. M.E.II, p. 339.

reality, God, he could not suffer or revolt so much against all attempts to close him up completely within this world[132].

It is because man already apprehends the presence of the Divine reality within the flow of experience that the idea of reality as mere process is so intolerable to him. Man's continual unrest and dissatis- faction with all purely immanent realities springs from the fact that he experiences this as immanent only in relation and in contrast to something other and permanent, transcending the mere process of the world. Because this contrasting other lies beyond this world and is experienced as its ground, man can no longer be happy with anything or any system which does not acknowledge this fact and allow him to act and develop himself accordingly. As von Hügel points out: "A man imprisoned in a railway carriage with the blinds all down, provided only there be no vibration, would be quite unaware of the train's movement, even if it ran through the country-side at sixty miles an hour or more. Only if, and because, he sees things fixed out of the windows, or, at least, things if they have any movement moving appreciably slower than himself, does he know he is moving at all"[133].

Similarly man experiences a sense of finitude, contingency, and in- sufficiency with all transitory reality and pure succession because he experiences also the simultaneous and abiding which raises him above all flux and relativity. Man suffers from this feeling of sheer contingency because he himself is, even potentially, beyond and outside this process. In other words, man's continual dissatisfaction with the finite can only be explained by the fact that he has a real though dim experience of the Infinite, the non-contingent. As the baron writes, it is because men "have the dim, inarticulate sense of what the Abiding means that the mere slush of change is so sickening"[134].

Ultimately then the restlessness and dissatisfaction with the contin- gent which sparks the desire for a certain permanence beyond and

132. Von Hügel stresses this when he writes: "Blessing, there is a fact which more and more impresses and keeps me steady... we remain as much, as, indeed more than ever, pained, oppressed, irritated by all *mere* contingency, all *mere* subjectivity, everything that is *simply my* fancy or *yours*. Why and whence is this? It is very certain that if we were really shut up within a stream or ocean of mere contingency, sheer happenings, simply intra-individual or even intra-human impressions, happenings, facts, we could not have this suffering, this driving force in our lives and that this suffering must come from our having however dimly, yet *most* really, most operatively, the experience and surely hence the requirement of the necessary, the Perfect, the Abiding, of Spirit, of God". Von Hügel to J. Mansel, 12 May 1911, SAUL.

133. R.G., p. 63.

134. S.L., p. 364. Against Goethe's dictum that "man never knows how anthropo- morphic he is" the baron simply reminds us that "it was a man, Goethe, it is at bottom all men, in proportion as they are fully, sensitively such, who have somehow discovered this truth; who suffer from its continuous evidences, as spontaneously as from the toothache or from insomnia". M.E.II, p. 282.

transcending the flux of existence is a concomitant of the presence within man's life of the non-contingent, the contrasting other, the infinite and transcendent reality of God. But the sense of the Infinite is not reached through some intellectual deduction upon finite data, nor can we attribute it to a specific mental category of the Infinite which would be evoked on occasion of man's knowledge or action on finite data. The experience comes, as von Hügel insists, from "the ontological presence of, and the operative penetration by the Infinite Spirit, within the human spirit"[135]. It is the presence of the Infinite Spirit within man which structures his humanity and produces on occasion of his contact with the contingent the keen sense of disappointment with everything finite[136].

2. *Dim Experience of God*

We must now examine the argument that negative theology, especially as articulated by the mystics, abolishes the fact of our dim experience of God. The *via negativa* arises from the fact that the Ground of our existence is not to be found among the things of the external world, it is not of this world. Some mystical positions, however, can become so extreme in their emphasis on negativity that they become almost agnostic. God's infinitude and incomprehensibleness is so conceived as to abolish all objective superiority between one experience or conception of Him and another. The baron finds this in some of the teachings of Pseudo-Dionysius, where Denis stresses that: "The Super-Unknown ... is altogether incomprehensible to all. ... To none is it permitted to celebrate the supremely Divine Essentiality either as word or power, as mind or life or essence, but only as pre-eminently separated from every condition"[137]. Elsewhere, especially in the third chapter of his *Mystical Theology*, the Areopagite speaks of grades of appropriateness in God's attributes. There are degrees of worth and approximation in the positive attributions and degrees of inapplicability and remoteness among the negative ones. As Dionysius writes: "Is He not, e.g., more nearly Life and Goodness than He is air or stone? And is He not further removed from debauch and wrath than He is from unspeakableness and inconceivability?"[138].

---

135. M.E.II, p. 282.
136. As the baron writes quoting C.P. Tiele: "But why should man torment himself with wishes which he never sees fulfilled around him, and which the rationalist philosopher declares to be illusions? Why? surely, because he cannot help it ... The Infinite, very Being as opposed to continual becoming and perishing, — or call It what you will, — *that* is the Principle which gives him constant unrest, because It dwells within him". M.E.II, p. 339.
137. E.T.II, p. 375.
138. Ibid., p. 376.

Von Hügel insists that such a scale of appropriateness would not be possible unless we had some obscure experience of or knew to some extent *what* God was. He reminds us that in his commentary on Dionysius' *Mystical Theology* Balthazar Corderius shows that all Denis's negative proportions, e.g. "God is not Being, not Life" presuppose a positive affirmation, namely that "God is Being and Life, in manner infinitely more sublime and perfect than we are able to comprehend"[139]. And Corderius gives arguments and authors from St. Jerome to St. Thomas for holding that we have some direct confused knowledge (experience as the baron terms it) of God's existence and nature quite apart from our reasoning and inferences from sense data.

According to von Hügel, St. Thomas himself offers a further proof that we have such an experience when after attempting to show that we can know *that* God is but not *what* He is, Aquinas admits that we do have some real experience of God himself. In his *In Librum Boetii de Trinitate* St. Thomas tells us: "In our earthly state we cannot attain to a knowledge of God Himself beyond the fact that He exists. And yet, among those who know *that* He is, the one knows this more perfectly than the other"[140]. Accordingly, while attempting to prove that we can only know *that* God is, St. Thomas admits that we have some knowledge of his nature. For if we could have knowledge only of the existence of a particular reality and not its nature, then no increase in knowledge of that reality's bare existence would be possible. The answer to the question of existence is simply yes or no. The difference of degrees which is presumed to concern only the bare existence of God is applicable only to a knowledge of His nature. The baron concludes therefore that Aquinas acknowledges that we have some confused knowledge (experience) of the reality of God. This being the case, von Hügel maintains that there can be no strict or real distinction between our experience of God's existence and His nature: both belong together. Consequently, we must replace the terms as to our utter ignorance of God's nature by indices expressive of an experience which, if not directly and clearly analysable by our reflective critical reason, is nevertheless profoundly real and indefinitely operative throughout all the realms of our life. Our endeavours in the first section of this chapter were aimed at describing this operative presence which we deemed to be the most universal and characteristic experience of the specifically human life. It is the sense of the mere contingency and finitude and the constant unrest, dissatisfaction and discontentment with all reality which we directly experience. We do not experience God's presence directly. However, His presence

---

139. M.E.II, p. 288.
140. Ibid., p. 289.

can be ascertained by its repercussions throughout our life and these experiences then act as the existential medium through which the immediate and direct presence of the Divine becomes fully conscious to us. The finite and the Infinite are really two poles of the one experience. We become aware of the Infinite only indirectly, i.e. on occasion of, as a contrast to and concomitantly with our direct experience of the finite. As we shall see later, there will be no inference from the finite to the Infinite, but a contuition of one, the Infinite, on occasion of and as a contrast to the other, the finite.

The position which von Hügel arrives at then is midway between deism "with its spatial outsidedness and distance of God"[141] and a pantheism where God is equally present within all things. According to the baron while nothing is God or part of Him, everything is in God, is penetrated and encompassed by Him. This panentheistic middle position "whilst ever holding the definite creaturelines of the soul, in all its reaches, puts God Himself into the soul and the soul into God, in degrees and with results which vary indeed indefinitely according to its good-will and its call, yet which all involve and constitute a presence ever profoundly real, ever operative before and beyond all the soul's own operations"[142]. We are actually touched and inhabited by God in whom we participate and yet this immanence involves no identity. The Divine prevenience and the essentially giving and gratuitous quality of God's love in our hearts along with the Divine Transcendence is thus preserved and reinforced. The baron stresses this "Divine anticipation, origination, preservation, stimulation" and speaks of a certain "Divine Self-Restraint"[143] which renders man's experience and response even possible. Because of this Divine indwelling and presence man feels the need and the desire to become more like that in which he participates. It is this transcendent dynamism which structures and intrinsically constitutes our humanity and which the sum total of all our immanent achievements will never satiate or exhaust. It is only the close identification of the seeking with the sought and the too exclusive realisation that what we seek has already been dimly found that lead many mystics in their expressions to evaporate the real quest and dynamism of the search and as a result to give the appearance of Pantheism.

3. Divine Transcendence

Against this pantheistic trend in religion it must be emphasised that within the specifically religious experience the Divine pole is experienced

141. F. VON HÜGEL, The Relations Between God and Man in The New Theology of the Reverend R. J. Campbell, p. 664.
142. M.E.II, p. 336.
143. Ibid.

not only as present within but also as Beyond, Other and Transcendent. While the religious consciousness proclaims the immense closeness, penetrating and transforming power of the Divine, it is simultaneously aware of the immense difference — a difference not only in degree but also in kind between itself and God [144]. It is important to note that the Divine Other maintains its reality for us only in relation to a contrasting relative series. If we take the Divine pole of the experience, treat our first vivid apprehension of It as a separate clear distinct idea and use this as the starting point and object of a strictly deductive system, then the living reality of religion crumbles before our eyes and we are left with mere formulae and abstractions. For the two poles experienced within the movement of existence are thereby hypostatised and erected into entities for systematic, logical and purely doctrinal deductions. Von Hügel demands that we distinguish very carefully between the dim concrete though real experience of the Infinite (always occuring in contrast to a relative series) spontaneously alive within us, and the clear abstractive idea of the Infinite which is purely intellectual and has little or no connection with living religion.

However, the other conveyed to us as a contrast to the relative is not always the specific religious otherness. Often the otherness which moves us or towards which we strive is of a mere quantitative kind, e.g. my particular science's progress, my nation's advancement, or some cultural achievements. These can and do furnish the otherness and the ideal for many people. Yet, they are but the outer shell of a still deeper otherness which is a difference not of quantity or degree but of quality and kind. It is experienced as an-other mode of being not simply distinct and above, but transcendentally and completely Other and Beyond us. And yet this central Transcendent Otherness is simultaneously felt to be the ground and condition of those othernesses which may be our better self but are certainly not God.

We shall briefly examine von Hügel's position on the specifically religious experience in so far as it contrasts with that of Friedrich Schleiermacher. In the baron's opinion, Schleiermacher gives us a brilliant description of the intuitive-emotional and experiential aspect

144. E.T.I, pp. 432-3. As the baron writes to George Tyrrell: "I have had for years, increasingly, a double sense: of the large, spacious, range of our ethical etc. capacities, and of the necessity and value of an ideal and indefinite exercise for them; *and* of all this not being God, not one bit, not one bit. Until a man feels this, sees this, till it pierces his soul: Eucken has this constant sense, Troeltsch has it; Seeley had it not, nor (I think) Comte: he has not, I think, waked up to the *specifically* religious consciousness, or at least, to the central point of its analysis. God is emphatically *not* simply our Highest Selves; heaven for us will *not* be a simple adequation or a simple identification (even in *kind*, apart from all degree) of our nature with God's; religion is *not* a simple or full intercourse between equals (in kind any more than in degree), where the movement from God to man can be understood by tracing it backwards, in the movement from man to God". S.L., pp. 124-5.

of religion and he is completely at one with the latter's sharp distinction between religion, metaphysics and morality. Von Hügel also believes that Schleiermacher's description of the central core of religious experience "as a sense both of contact between finite realities and of the Infinite Reality within, and in contrast to, those finites"[145] is admirable. However, it is on this fundamental point the baron feels that Schleiermacher's critical subjectivism prevents him from being fully satisfactory in two important respects. Firstly, Schleiermacher accepts that we can know the universe as such, but von Hügel believes that he is so afraid that our perception distorts it as it is in itself that he will not affirm anything ontological of it. In his theory of knowledge then Schleiermacher, like the critical Kant, permits only a real knowledge of human knowledge generally and not of objects as such. As a result, the baron concludes that in religion Schleiermacher brings us to "a genuine feeling only of human feeling generally"[146] without any real acceptance of a distinct object which is the cause of such feeling. For von Hügel on the contrary the specifically religious experience resides ultimately in "an intuition and feeling of Reality as distinct from, as prior and subsequent to, as indefinitely more than, and as the cause of, the activities through which we apprehend it"[147]. Basically the religious experience is an experience of a Transcendent reality and not of any system of abstract principles. Religion is essentially metaphysical and dogmatic and, as the baron says, "if all Ontology is illusion, then all Religion is so likewise"[148].

With von Hügel's second criticism we come to our particular problematic. According to the baron the specific religious sense is one "of *a depth of Reality greater and other than*" ourselves or of the universe as a whole, while Schleiermacher's sense is more one of a "Spatial Infinite"[149]. The Infinite to which we are awakened, on occasion of our contact with the finite, in the religious experience is for von Hügel not a boundless extension of the finite, but "a Reality contrasting with, whilst partially expressing Itself in, those finitudes, a Reality helpful towards, because Itself possessing, in an unspeakable manner and degree, all that is highest in ourselves"[150]. In this the baron agrees with all the great Christian mystics who have been restless for a Divine reality present everywhere within, though also transcendent and beyond the world.

145. E.L., p. 186.
146. Ibid., p. 187.
147. Ibid..
148. Ibid., p. 188.
149. Ibid..
150. Ibid..

4. *True Mysticism : One Element of Religion*

There is no specifically distinct, purely mystical mode of apprehending reality. To believe in a separate, self-supporting mystical experience is to fall into the error which the baron terms exclusive or false mysticism. According to von Hügel, even the most exclusively mystical soul always requires some contact with finite, contingent, spatio-temporal reality and with society, since the mystical sense is evoked only on such occasions. The Christian mystic must be in the world but not of it. He lives on two levels, in the world of time and of eternity. Neither can be separated since they are polar aspects of the same experience. It is only by living on both levels and allowing the creative tension between them to fructify his life that the mystic develops. Ultimately all this rests on the fact that man experiences himself to exist in a "rich middle position, of an admittedly ever unfinished movement, tension, and mixture"[151] of life and death, time and eternity, this world and the other. As we shall see later, life must not be seen as a circle round a single centre, but as an ellipse with two foci, e.g. God and man, divine and human, grace and nature, the other-world and this-world. Our ideal end is to make ourselves into a rich organic personality by a maximum of multiplicity and this-worldly attachment permeated, purified and harmonised by a maximum of unity and other-worldly detachment. Precisely in the tension between these contrasting poles lies the richness and fruitfulness of life and the source of its "perennial youth and renovative power"[152].

The mystic as mystic ever strives to be recollective and to ignore or neglect the absolutely necessary contact with the world of sense in the hope that he can thus give himself more fully to God. Yet, in attempting to detach oneself from the things of this-world one runs the danger of losing all contact and interest in the visible, material world and in the process denying one's own existence as an embodied-spirit-in-the-world. However, by absorbing oneself completely in this-world one can become so caught up in material, immanent matters that one gradually becomes assimilated to them. Mysticism therefore is only true when it is not everything in anyone but something in everyone. In other words, when it is a mixed or partial mysticism and not exclusive.

Pure mysticism must be rejected because we can acquire and retain a vivid sense of the religious Infinite only through close contact with finite reality. As we shall see, it is especially through our encounter with God's self-manifestation in particular finite beings

151. R.G., p. 195.
152. E.L., p. 315.

and in a supreme way in Jesus Christ that a full personal and concrete religion is developed. What the baron demands is an incarnational mysticism, as Christianity proposes. And while he stresses the importance of man's going out into the external world, he fully realises that the interior, incoming recollective movement is not only essential but ultimately the more centrally religious, of the two movements necessary for the acquisition of spiritual experience and life.

Because the more neo-Platonic type of mystic flees the temporal world to be alone with the Alone, the impression is given that he has no need of any mediations, in other words that the mystical experience is a pure immediacy. This view was challenged by Ernst Troeltsch who maintained that in comparison with historical, institutional religion, mysticism is always secondary and reflective. Von Hügel came to agree with this and to hold that the mysticism which regards itself as primary and immediate always results from the elaboration and assimilation of some positive historical religion. Nevertheless, the baron feels that because the mystical interpretation always succeeds the external events of religious history in time, it does not follow that it is simply an addition or a substitute for the original historical event. While agreeing that the mystical type of religion is secondary and reflective, von Hügel is convinced that there is some element of immediacy in the mystic's experience. Ontologically there is a real, direct relationship between the soul and God. However, we do not grasp the Absolute separately or alone but only concomitantly with, on occasion of and as a contrast to our apprehension of the finite. Our consciousness of our finitude and contingency acts as the existential medium, (there is no discursive inference), through which we become aware of the immediate presence of the Infinite within us. Ontologically the priority must be given to the immediate presence; logically and psychologically it belongs to our existential consciousness of finitude and contingency. In a real sense than we can speak of our knowledge of God as a mediated-immediacy.

CHAPTER V

THE DEMISE OF THE MYSTICAL ELEMENT

1. *Religion and Morality*

Among philosophers von Hügel holds Kant responsible, in a large measure, for the demise of the mystical element of religion. As he tells us, Kant in 1793 had held that: "Such a feeling of the immediate presence of the Supreme Being, and such a discrimination between this feeling and every other, even moral, feeling, would imply a capacity for an intuition, which is without any corresponding organ in human nature"[153]. Kant therefore felt that the mystical sense ought to be replaced by a compound of moral interest and a striving for happiness. While the baron realises that these elements are connected with religion, an examination of religious experience and history, he believes, shows that the essence of religion lies elsewhere. Kant's one-sidedness in basing religion on morality (oughtness) to the neglect of ontology (being, presence) undermines von Hügel's conviction of the *sui generis* character of religious experience. As we shall see, the baron will hold emphatically to the distinction between ethics (oughtness) and religion (isness).

According to von Hügel, the non-identity of religion and morality can be seen from the fact that though both influence each other, they never follow the same line of development in the history of a particular human being or of humanity in general[154]. While admitting that the development of the religious life always presupposes certain moral values and training the baron asserts that the specifically religious sense is not derived from a sense of duty but rather from one of presence. And although this presence implies certain obligations, it is basically not directed towards obligation, but to a sense of peace and joy which it brings to those who acknowledge it. In spite of the

---

153. M.E.II, p. 260.
154. The baron elucidates his position in a letter to a Mr. Malcolm Quin when he writes: "You appeal with A. [uguste] C. [omte], to righteousness, to the hunger for moral perfection, as the easy, true, way to religion, and Catholicism, — and this as though there were an identity between morality and religion. I should answer; 'for propaedeutic purposes, yes; intrinsically, no'. I feel confident that the two are not, *at bottom*, the same thing, nor even different stages of the same thing. ... Religion, I feel more and more, is (in contrast with Ethics) essentially concerned with what *already* is and most speedily will be, and with what is indeed environing and penetrating man ever on and on, but yet as superhuman, other than simply human, as truly transcendent, and not only immanent". S.L., p. 174.

intrinsic relationship, religion must be distinguished from morality because ultimately it proclaims not a sense of "oughtness" but of "Isness". Religion is primarily evidential, it intimates a supernatural world and reality and it affirms a real contact with this reality which is felt to be within and yet beyond our experience[155]. Von Hügel believes that the deepest characteristic of the specifically religious outlook lies in the profound sense of the presence of an over-flowing reality, with its element of "Otherness", "Over-against-ness", "Contrada"[156]. Within religion man recognises that his basic movement towards God is primarily a response to and an effect of the Divine reality which, through Its presence, awakens man to Its existence and draws him to Itself. Religion therefore, according to the baron: "Affirms as supreme *Isness*, a Reality or Realities other and greatest in man, as existent prior to, and independently of, the human subject's affirmation of It or of Them. Indeed this Reality is held to occasion such affirmation and to express Itself, however inadequately, in this human response"[157].

While religion is related to morals and to all other areas of human life no intimation or experience within these areas can replace the super-human reality given within the specifically religious domain. Religion ultimately is not concerned with morals, laws, social advancement, or scientific discovery, but as the baron writes, "with fear, propitiation, love, adoration of what already is"[158]. And even where religion seems to be simply about morality or human values, it always envisages them within a deeper context. For example, while morality proper stresses the primacy of "Responsibility, Prudence, Merit, Reward, Irretrievable-ness"[159], religious ethics emphasises "Trust, Grace, Heroism, Love, Free Pardon, Spiritual Renovation"[160]. As we shall see later within the truly Christian life, neither area can be neglected, for it is only

155. The baron maintains: "that the natural, external world (especially in so far as it is organic) and our knowledge of it possess certain characteristics which bring them *nearer* to the central characteristics of religion than do the ethical world and our apprehension of it. This because religion, at least among the mystics (and I believe that, on this point at least, the mystics merely dive deeper into and bring out more explicitly the sap or the central core of the religious passion), consists centrally in the sense of Presence — the sense of an overflowing Existence distinct from our own and in the Adoration of the same. True, this Presence, this Existence, is apprehended as All Good, as Beatific because All Good ... Yet it is equally true that even sheer Perfection leaves him cold so long as it claims to exist, or may possibly, after all, exist, only as an idea within our own mind, or even within the mind of mankind at large". R.G., p. 71.

156. E.A.II, p. 248.
157. E.A.I, p. 23.
158. Ibid..
159. M.E.II, p. 274.
160. Ibid..

through their creative tension that ethics becomes deepened and religion broadened. However, we must now proceed to analyse the theological repercussions of this Kantian retreat from the mystical element in religion.

2. *Non-Mystical Religion*

In the second half of the nineteenth century Kant's impoverishment of religion was reflected in Ritschlian theology and especially in one of the chief exponents of this school, Wilhelm Herrmann. While Kant derived belief in God from an analysis of goodness and happiness, (God being the unifying principle of both), Herrmann continued his stress on the categorical imperative but replaced the desire for happiness with the historical Jesus. For Herrmann complete religion is based on the acceptance of two experiences. First the categorical imperative of moral conscience and secondly on the historical Jesus who is seen as the unique perfect realisation of this imperative and so as the perfect revelation of the meaning of reality and the unique help in our response to that imperative.

Mysticism is therefore excluded from the life of faith. As Herrmann says : "True, outside of Christianity, Mysticism will everywhere arise, as the very flower of the religious development. But a Christian is bound to declare the mystical experience of God to be a delusion. Once he has experienced his elevation, by Christ alone, above his own previous nature, he cannot believe that another man can attain the same result, simply by means of recollection within his own self. ... We are Christians precisely because we have struck, in the person of Jesus, upon a fact which is incomparably richer in content than the feelings that arise within ourselves" [161]. What Herrmann has done is to whittle down what we termed mixed, partial or true mysticism (the Christian conception) to the sub-reality of pure, exclusive or false mysticism (in the neo-Platonic sense). After replacing the total reality by this partial notion, he proceeds to emphasise the falsehood of this latter conception and to erect his own position on the portion of reality this view neglects, i.e. the exterior historical aspect of religion. It becomes quickly evident, however, that this position is one-sided and unbalanced. For instance, he believes that we would not recognise any gift of God throughout history or in our personal life, except "God appeared to me in the historic Christ" [162]. But as we saw earlier, no purely exterior event or appeal could elicit or evoke a response or commitment from us unless we already possessed a sense which could appreciate and recognise this appeal and so afford us the possibility and the desire

161. Ibid., pp. 263, 332.
162. E.T.II, p. 366.

to respond and answer it. And all the great representatives of the historical religions have witnessed to the presence of such a sense and affirm having such a vague but most real experience of the Infinite "to which the historic revelation comes as the ever more or less necessary, full stimulation, expansion, response and transformation"[163].

Herrmann's protest may be seen as a legitimate reaction to all empty sentimental subjectivism or false mysticism and a reaffirmation of the importance of the concrete, of the historical and of the centrality of Jesus Christ's place in Christianity. However, we may not presume it to have abolished the necessity and reality of true mysticism. Against his charge that the mystic's experience is sentimental subjectivism we would remind the reader that, as we saw earlier, our authentic experience is always an experience of reality from the start, there is no such thing as the purely objective or the purely subjective. These two poles are later differentiations within experience which cannot be separated, isolated or hypostatised without destroying the reality of experience. Herrmann is so afraid of falling into subjectivism, that he refuses to acknowledge the legitimacy of the subjective factor in experience and consequently "he is driven to follow the will-o'-the-wisp ideal of a pure, entirely exclusive objectivity"[164]. Drawn by this need for pure objectivity Herrmann is compelled to define all mysticism as exclusive (as pure subjectivism). Mysticism consists according to him "solely in an interior experience of the individual soul... without any exterior being apprehended"[165]. But as we have shown, true mysticism is never simply exclusive, i.e. a purely interior experience but ever partial, mixed. It presupposes a real contact with the religious reality through some mediation and contact with the external world, history and community. We acknowledge the illusionary character of such a self-sufficient exclusive mysticism which can only arise when the polarity of the original experience has been rent asunder. What Herrmann has done therefore is to substitute a deformed sort of mysticism for the true one, shown up the flaws in the substitute, (which we are supposed to see as the real), and expected us to conclude from this that all mysticism must be rejected. This trick is also used by all projectionist theoretists. They refuse to work with a broad and open conception of experience within which objective reality is immediately given. They obscure this fact, confine themselves within a closed sub-field which excludes one pole of experiential truth and expect us also to operate within their warped world. If we enter this world, we lose the only thing worth having, namely reality itself. There is no way out, the only escape is to refuse to enter.

163. Ibid..
164. M.E.II, p. 264.
165. Ibid..

For the rest the baron can agree with Herrmann that God reveals himself fully and personally in human history alone and "in a supreme and normative manner, in the life and teaching of Jesus Christ"[166]. Naturally it would be against the whole plane of salvation for us to neglect or ignore God's own condescensions. However, von Hügel believes that even this essential historical element in Christianity is endangered by Herrmann's excessive christocentricism, his "Pan-christism"[167], as he calls it. According to Herrmann "right prayer is a work of faith, and only a Christian can perform it"[168]. And again he tells us: "I should have failed to recognize the hand of God even in what my own dead father did for me, had not, by means of my Christian education, God appeared to me, in the Historic Christ"[169]. If this be so, von Hügel warns us, then none of the great prophets, nor any of the many devoted people in the earlier non-christian religions could have experienced anything of the divine providence in their human father's love for them, nor have even had any real experience of the true God. As he writes: "if Christ Himself be 'the true Light that enlighteneth every man that cometh into the world,' He cannot be this Light solely by means of men's historic knowledge of the historic Christ, since even now the large majority of men have no such knowledge of Him"[170]. As the baron sees it there is "a divinely-implanted innate tendency towards this light, extant in man prior to the explicit act of faith, and operative outside of the Christian body"[171]. If this were not so, he maintains, we would make Our Lord into so exclusive a centre of the Divine that he would come into a completely God-forsaken world. And Christianity would then have no affinity with the universal unrest and religious seeking and revealing of the Divine present "in various degrees and ways, in every place and time"[172]. Von Hügel therefore demands a real interdependence and connection between what he terms diffused religiosity and concrete, historical, characteristic religion which, after an indefinitely long series of lesser manifestations, reaches its supreme term and culminating point in the person of Jesus Christ who is "the central Revelation, the final Incarnation of God in man"[173].

Thus the prior existence of the light in the world allows people, in various preliminary degrees and ways, to believe in the Divine without an explicit knowledge of the historic Christ. It is only as a conse-

166. Ibid..
167. Ibid., p. 266.
168. Ibid., p. 263.
169. Ibid., p. 332.
170. E.T.II, p. 366.
171. M.E.II, p. 79.
172. Ibid., p. 267.
173. E.T.II, p. 363.

quence of this that Christ Himself is recognised as really "the very centre, and sole supreme manifestation and measure of all this light"[174]. Moreover for Christianity to be the culminating and fullest form of religion, it must after all have something to crown and measure. In other words, this conception of Christianity demands that we acknowledge some fragments, stages and degrees of truth and goodness in religion outside the specific confines of Christianity. This implies no trace of indifferentism or naturalism. For although there is some light everywhere it varies immensely in different ages and places, among various groups and between particular individuals. And over and above these involuntary genuine differences, there are also those which result from man's intentional cowardice and opposition to the degree of light given to him personally. Consequently, God's universal gift of Love which allows various degrees of true religious experience to be scattered everywhere is not equally present nor brought to equal fruition everywhere or by everyone.

However, before going on to examine the degree and kind of light present in the various non-chistian religions, we would like to stress that one of the most important contributions of the mystical element is that it helps keep alive and reminds us continually of the universal prerequisites and affinities in man for the apprehension of the concrete historical aspects of religion. Such special personal revelations and their dogmatic expressions as are found in the historical religions and in a supreme manner in Christianity, are necessary for the preservation, development, communication and consolidation of the religious message. But they "ever presuppose a general, usually dim but most real, religious sense and experience, indeed a real presence and operation of the Infinite and of God in all men"[175].

3. Christianity and Other Religions

One of the great difficulties resulting from our adherence to one particular religion, (however necessary this be for the growth of the spiritual life) is that we are almost naturally inclined to endow it with all truth and goodness and to class all other religions as false. And the more fervent religionists we are, the greater the danger becomes of believing that our religion is the only true one. According to the baron, St. Paul in some elements of his teachings furnishes a remarkable example of this. After his conversion he tended to regard the whole Old Testament religion simply as a sign of our sinfulness and as having no power of effectuating salvation for us. We

174. M.E.II, p. 268.
175. Ibid., p. 332.

confront here not only a perennial phenomenon in the history of
religion, but in all history. For after almost every great change, personal
conversion, social or political revolution, etc. man concentrates on
the new discoveries and even delights in denigrating and deepening
the gulf between this new insight or way of life and what he held or
was before. There is a real problem here, since the distortions
spring from a kernel of truth in the proponent's experience, e.g.
Christianity and Judaism are really different. However, with a special
eye to balancing this Pauline one-sidedness von Hügel introduces
the Synoptic tradition which recognises "certain true elements in the
pre- and extra-Christian religions"[176]. In line with this Synoptic view
he reminds us that the more authentic Catholic tradition has always
refused to confine itself entirely to the novel aspects in revelation, but has
ever attempted to embrace the manysidedness and complexity of
Christianity as a synthetic whole.

In this perspective von Hügel considers it a true blessing that
Christianity historically sprung from another religion, namely Judaism,
since this obliges it to deeply respect at least one other religion. As a
matter of fact, Christianity was faced with this problem and alternative early in its history when the Montanists held that the New
Testament was from God and the Old from the devil. The Church
authorities intervened and declared that both testaments were of
Divine origin. In the baron's opinion this decision committed
Christianity and Catholicism to a broad, tolerant, open position and
to the recognition of different degrees and kinds of truth in other
religions and to various phases of growth and development in the
Divine light.

Von Hügel constantly refers to Juan de Lugo[177] to reinforce his
position regarding the degrees and stages of truth in other religions.
According to de Lugo, Catholic doctrine teaches us that "God gives
light, sufficient for its salvation, to every soul that attains to the
use of reason in this life"[178]. And although he admits that God
could reveal himself by strict miracle to each individual, he contends
that this is not strictly necessary nor is it the normal means of
revelation or salvation. Usually the sincere soul, under the influence

---

176. Ibid., p. 118.

177. Von Hügel tells us: "De Lugo (A.D.1583-1660), Spaniard, post-Reformation
Roman Catholic Jesuit, Theological Professor, and a Cardinal writing in Rome under
the eyes of Pope Urban VIII, teaches that the members of the various Christian
sects, of the Jewish and Mohammedan communions, and of the heathen religions and
philosophical schools, who achieve their salvation, do so, ordinarily, simply through the
aid afforded by God's grace to their good faith in its instinctive concentration upon,
and in its practice of, those elements in their respective community's worship and
teaching, which are true and good and originally revealed by God". E.A.I, p. 2.
Cf. also E.A.I, p. 63; E.L., pp. 350-1.

178. E.A.I, p. 252.

of grace, seeks and finds God and His truth within the religious
and philosphical environment, the culture, institutions, community,
and tradition in which he is brought up. In the baron's opinion
this view, while acknowledging man's profound need of tradition and
institutional training, also recognises the subjectivity and dispositions of
the individual and the variety of God's special graces to individual
souls and their response. Only in this way, he maintains, do we "attain
an outlook, generous, rich, elastic; yet also graduated, positive, unitary,
and truly Catholic"[179].

What makes this broader position often difficult to hold for a
Catholic, according to von Hügel, is not so much the sacramental
system as such, but a particular conception of it which has gradually
come to the fore. As the baron sees it the sacraments can be
viewed in two ways. We can regard Baptism and the Eucharist
either as the apex of a rich totality of many visible gifts and
helps given to different people in various traditions by God; or
we can see them as being so exclusively the vehicle of grace that
whoever does not partake of them, remains without any supernatural grace whatsoever. This latter position has never been traditional
Catholic teaching, since it would exclude approximately four-fifths of
mankind from the possibility of salvation. As the baron reminds
us, even the strictest Catholics have always spoken of a Baptism of
desire which in special circumstances can take the place of the sacrament. And the desire mentioned here is not for the sacrament as
such, i.e. for its specific matter and form, but is rather a "deep and
sincere longing for purification from all sin and sinful inclinations by
God"[180].

Of course, there is a form of apologetic which tries to combine the
strictest sacramentalism with the widest possible operation of grace.
This sees the saintly priest, through some special divine intervention,
being brought hundreds of miles to the deathbed of someone
longing for Baptism. Not that this can be completely excluded,
but with de Lugo, von Hügel feels that this makes what is really
extraordinary into the normal means of God's ordinary providence.
Furthermore, although every human being receives sufficient grace
for his salvation, this in no way means that all receive it equally or
respond to it in the same degree. There is also he believes a profound
difference between the various religions. So, while being open to
the truth of each, we must be constantly aware of the danger of
all indifferentism, of a levelling-down of all to a common denominator.
Against this trend the baron insists on different grades of "God's
upward-moving self-revelation"[181]. "This would constitute an attempt

179. Ibid., p. 253.
180. R.G., pp. 148-9.
181. L.N., p. 57.

to level up"[182], it would mean an effort at erecting an ascending order of religious values by an impartial study and then to see their numerous increasingly adequate and comprehensive representatives and embodiments. In this view, for example, the Sikh religion would be higher than unreformed Hinduism, Judaism fuller and deeper than this and, of course, Christianity, for the baron, would be the full realisation and fulfilment of the various upward movements of God's light and grace. And, as von Hügel argues, only when Christianity is regarded as the fulfilment of a series of varyingly lesser manifestations can it truly be seen as the crown, goal and measure of them all and as such the religion of all religions.

Despite his openness and tolerance the baron does not hesitate to persist in his belief in the universality of the claims of Christianity. According to him it is precisely because we see Christianity and Catholicism especially as having a message and a meaning for all men that both it and we must be large and many-sided, because both it and we have to answer to an indefinite variety of souls and needs. In fact, the moment we treat Christianity or Catholicism as one among many means to salvation established by God which will continue until the end of time, then, von Hügel contends, there will be no real reason for keeping our outlook broader than our own particular denomination, since after all it is only as necessary, as good or bad as all the rest. If this situation was allowed to develop, Catholicism would become simply a narrow religion of sacristans cut off from the rest of life. Accordingly the baron demands that Catholicism must never give up its ideal of becoming the one universal Church, but as he sees it this is realisable only if we recognise "the rudimentary, fragmentary, relative, paedagogic truth and worth in religions other than our own"[183].

4. *Christianity: Mystical and Historical Religion*

As we saw, God reveals himself to man in a twofold manner : vaguely but most really through his operative presence in man's dim, obscure experience and concretely and personally in and through the great revealers of religion, the prophets and especially Jesus Christ[184]. Man's

---

182. E.A.I, p. 7.
183. Ibid., p. 63.
184. Von Hügel exemplifies this in his own amicable fashion in the following analogue : "Some years ago alarm grew rife, concerning the safety of Winchester Cathedral, discovered to be undermined by water-courses; and expert divers, ... plunged down through the springs to the swamps and sands ... The divers found the great oaken beams, as laid by those first builders upon those shifting natural foundations, still, for the most part, serviceably sound. Yet some of these beams required replacing; and the

dim confused sense of God is, as we emphasised, awakened on occasion of and as a contrast to his experience of the finitude and contingency of ordinary reality. This sense expresses itself as an existential unrest. However, this unrest and the search which issues already carries the soothing answer within the luminosity of its movement. In other words, man is moved, attracted and drawn in his search of the Ground by the Divine ground of which he is in search. This Ground cannot be regarded as purely immanental because in the specific religious experience the central experience is of something beyond, other and transcending all contingent reality. Nevertheless, in real life this dim sense is never a merely formal dynamism but it always encounters clear concrete and personal embodiments of what it seeks, in the traditions, history and visible institutions of the various religions. In this way the initial confused experience becomes more clear and concrete, fully realised, even transformed. For although in some sense we already know the end from the beginning of the search, the final discovery so surpasses all our wildest expectations that it is something really new. Thereafter we are still the one man but no longer really the same.

It is sometimes felt, especially by institutional religionists, that this dim experience or the sense of the Infinite, which we treated earlier, is but a sort of religiosity whereas religion proper resides in the specific religious institutions and their sacramental and dogmatic systems. Some thinkers even see a conflict and opposition or at best no interconnection whatsoever between the sense of the Infinite and faith in God. These men are convinced that while philosophy may arrive at an Infinite in the general, cosmic, non-personal sense, religion alone can bring us to a Personal God. For such people "these two objects and man's respective approaches to them ever remain parallel and distinct, and never succeed, stimulate or supplement each other"[185]. For the baron however, while there may be little or no connection between our reflective, clear, purely intellectual idea of the Infinite and the actual reality of God, this is not true of our confusedly concrete sense of the Infinite. For this latter more confused universal sense of the Infinite ever arises only on occasion of and as a contrast

---

guardian architects decided to replace them all by great concrete piers. We too, in this study, have been probing foundations — those of Religion. But here we have found the foundations to consist of rock — two interdependent, interclamped rock-masses : the general, dim and dumb Religiosity — the more or less slumbering sense and need of the Abiding and Eternal; and the concrete, precise and personal Religion — the clear answer, the now keen articulation of that dim demand. And both that general dull sense and this special definite presentment were found by us in actual life, — found by us there as Givenness of an evidential, revelational, an other-than-human, a more-than-human quality". E.A.I, pp. 65-6.

185. E.T.II, p. 364.

to our apprehension of finite realities which "are simultaneously felt as surrounded and fulfilled by and manifesting that Infinite"[186]. And this sense and experience is recognised as manifesting some of the self-manifestation of the Infinite which becomes so concrete and personal at the stage of historical revelation. It is the same God then who through His inner presence within man initiates our whole search (in our philosophical questioning) and who, when the end has provisionally been reached (in religion), is recognised now really for the first time as He Whom we sought from the very beginning.

In this manner von Hügel steered a middle course between pure immanentism and simple extrinsicism. He reacted against an immanentism which saw the religious and Christian experience springing purely from within the obscure depths of human consciousness. On the other hand, he refused to accept an extrinsicism which so emphasised the external aspect of revelation as to exclude all interiority regarding the exterior fact as requiring to be automatically accepted by a purely passive subject. Maurice Blondel categorises these as two similar kinds of monophorisms. Against these extremes both Blondel and von Hügel hold for a double aspect in all Christian revelation. As the baron writes: "everywhere, within human souls, is there an unrest — a demand, which, at deepest, are of grace and divine, and which are met and satisfied by graces, revelations from without, — a supply"[187]. But no amount of exterior factors could evoke a response or commitment from us, "unless we already possessed ... a sense and apprehension which could answer to those attestations or appeals"[188]. There are always two poles, one internal and the other external, in the Christian revelation[189]. It is the Divine inner presence of the Unincarnate God which offers and affords us the possibility to recognise and respond to the external historical Jesus brought to each generation anew within the Christian tradition. Or to put the matter

186. Ibid..
187. E.A.I, p. 236.
188. E.T.II, p. 365.
189. As von Hügel writes: "God is indeed the beginning, the middle and the end, the ceaseless presupposition, of all Jesus' teaching... Yet it can be wisely maintained by us only if we simultaneously remember that, however truly God revealed Himself with supreme fullness and in a unique manner in Jesus Christ, yet that this same God had not left Himself, still does not leave Himself, without *some* witness to Himself throughout the ages before Christ, and throughout the countries, groups, and even individual souls, whom the message, the fact, of the historic Jesus has never yet reached, or who, in sheer good faith, cannot see Him as He really is. The Unincarnate God has thus a wider range, though a less deep message, than the Incarnate God; and these two Gods are but one and the same God, Who, mysteriously, mostly slowly and almost imperceptibly, prepares or supplements, expresses and otherwise aids Himself, in each way by the other way". E.A.I, pp. 134-5.

another way, the interior mystical sense or element of religion in each of us, if accepted, moves us to seek and allows us to recognise, accept and commit ourselves to the exterior historical concrete person of Jesus who lived, died and now lives again in glory with God and in the Christian community today.

Usually the baron speaks of this more general interior stage, i.e. the inarticulate demand, in Rudolf Eucken's category of "universal religion", and again with Eucken he terms the specifically historical stage, the clear supply, "characteristic religion". He therefore sees religion within an organic conception of two interdependent stages, with universal religion demanding what characteristic religion supplies. Neither of them is a matter of mere reasoning. Both arise from and respond to man's concrete nature, though at different levels. As in the case of man's sense of the Infinite and the historical religionists' knowledge of God, von Hügel here again departs from the old more static abstract viewpoint which conceived of man arriving at a natural religion by the use of reason and then having supernatural religion revealed to him and accepted in faith. From the baron's more concrete position both are seen from within the dynamic unity of the subject and so their interdependence, interstimulation and continuity rather than their difference is stressed. Ultimately there is a basic similarity since both are given. They are dissimilar in the sense that they represent different degrees of differentiations within the one givenness and self-revelation of God and so may be distinguished but not separated. The two givennesses therefore require each other and only together render possible the act of Christian faith.

Like Eucken then von Hügel replaces the notion of natural and revealed religion by the terms universal and characteristic religion, because he believes that we nowhere find a religion of pure natural reason bringing us so far from the human standpoint and then another one coming on top of this directly and exclusively from God[190]. In concrete existence religion always comes from God, produces in man a desire for Him and itself fulfills that desire[191]. However,

190. Elsewhere the baron writes: "In actual life Natural or Rational Religion or Pure Theism exists as the mirage after the setting, or as the dawn before the rising, of an Historical Religion. And such Historical Religion always claims to be, not Rational but Revelational, and not Natural but Supernatural; and such a Religion is never purely Theistic, but always clings to a Prophet or Revealer of God and to a Community which adores God and worships the Revealer". E.A.I, p. XVI.

191. As von Hügel tells us: " 'Universal Religion' is at work, as an often obscure yet (in the long run) most powerful leaven, throughout all specifically human life, — Science, Art, Philosophy, and Ethics, calling for, and alone satisfied with, the answering force and articulation of 'Characteristic Religion', each requiring and required by the other, each already containing the other in embryo, and both ever operating together, in proportion as Man and Religion attain to their fullness' ". M.E.II, p. 269.

while characteristic, historical religion is the crown and answer to the universal stage, it brings with it all the perplexities, tensions and abuses connected with historical events and persons, authoritative institutions and hierarchies, dogmas and theologies but also all the benefits of a concrete personal social and communal form of religion.

CHAPTER VI

GOD MAN SOCIETY AND THE WORLD

1. *Love of God and Love of Man*

Von Hügel is in general agreement with George Tyrrell's attempt in "Poet and Mystic" to move away from the more common ascetical conception of the relationship between man's love of God and of his neighbour. According to Tyrrell the popular view pictures God more as the first and highest creature who competes with the rest of creation for man's love. God is seen, as it were, alongside other creatures and any love man bestows on them must, it seems, automatically detract from his love of God. To love God then man must exclude all other loves. Against this either/or position Tyrrell proposes that we conceive of God not alongside, but rather behind other creatures, shining through them and bringing them whatever depth and lustre they may possess. Thus in acknowledging the beauty and goodness of our fellow creatures and in loving them as such we would simultaneously love God. God is loved not apart from, but with, through and in his creation [192].

However, the baron was not entirely satisfied with this solution of Tyrrell and in an unpublished letter to him he exposes his own position. As von Hügel conceives it everyone should endeavour to cultivate a love of God in and through his fellow-men and a love of God apart from and in contradistinction to them [193]. Von Hügel believes that the necessity for such a polar relationship can be substantiated simply by concentrating exclusively on the demands of either one of these two loves and showing the inadequacies of the resulting position. For just as the suppression of all vocal prayer even in the highest states of perfection was condemned by the Church (though we must admit that it is hard to find such prayer in many of the Fathers of the Desert) so also the Church would condemn any

192. As Tyrrell writes: "The love of Him is the 'form', the principle of order and harmony; our natural affections are the 'matter' harmonized and set in order; it is the soul, they are the body, of that one Divine Love whose adequate object is God in, and not apart from, His creatures". G. TYRRELL, *Poet and Mystic*, in *The Faith of the Millions*, London, 1901, p. 53.
193. According to the baron: "every soul not only may have, but actually has, and ought to have *some* direct, spontaneous affection for its fellow-creatures, and again, *some* love ... direct and spontaneous for God: and that the latter has to penetrate and elevate and unify and spiritualise but never to simply and finally *suppress* and *supplant* the former". Von Hügel to M. D. Petre, 20 April 1902, SAUL.

exclusive love of God, which in practice would mean the complete suppression of all affective love of our fellow men (though again we must concede that the presence and growth of such affective love would be difficult to prove in the life of many a saint). Nevertheless, the baron contends that even the most systematically detached and neo-Platonic of saints always allow for some attachment, in fact lay great stress on the polarity within an original unity of such loves.

This principle of polarity, this double law of attachment and detachment runs, according to von Hügel, throughout the whole of life. There exists no object, act or affection however right or necessary for the perfection of man which does not require some alternation of attachment and involvement alongside its movement of detachment and abstention. As the baron writes : "this general law applies as truly to Contemplation as it does to Marriage"[194]. In both cases, as throughout life, detachment and renunciation are the universally necessary means, conditions and even constituent factors in all development, growth and life. The element of detachment therefore must be at the very centre of our lives penetrating and purifying from within all our attachments, "even the attachment to detachment itself"[195]. However, while detachment and renunciation are essential and are regarded as the more difficult and spiritual element of the soul's movement, they are such only on condition and in proportion as they preserve the element of attachment. Here as throughout life von Hügel reminds us "there is no good and operative yeast except with and in flour; there can be no purification and unity without a material and multiplicity to purify and unite"[196]. Both aspects and movements are necessary for while detachment purifies and spiritualises our attachments it can do so only in so far as there exist certain right attachments which act as the necessary material for a fruitful and enriching purification.

As we saw earlier, the neo-Platonic type of mystic flees from all multiplicity and materiality (his fellowman and the world), regarding them as so many distractions from his true goal, the purely individual, spiritual love of God. The imbalance and one-sidedness here results from the mystic's confining himself to the element of detachment and erecting this movement into the exclusive means and measure of a person's spiritual perfection and sanctity. Of course, the Church by her idealisation of the monastic life has also helped to reinforce the belief that the ultimate criterion of all Christian perfection lies in "a flight of the soul from the body and the world"[197]. However as the baron insists

194. M.E.II, p. 354.
195. Ibid..
196. Ibid..
197. Ibid., p. 127.

the Church has never endorsed such onesidedness but, on the contrary, has always regarded detachment as but one of the two essential movements of the human soul[198]. Attachment and involvement with our fellowmen in the world then provides the substance and material for spirituality to form and leaven while detachment furnishes us with the power to penetrate, harmonise and integrate the variety of our this-worldly interests so that in the process a fully rounded, broad and deep, truly human, spiritual personality may develop[199].

It is only in the polar movement between man's almost complete involvement in the multiplicity and variety of his wordly activities and, on the other hand, his detachment, renunciation and almost total withdrawal and rejection of the exterior world in favour of interiority that we achieve "a sufficient other-worldliness without fanaticism, and a sufficient this worldliness without philistinism"[200]. As von Hügel never tires of reiterating: "The great rule is, *Variety up to the verge of dissipation: Recollection up to the verge of emptiness*: each alternating with the other and making a rich fruitful tension"[201]. The aim of the fullest type of human life then must be to introduce an ever greater unification and harmonisation into the multiplicity and variety of its actions up to the point where this unity's constituents would, like the positive and negative poles of an electric battery, become so overcharged or integrated that a fruitful interaction would no longer be possible. Simultaneously, of course, we must continue broadening and enlarging this unity by allowing it to embrace an ever wider variety of activities until these in turn begin to seriously impar or weaken the true recollective spirit.

The Christian therefore must be involved in the world with his fellowmen, transforming it and in the process developing himself. The baron is adamant that in our modern world "any exclusive Other-Worldliness, all quietistic suffering and listless waiting, would be treason against both man and God"[202]. After all, if Christianity

198. Detachment must be regarded according to von Hügel: "as but one of two great movements, of which the other, the Positive movement, must also ever receive careful attention: since only between them is attained that all-important oscillation of the religious pendulum, that interaction between the soul's meal and the soul's yeast, that furnishing of friction for force to overcome, and of force to overcome the friction, that material for the soul to mould, and in moulding which to develop itself, that alternate expiration, upon which the soul's mysterious death-in-life and life-in-death so continuously depends". M.E.II, p. 366.

199. As the baron writes: "Only in the rhythm of action and reaction, of the going out to these things to the verge of abiding distraction, and of the coming back from these things to the verge of persistent emptiness, is the soul's normality and development attained". E.A.II, pp. 100-1.

200. E.L., p. 255.

201. L.N., p. XXI.

202. E.L., p. 316.

with its central belief in the Incarnation, (the ultimate and perfect expression of the principle of polarity which runs throughout life), turns its back on one of its constituent elements it becomes a contradiction unto itself. No one can become a christian saint then who has not achieved a profound unification and spiritualisation of the multiplicity and materiality with which each of us must be involved. Naturally for some the unity, the detachment and withdrawal from the world will distinctly surpass, though hopefully never eliminate the multiplicity of attachments and interests. With others it will be the variety and breadth of their involvements, their being completely in the world, though not of it, which first strikes us. Both groups witness however to the constant necessity of the two movements and exemplify "the immensely fruitful friction and tension which their well-ordered alternation introduces into the soul's inner life"[203]. "The life", as von Hügel tells us, "which can englobe and organize both these movements, with their manifold interaction, will have a multitude of warm attachments, without fever or distraction, and a great unity of pure detachment, without coldness or emptiness"[204].

Because of the limitations attached to all individual embodiments of this ideal of perfection and of the universal necessity and difficulty of its exemplifications, it is obvious that some groups of people will be drawn specially to personify a maximum form of detachment or perform the most difficult kinds of renunciation. So for example, the monk would represent a living example of the necessary element of detachment, purification and constant spiritualisation of those worldly interests and personal affections which humanity at large exercises to a greater extent and degree than he, but which even he cannot totally neglect. In this way each and every person would help to complement, correct and supplement the others through a generous exchange of specific gifts and duties so that by means of the creative interplay between the various constituents an ever greater, wider yet richer and deeper organism would be continually in the making[205]. Because of the inexhaustibleness of the possibilities, even for mankind as a whole, they must be interspersed and shared among different individuals and various groups who have special attractions or abilities in one particular sphere or another. It must be emphasised, however, that this specialisa-

203. M.E.II, p. 129.
204. Ibid..
205. As von Hügel summarises it : "if the minority will thus represent a maximum of 'form', with a minimum of 'matter', and the majority a maximum of 'matter', with a minimum of 'form' : yet some form as well as some matter must be held by each; and the ideal to which, by their mutual supplementations, antagonisms, and corrections, they will have more and more to approximate, our corporate humanity will be a maximum of 'matter', permeated and spiritualized by a maximum of 'form'". M.E.II, p. 355.

tion and subdivision of tasks avoids the danger of one-sidedness and
extremism only when they are accepted and recognised as such
subdivisions. Each individual or group must constantly "retain and
cultivate some sense of and respect for, the chief human activities
not primarily its own"[206]. We must also be tolerant of certain onesidednesses provided these do not cut themselves off completely from
the whole.

Religion is thus essentially social. Each particular person is intended
to realise his own specific and unique possibilities and functions within
a social organism. He is not expected to be a jack-of-all-trades
but simply to develop his own special attraits, offer these as his contribution to that larger whole and be always willing to have them
contested, purified and supplemented by those of his fellows. Consequently, "the striving of any one soul can thus be peaceful, since
limited in its range to what this particular soul, at its best, most
really wants and loves"[207]. The essence of true human action lies
not in competition but cooperation[208]. Within this vision religious
society is regarded as a body, an organic unity, in which each organ
has its own particular function "each different, each necessary, and
each influencing and influenced by all the others"[209]. The complete bride
of Christ then is never the simple individual but the full organism of
all the faithful throughout time and space. And the individual can be
seen as the bride only in so far as he is an operative constituent of the
total organism, the Christian community — the Church. This organic
conception also repudiates the untrue and unchristian doctrine of the
exclusion of any one group of men from all the rest or the separation
of some activities, e.g. contemplation from an interest in our fellowmen.
It brings us back once again to "the beautifully humble, rich,
and true view of a constant, necessary interchange of gifts and duties
between the various constituents of a highly articulated organism"[210].

206. M.E.II, p. 361.
207. E.L., p. 395.
208. As the baron writes : "Only by all and each joining hands and supplementing each
other can all these numberless degrees and kinds of call and goodness, together, slowly,
throughout the ages, get nearer and nearer to that inexhaustible ideal which lies so
deep and ineradicable within the heart of each and all. And thus will the two
fundamental movements of the soul, as it were its expiration and its inspiration,
the going out to gather and the coming home to garner, be kept up, in various
degrees, by every human soul, and each soul and vocation will as keenly feel the
need of supplementation, as it will apprehend the beauty and importance of the
special contribution it is called to make to the whole, a whole here, as everywhere,
greater than any of its parts, although requiring them each and all". M.E.I, p. 249.
209. M.E.II, p. 356.
210. Ibid., p. 357.

2. The Polarity in Christianity and Human Life

As we have seen in the previous section, at every critical stage in religious philosophy and in Christianity the movement is not of a circle round a single centre — detachment, but rather of an ellipse around two centres — attachment and detachment. It is precisely in the difficult but immensely fruitful oscillation between both these poles that the culminating richness and perfection of Christianity resides. The tensions inherent in this polarity are, according to von Hügel, particularly evident in our modern society where non-religious, this-worldly activities and sciences are regarded as autonomous, with specific methods, aims and ends proper to themselves, independent of religion. Because religion ultimately points to an other-world, because it demands a completely other orientation certain conflicts and antagonisms quite naturally arise. In fact the specific peculiarity of our modern civilisation is that it accepts this fact and attempts to discover a richness and creativity within this conflict. Only through such inner tension and interaction can we achieve "the deepening of the Humane Ends by the Christian Ethics, and the humanizing of the Christian End by the Humane Ethics, so that life may become a service of God within the Cultural Ends, and that the service of God may transfigure the world"[211].

Should the tension between these two poles and movements collapse as happened in the Hegelian system and in the philosophies of the eighteenth century, we witness a derailment either into the divinisation of man and human culture or the humanisation of God. Only when the existential tension experienced at the centre of our humanity is acknowledged and allowed to play its essential role in keeping the two poles firmly apart do we escape the danger of the clever ideologues' attempts to bring about the immanent actualisation of the Divine transcendent pole. So while the human and Divine poles are continually fertilising each other and the friction is in a continual process of reconciliation, the basic tension cannot be resolved or abolished without the destruction of the fundamental structure of our humanity which exhibits at its central core the specific religious experience of the otherness and transcendence of the Divine pole. In this world then, only the penultimate, never the last word can be spoken.

Christianity, of course, embraces and manifests this fundamental tension but ultimately the polarity. stems from the metaphysical

211. Ibid., pp. 273-4. As the baron writes elsewhere: "Only the two movements of World-flight and of World-seeking, of the Civilising of Spirituality, and of the Spiritualising of Civilisation: only This world and That world, each stimulating the other, although in different ways, from different sources and with different ends: only these two movements together form man's complete supernaturalised spiritual life". E.A.I, p. 270.

constitution of man's being. As the baron tells us: "Man is incurably *amphibious*; he belongs to Two Worlds — to two sets of duties, needs and satisfactions — to the Visible or This World, and to the Invisible or the Other World"[212]. The notion of the tension between the multiplicity of man's this-worldly interests and the unifying principle of the divine detaching pole finds its fundamental source here in the "(metaphysically) intermediate position of man's soul"[213]. Life as we said is not a circle round a single centre but an ellipse with two foci, man and God, the human and Divine, the immanent and transcendent, attachment and detachment, this-world and the other-world, nature and grace, time and eternity, etc. If we confine ourselves to either one of these poles or even take the two but treat them as independent, separate or isolated entities we sterilise our being and parch the sources of real life. We must accept the tension and the sharper the conflict, the more painful the friction and the more difficult the unification and harmonisation, so much more complete and profound will be the victory and the personality thus achieved and won. For precisely in this immensely fruitful oscillation, rhythm and tension between these two contrasting poles lies the richness and fullness of life and the source of its "perennial youth and renovative power"[214].

3. *The World: A Means of Purification*

History witnesses to the various fluctuations and oscillations between the two poles of man's existence. At one moment we have great movements of world-flight, in primitive Christianity, early and eastern monasticism, neo-Platonism and Buddhism, and at another the world-seeking movement is to the fore as e.g. in classical hellenism, the renaissance and modern times. Within one's own life the same tendencies can be observed at various stages. There is also the constant attempt by each pole to dominate and even exclude the other to the detriment of the whole movement. Furthermore, by emersing oneself fully, for example, into one's work within the world there is always the danger that we become unconsciously assimilated to the things of the world. Nevertheless, without this involvement in concrete reality one loses the necessary materiality and means for humility and correction, for expansion and creativity, for conflict and renovation which are essential to the growth and development of true personality.

But it is precisely this latter movement which seems, in theory at

212. E.A.II, p. 246-7. Elsewhere the baron describes man as "a denizen of two worlds and a link between them". E.L., p. 312.

213. G.S., p. 116.

214. E.L., p. 315.

least, to be denied by some mystics. Some of them speak as
though man purifies and becomes his true self by turning away
from the particularity, the concreteness of creation and absorbing
himself in an abstract, pure spirituality, in the simplicity of the
Creator. Within this perspective there is no logical place for the
world and its scientific observation, indeed all motive and necessity for
transforming the world for the benefit of our fellow-man is removed.
According to the baron however, the orthodox mystic's practice is
usually quite satisfactory for, as he contends, "they have sayings
about the purifying irreplaceable quality of true work that sound as
though spoken by Carlyle"[215]. In company with these mystics von
Hügel believes that work can become a unique means of purification
and discipline and can positively contribute to the development and
establishment of true, authentic selfhood. Contrary to the previous
insistence on the spiritual value of fleeing the world, man's involvement
and occupation with his fellowman in the world would be seen as the
normal and necessary means of spiritualisation. Christians would be
taught that through study and work they not only avoid the dangers
of idleness and escape the strain involved in pure spirituality, but
allow the other, the immanent pole to play its legitimate part in the
development of a full, truly human spirituality.

It was especially under the influence of what he believed to be
St. Catherine of Genoa's conception of spirituality that the baron
came to stress the essential role of our immanental activities, especially
of the physical and mathematical sciences as means of purification.
As a result of his study of the life of St. Catherine von Hügel
distinguished three stages in the growth of spiritual personality and
correspondingly three distinct types or classes of persons. The first
stage or type comprises of those individuals who continue to live
their lives on the naturalistic, selfish individualistic, almost physical
place on which they began[216]. In a second stage or class, duty, obligation
and objective law are accepted as the means of serving God and
developing the self. Consequently all subjectivity, personal originality
and uniqueness are viewed with suspicion and sacrificed to the objectivity
and uniformity of external law. We thus reach the "universalistic,
uniformative type and class"[217] to which the majority of people in
every age belong.

215. F. VON HÜGEL, *Caterina Fiesca Adorna, the Saint of Genoa, 1447-1510*, in
The Hampstead Annual (1898), p. 81.
216. The baron characterises these as : "Individualistic, unmoral or even anti-moral
men, who, however gifted and cultivated as artists, scholars, philosophers and statesmen,
must yet be counted as essentially childish and as clever animals rather than as
spiritual men". M.E.I, p. 242.
217. Ibid..

The third and final stage is attained by a comparably small group of people. On this level and with this class of people the uniformity, universalism and objectivism of law in the second stage is internalised and issues in the originality, uniqueness and subjectivity of self-determining spiritual personality which lies at the opposite pole to the selfish natural self which reigned supreme before the intervention of the intermediary stage of obligatory law. The spiritual life now far from being a law to be adhered to objectively, becomes a reality and a life subjectively and personally appropriated[218]. We witness here the full shift to interiority or inwardness as Kierkegaard called it. However, in order to guard against the possible misinterpretation of such a statement as Kierkegaard's "that subjectivity, inwardness, is the truth"[219], the baron insists that if the selfish egoism of the first stage is to be surmounted and eliminated from the third personalist level, we must retain within this level all the essentials of the second stage. Thus, while the second stage attempts to exclude the first, the third sublates the second, in the sense that we must constantly discipline our selfishness by traversing the intermediate level of an objective system of laws, felt to be interiorly binding upon the self, if the true self is to emerge and continually develop.

Because of the central position which images derived from the natural elements, e.g. sun, light, fire, air, ocean occupy as purificatory agents for the selfish self on the second, intermediate stage in St. Catherine of Genoa's teaching, the baron concludes that she believed: "that she must continuously first quench and drown her feverish immediacy, her clamorous, claimful false self, and must lose herself, as a merely natural Individual, in the river and ocean of the Thing, of Law, of that apparently ruthless Determinism which fronts life everywhere, before she could find herself again as a Person, in union with and in presence of an infinite Spirit and Personality"[220]. Although St. Catherine's central idea of "the soul's voluntary plunge into a painful yet joyous purgation"[221] ultimately refers to the purifying love of God, her use of such thing-like metaphors as light, fire, water,

---

218. As von Hügel writes: "Yet now all this, in these rare souls, leads up to and produces a living reality bafflingly simple in its paradoxical, mysterious richness. For now the universality, obligation, and objectivity of the Law become and appear greater, not less, because incarnated in an eminently unique and unreproduceable, in a fully personal form". M.E.I, p. 243.

219. Søren KIERKEGAARD, *Concluding Unscientific Postscript*, Princeton, 1971, p. 266.

220. M.E.I, p. 246. The baron's conclusion here from St. Catherine's use of material symbols to the unique place of determinist science in the development of personality is somewhat arbitrary and *a priori*. His argument that the use of these images were due neither to Catherine's psycho-physical condition, nor to the failure of her personal relationship within marriage leaves one unconvinced.

221. M.E.II, pp. 385-6.

etc. along with von Hügel's own belief that modern man must be involved in physical, mathematical sience, led the baron to allot an essential role within the spiritual life to science or, as he says, "the seemingly ruthless Determinism of Law, in which the little individual is lost for good and all, and which only the spiritual personality can survive"[222]. Accordingly, von Hügel stresses that man must remain in constant contact with "the Thing-world, the Impersonal Element, Physical Science and Determinist Law"[223] for he believes that it is only by continually passing through these caudine forks that the immediate, false egoistical self is purified and the true, spiritual personality emerges.

Man comes into the world as a selfish sensual mere individualistic unit who can remain such but who has also the mysterious capacity for constituting himself into an unselfish, spiritual, fully personal organism. But he can only realise this by detaching himself from his egoistical tendencies and to accomplish this the baron proposes that he retain at an intermediate level the ruthlessly impersonal world of science with its purifying zone of objective laws in which he must be engaged and through which his surfacy selfishness and individualism is continually confronted and made to bend and submit. Moreover, because the inner tension between self-attachment and self-interest and detachment and disinterestedness remains throughout life, some such purifying medium is always necessary if the battle against the petty self is to be won.

In early Christianity the purifying detaching function which modern science can play in the spiritual life was, in the baron's opinion, exercised by the immanent expectation of Our Lord's Second Coming, the Parousia. From St. Augustine's time onward a similar function was discharged by the conception of Original Sin and its effects. Both of these helped to instil in man a negative and pessimistic attitude towards the world and to create in him a longing either for his prehistorical beginnings or for a new definitive age which would eclipse anything this world had to offer. Von Hügel is convinced that the all-pervasive detaching power once exercised by the Parousia and Original Sin is now available to modern man through his scientific endeavours. Here in the midst of his activity in the world he discovers and is constantly confronted by a detaching, purifying barrier and medium "necessarily painful to the false, surface, immediate, animal man, and necessarily purifying (where willed and accepted) to the true, inner, remoter, spiritual self"[224].

222. Ibid., p. 386.
223. Ibid., p. 378.
224. *Von Hügel and Tyrrell*, p. 32.

By way of conclusion to this rather difficult aspect of von Hügel's thought we would like to emphasise that although the baron's conception of science as deterministic is somewhat positivistic, this does not really invalidate the purgatorial function he allots to it within his general theory. Since von Hügel believes that all the sciences, no matter what our ultimate view of them are alike "if taken as means of purification for the soul bent upon its own deepening"[225]. For us it is the special virtues of sensitivity, sincerity, selflessness, conscientiousness, generosity etc. demanded by the methods and procedures of all genuine scientific endeavour rather than mathematical or physical science itself which are the true means of purification and growth.

Finally it must be admitted that the baron's emphasis on the purifying function of science seems somewhat intellectualistic and elitist. He himself counters this criticism by emphasising that "every however simple mental attention to *things* and their mechanism, their necessary laws and requirements"[226] can act as a purifying medium. For example, he maintains that any simple washing-woman, farm-labourer, black-smith or miner, etc. who attend faithfully to the require-ments and laws of their specific occupation would fulfill the required conditions. We would only add that it is not just mechanical, deterministic science, but all man's authentic immanent, worldly and secular activities, in so far as they demand certain sacrifices on the part of the selfish self, which furnish man with a purifying buffer zone through which he can continually pass in the effort to leave the narrowness and selfishness of his false self and gain the openness and selfless love of his true authentic selfhood from which alone can issue real peace and joy.

4. *Purification and the Constitution of Personality*

As we saw in the previous section man begins by finding himself in the world on the level of mere physical existence. In as much as he directs all his energies towards his simply physical, generally selfish advancement, his growth must be conceived as purely quantitative. However, from the start man is also endowed with certain rudimentary spiritual aptitudes and capacities which he can actualise and make his own. In fact, their actualisation constitutes his selfhood. But we must also realise that man's possibilities, his inclinations and attractions are both upward and downward, and consequently through his actions he can in-crease or decrease as a man, gain or lose his true selfhood. As we already mentioned man lives in a rich middle position of an ever unfinished movement between truth and falsehood, good and evil, the

225. M.E.II, p. 383.
226. M.E.I, p. 78.

holy and the unholy. Because of the luminosity of this movement a direction is unveiled which precedes and casts its light over all man's particular choices and actions and remains alive afterwards as an existential judgment on the course of action or life taken. When man follows the right direction discovered within the movement of existence, he lives an authentic life and becomes his true self. By taking the wrong course one does not make it right but slips into a false, inauthentic form of life where the selfish, sensual tendencies are strengthened and expanded and the resultant weakening and contraction in the true self can lead to an abiding personal disintegration and a living death of the real self.

But no matter which direction we follow, the fundamental tension of existence always remains [227]. Throughout the whole of life man is continually attempting to build up his character and personality by the successive conquest of the lower, selfish self on the various levels of existence he attains. And this constant exodus from the present self, in so far as it begins to appear below the subject's own desired achievement and anticipation in the growing light of conscience and the increasing actualisation of his moral personality, demands a daily death to self, and a perpetual purification.

We attain here a profoundly open, creative, positive notion of personal and spiritual life in which tension and constant purification play a constitutive role. The earlier static conception of man's spirit as a substance of a definite, final shape and size from the start which requires only the removal of disfiguring impurities to preserve or restore it to its original pristine and perennial beauty is now eliminated. For purification, holiness, the development of a truly human spirituality is seen to consist not primarily in the absense of blemishes but to reside in something positive, the growth, development and establishment of the true self through acts of pure, disinterested, selfless love. This love, of course, would be in constant tension and conflict with impure, interested, selfish love — concupiscence, which, as a contradiction of man's true selfhood, leads him into all sorts of *divertissements* and inhumanities. So the notion of purity and man's purification (far from being the removal of bodily stains, a negative act not needing repetition) is seen here as something positive, open to continual growth and renewal. For purification, being ultimately a movement away from impure false self-love and toward true selfless love (really our true self-love) "has", as St. Thomas says, "no limits to its increase, for it is a certain participation in the Infinite Love, which is the Holy Spirit" [228].

227. As the baron writes: "up to the end, there will be no standing still, but only the alternative between shrinkage and expansion; between the deteriorating ultimate pain of self-seeking and self-contraction, and the ennobling immediate pangs of self-conquest and self-expansion". S.L., p. 89.
228. M.E.II, p. 301.

Following St. Catherine of Genoa, von Hügel regards man's purification as occuring fundamentally by a voluntary plunge of the self
into God as all-pure and all-purifying Love. God Himself is the ultimate
purifier and his Love is the initiator, the means and the adequate end and
fulfillment of all man's deepest desires. As von Hügel, quoting St.
Catherine of Genoa, tells us: "When God created man, He did not
put Himself in motion for any other reason than His pure love
alone. And hence, in the same way as Love Itself, for the welfare of
the loved soul, does not fail in the accomplishment of anything,
whatever may be the advantage or disadvantage that may accrue from
thence to the Lover, so also must the love of the loved soul return
to the Lover, with those same forms and modes with which it
came from Him. And then such love as this, which has no regard
for ought but love itself, cannot be in fear of anything"[229]. We
have here a relationship "begun and rendered possible by God's
utterly prevenient, pure, *ecstatic* love of Man"[230]. And this *amicitia*
between God and man is not just a particular gratuitous act of
God but, expressive of God's intrinsic nature, the relationship informs,
nay, transforms man's nature. For the love with which man returns the
Divine Love can be so perfect and all-fulfilling because it is a participation
in God's own love, in God Himself. In accepting the offer of
Divine love man is swept up by the moving power of love itself to
respond to God's love with "the very love with which God Himself loves"[231]. And this pure love of God constitutes man's absolute
perfection because in it man shares in the beginning and end of all
Love, Perfection and Being, the very nature of God Himself. As
St. Catherine of Genoa teaches: "The love of God is our true self-
love, the love characteristic of and directed to our true selves,
since these selves of ours were created by and for Love Itself"[232].

Within the depth of the notion of Pure Love we uncover not only the
fundamental principle underlying the formal dynamism which structures our humanity, but the basic concrete personal love relationship
which structures the whole mystical, christian and truly human life.
In this relationship the dynamic conception of personality chartered
in our third chapter is concretely grounded and at the same time
crowned with the almost infinite possibilities for authentic personal
realisation now offered and demanded of man if he is to co-operate
with and respond to the initial free gift of Divine love bestowed
on each and every person in all times and places. Only here is human
personality seen for what it is and allowed to become what it

229. M.E.I, pp. 261-2.
230. M.E.II, p. 335.
231. E.A.II, p. 154.
232. M.E.I, p. 262.

truly has to be. For no purely immanent or intramundane actualisation of his potentialities can really satisfy or fulfill man. Ultimately man's true happiness lies in an ever deeper and fuller growth into the infinite love of God and, through and in this, the love of his fellow-men for the sake of their own true selves.

God and religion then, far from stunting man's freedom and personality, allow them almost infinite scope for expansion. For not only are human personality and a Personal Infinite Being not mutually exclusive but they are metaphysically so intrinsically united that it is only because of our participation in the Infinite that we are persons at all[233]. We must conclude therefore that the emergence of personality, the love of God and the love of our neighbour are so intrinsically connected that the one cannot grow without the other.

233. As von Hügel writes quoting Hermann Lotze: "these hindrances to a perfect 'Personality' are the necessary consequences of our finitude, so that perfect personality not only is compatible, but is compatible *only*, with the conception of an infinite Being, and is only more or less approachable by finite ones". E.T.II, p. 365.

CHAPTER VII

PERSONAL RELIGION

The Three Elements of Religion

Because of the centrality of personality in von Hügel's religious philosophy and because man's reception of all reality including the Divine Reality is always personal, i.e. sensational, emotional, cognitional and volitional — a response of the whole man, we would expect that religion, being the most profound form of life, would appeal and demand a commitment of the entire personality. This, not surprisingly, is precisely the baron's contention. As he tells us: "Religion ... in its completeness, is simultaneously Historical and Institutional, Critical and Speculative, Mystical and Operative, thus calling into play the whole man and his various faculties — sense-perception and memory; analytic and synthetic reason, and feeling; intuition, and volition"[234].

Although von Hügel's conception of religion as a dynamic, organic unity of three elements follows from his general theory of the multiplicity within unity of all reality and from his conception of experience as always sensational, emotional, cognitional, volitional, i.e. fully personal, the baron was nevertheless directly influenced in his articulation of these elements, as we mentioned, especially by Newman's Preface to *The Via Media* and William James' "Reflex Action and Theism".

While Newman's Preface deals specifically with the threefold office of Christ as priest, prophet and king as this is continued within the Church, the baron's primary concern all along was in the broader reality of religion and its mystical, intellectual and institutional elements. As such, von Hügel's treatment is more ecumenical and indeed more relevant for the contemporary situation. To a certain extent the baron's interest is more existential also. For while Newman focuses primarily on the differing functional utility of the various offices within the Church, the baron concentrates specifically on the individual's personal appropriation, integration and embodiment of these elements at the different stages of his religious development. In the formulation of these latter insights the baron was aided especially by William James' theory of the three aspects of reflex action from his essay "Reflex Action and Theism". From a study of this essay von Hügel concluded, as we saw, that all man's knowledge and

---

234. F. VON HÜGEL, *The Papal Commission and the Pentateuch*, p. 46.

activity begins with sense-impressions, then moves through a central
process of reflection and ends finally in the discharge of will and
action[235]. In a similar fashion the baron contends that religion is
comprised of three elements and he proceeds to trace its "three
modes of apprehension and forms of appeal and of outlook"[236]
throughout the differing phases of the individual's development.
However before proceeding with our exposition we would like to
reiterate that there never exists a trace or semblance of any one
of these elements or functions without the joint-presence of the other
two. In reality we always begin with an organic whole in which
each is present to a greater or lesser degree. Within life man always
moves as a whole and never as an extrinsic mixture of separate
or independent parts. Nevertheless at various stages of his life or
religious development specific functions or elements predominate and
it is to this phenomenon we must now turn.

Von Hügel distinguishes at a first stage in the growth of all
knowledge and religion, the child's more passive reception of external
sense data along with the traditional, social interpretation of reality they
incorporate. These data and their interpretation come to man from
outside and impose themselves on him with the authority and certainty
of their unbroken centuries of traditional embodiments and as such
demand his unquestioning obedience. Since the individual needs this
larger stream of experience for his own development, he must, in the
beginning at least, accept and trust in the various external, social and
institutional structures which channel these wider possibilities to him.
At this stage then, "the External, Authoritative, Historical, Traditional, Institutional side and function of Religion are everywhere
evident"[237].

Soon another human activity and requirement arises and the
corresponding element of religion responds. Gradually with the
emergence of one's own individuality and the consciousness of one's
autonomy one begins, as a youth, to question and challenge the
previously acceptable traditional truths and to reject some. The testimony
of the individual's own direct experience and reasoning alone is now
accepted as a valid justification for holding any particular view. Though
truth is still seen as something external and the subject is regarded
more as mind and intellect than as a person, reality must nevertheless

235. As the baron writes: "All the activities of specifically human life begin with a
sense-impression, as the first, the one simply *given* element; that they move into and
through a central process of mental abstraction and reflection, as the second element,
contributed by the mind itself; and that they end, as the third element, in the
discharge of will and of action, in an act of free affirmation, expansion and love". M.E.I,
pp. 57-8.
236. M.E.I, p. 51.
237. Ibid..

be seen to fulfill certain subjective, though rational requirements before it can be assented to by the individual. We come here to "the Critical-Historical and Synthetic-Philosophical element of religion"[238], history, philosophy and theology now begin to play an ever more important role in our religious lives.

All this time, however, a third and final stage is in preparation. Here we reach the true autonomy of reason and the full maturity of personal experience. For tradition is no longer simply acquiesced in on the authority of others, nor challenged or rejected in favour of a pure rationalism or the direct autonomous experience of the individual, but is now accepted as a first principle of existence without which man cannot develop. However, although tradition broadens and deepens the individual it is the latter who, in embracing it, modifies, renews or at the very least interprets and integrates the former's insights within the organism of his own personality in such an original fashion that his personal embodiment and manner of communication become his unique contribution to society[239]. With this personal appropriation of truth, religion, far from being something out there or a truth objectively known, becomes a life subjectively appropriated and lived. At this stage man's emotional and volitional, his ethical and spiritual powers are in full movement and they are "met by the Mystical and the directly Operative element of Religion"[240]. As the baron writes : "Here religion is rather felt than seen or reasoned about, is loved and lived rather than analyzed, is action and power, rather than either external facts or intellectual verification"[241].

We would like to emphasise this operative, existential, active dimension of the third element or level since, unfortunately, mysticism is often equivocated with pure passivity or quietism. James B. Pratt's friendly criticism of von Hügel's triple division of religion into "(1) the traditional or historical, (2) the rational, and (3) the volitional or mystical"[242] as too simple because it fails to account for the fact that "the will to believe and the active, volitional, practical expression of religion are as far removed from the mystical form of religion and belief as they are from the intellectual"[243] is not really valid. For

---

238. M.E.II, p. 389.

239. As George Tyrrell wrote in his review of *The Mystical Element*: "This personal twist that we give to the traditional mind is a sort of toll paid to society. Else tradition would be but a mechanical printing-off from stereotype, not the transmission or persistence of a growing idea". G. Tyrrell, The Mystical Element of Religion (Review), p. 108.

240. M.E.II, p. 390.

241. M.E.I, p. 53.

242. J. B. PRATT, *The Religious Consciousness : A Psychological Study*, New York, 1921, pp. 13-4.

243. Ibid..

although one must admit a certain inner tension between mysticism in its tendency towards interiority and quietism and the volitional stress on externality and activity, the essentially polar and incarnational structure of Christian mysticism runs the risk of a reduction to the pure flight from the world or a desire to be alone with the Alone type of neo-Platonism if the mystical element is distantiated too much from its operative aspect. Stressing their close and essential interrelatedness von Hügel rightly speaks therefore of "the emotional and volitional", "the ethico-mystical", "the Experimental and Mystical" or again of "the Mystical and the directly Operative element of Religion"[244].

Furthermore we must reiterate that the religious person does not simply move from one more elemental stage to the higher. From the very beginning all the elements are present to some degree and must be retained throughout the whole of life if there is to be a full, balanced development. The first two stages are sublated then not by the Hegelian device of their reconciliation in a third, but through the retention and higher integration of their accumulated values and insights in an ever deepening, ever growing personal unity within the subject. However, the constant tendency within each element to eliminate or partially suppress the others to the detriment both of itself and the religious organism as a whole always remains and it is to this we must now turn our attention.

As we saw every living unity is constituted and must finally be evaluated by its integration and harmonisation of an ever greater variety of often conflicting elements. Because religion reveals itself as the most fundamental and ultimate example of what is disclosed to a lesser degree on every other level of existence and experience it follows that, as von Hügel writes: "Religion ... requires the fullest action and co-operation, the most perfect unity, in and through diversity, of all the soul's powers"[245]. While the elements of variety and multiplicity and of unity and harmonisation always cost a great deal to secure and maintain, there are specific difficulties inherent in each of the three elements of religion which tempt them to minimise or suppress the other two to the detriment and impoverishment of the whole. For example, since all concrete religiousness is evoked in us first by some previously extant religion, man's first contact with religion is normally through the medium of its external historical, traditional, social and institutional element. The danger however is that what appears first is accepted and cherished by the recipient as the one and only element of religion. And because of the supreme importance for the religious man of the truth embodied in this traditional, institutional

244. M.E.II, p. 390.
245. Ibid., p. 116.

form he feels obliged to preserve it intact in its totality, to defend it from all incursions and to pass it on as received to future generations. Of course, should man falter in this task religion can always rely ultimately on the guardians of the institutional truth, the authorities, to make sure that the truth is safeguarded and transmitted intact to posterity[246].

This is what Blondel called the extrinsicist or fixist view of revelation and tradition, what we might now label as essentialism. This danger is constant in religion since it flows from the abuse, the one-sidedness and exaggeration of the essential external and authoritative character-istic of all true religion. But although official organisation and authority are a necessary part of a living and fruitful spiritual life, they are nevertheless only a part, never the whole. Man is bound to them only as instruments for his own spiritual development and community relationships. In the baron's opinion "official organisation and Authority are ever means, necessary means, of life; means, not ends; of life, not of death"[247]. And although this "unanalytic, unspeculative, unmystical, thing-like, rock-solid faith"[248] with its monolythic organisa-tion and central authority has never been actualised in history, the political Catholicism and narrow absolutist neo-ultramontanism of the baron's own day made von Hügel fear that such an eventuality could overtake Catholicism.

With reference to the second, the intellectual element, the baron agrees that : "Though no amount of talk can, otherwise than harmfully, take the place of life, yet observation and reflection can help us to see where and how life acts ... and can thus supply us with aids to action, which action will then, in its turn, help to give experimental fulness and precision to what otherwise remains a more or less vague and empty scheme"[249]. Within religion the need to analyse and

246. As von Hügel tells us : "Religion will here be conceived as a thing to be kept literally and materially identical with itself, and hence as requiring to be defended against any kind of modification. Conceive it as a paste, and all yeast must be kept out; or as wine, and fermentation must be carefully excluded". M.E.I, p. 71.

247. E.A.II, p. 17. The baron never identifies the authority within the Church with the total Church. As he writes : "And Church officials are no more the whole Church, or a complete specimen of the average of the Church, than Scotland Yard or the War Office or the House of Lords, though admittedly necessary parts of the national life, are the whole, or average samples, of the life and fruitfulness of the English nation". Ibid. Nor again would von Hügel identify the visible Church with the whole Church. As he writes : "Well, the later Catholic Christians saw and see the Invisible Church in the Visible Church and connected with it, but certainly not as simply identical or co-extensive with it. 'There are many souls within the Visible Church that do not belong to the Invisible Church; and there are many souls not within the Visible Church that belong to the Invisible Church' is still a thoroughly orthodox and common saying". E.L., p. 356.

248. M.E.II, p. 388.

249. M.E.I, p. 50.

synthesise, to question and deliberate, to clarify, express, state, restate and communicate, to give meaning and significance to the external signs and events to which man adheres, to integrate them coherently among themselves and within a general world view is absolutely essential for every man and every religion. But of itself the intellectual element neglects all emotion, feeling, intuition and, while it consolidates the original experience and clarifies its dimness and obscurity, it depersonalises it and tends towards a static abstract system of clear and readily transferable ideas. A further danger arises when these conceptualisations are regarded as adequate articulations of experiential reality and so, far from being means, are seen as ends in themselves and thus become the starting points and first principles of a logical deductive theology. The inevitable result of the intellectual faculty or element's detachment from its proper function within the total organism and its suppression of the other elements, is that logical formulae replace existential reality, our theology becomes purely speculative and abstract and our religion purely rational.

To rescue man and religion from this fate we require the emotional, intuitive and volitional aspect of man's character and the corresponding experiential, mystical and operative element of religion. The stress here is on interiority and subjectivity, on a : "dim yet direct and (in its general effects) immensely potent, sense and feeling, an immediate experience of Objective Reality, of the Infinite and Abiding, of a Spirit not all unlike yet distinct from our own, which penetrates and works within these our finite spirits and in the world at large"[250]. There is the danger, however, that the subject clings so exclusively to the immediacy and directness of his contact with the Divine reality that all else is eliminated or relegated to insignificance. We arrive then at the pure interiority of exclusive or false mysticism with its disregard for historical occasions, externality and its repugnance to all exterior activity[251]. Although there is a certain one-sidedness here which flows from the elemental primacy and immediacy on the ontological level of the mystical element of religion, it is important to realise that concretely, historically, logically and psychologically mysticism is always mediated and so to an extent is secondary to the historical, traditional and institutional elements. Furthermore, in so far as the soul rests in the composure and simplicity of its emotional and intuitive experience of God, it will instinctively shrink from all reflection and analysis of this relationship, regarding it as so much botanising on

250. M.E.II, p. 390.
251. As the baron writes : "yet each such experience tends to obliterate the traces of its own occasion. Indeed the interior feeling thus achieved tends, in the long run, to make the return to the contact with the fact that occasioned, and to the act that produced it, a matter of effort and repugnance". M.E.I, pp. 73-4.

one's mother's grave. But without the normal correctives afforded by the other elements the individual's psychological and subjective activities receive a free hand and can easily lead to all forms of illusions or degenerate into pure sentimentality or emotional fanaticism [252].

Not realising that it is only in conjunction with all the other elements that both itself and they flourish and develop into an ever rich living whole, each element tends to claim for itself the exclusive monopoly of the religious reality. Each must learn that it can influence and be influenced, contribute and have itself corrected and supplemented by all the other elements only if it remains within the bounds of its own intrinsic nature and legitimate range. Hence, as the baron tells us: "here as elsewhere, but more than anywhere, our ideal standard will be the greatest possible development of, and inter-stimulation between, each and all of the religious elements, with the greatest possible unity in the resulting organism" [253]. The final aim must be the fruitful interaction and eventual harmonisation through a creative tension and cooperation of the maximum number of elements and functions within one great living organism. And the more perfect the organism becomes the more it approaches the personal. For there is no self-subsistent stage, function or element in man or his religion out there looking to be attached to some others. As we have seen, the elements cannot be separated or viewed apart from their function within the whole. And this whole is not some abstract unity but the pulsating, dynamic, organic unity of the concrete living person [254].

As we have continually intimated, the only true solution to any faculty psychology or to the ascendency of one particular element of religion over the others is to be found, as the baron tells us, "in an ever fuller conception of Personality, and of its primary place in the religious life" [255]. And Christianity, the highest and deepest of all religions, witnesses and exemplifies this. As von Hügel writes in a beautiful passage in his *Mystical Element* [256]:

252. As von Hügel reminds us: "the emotional-experimental force will, in its turn, be tempted to sweep aside both the external, as so much oppressive ballast; and the intellectual, as so much hair-splitting or rationalism. And if it succeeds, a shifting subjectivity, and all incurable tyranny of mood and fancy, will result, — fanaticism is in full sight". M.E.I, p. 55.

253. M.E.II, p. 116.

254. As the baron writes: "And this whole series of ... movements exists only in Persons; it begins with an at least incipient Person and ends in the fullest self-expression of Personality". M.E.I, p. 86.

255. M.E.I, p. 76.

256. Ibid., pp. 26.

For it's [Christianity's] originality consists not so much in its single doctrines, or even in its teaching as a whole, and in the particular place each doctrine occupies in this teaching, as in its revelation, through the person and example of its Founder, of the altogether unsuspected depth and inexhaustibleness of human Personality, and of this Personality's source and analogue in God, of the simplicity and yet difficulty and never-endingness of the access of man to God, and of the ever-preceding condescension of God to man. Hence if Christianity is thus throughout the Revelation of Personality; and if Personality is ever a One in Many, (and more deeply One and more richly Many, in proportion to the greatness of that spiritual reality): then we need not wonder at the difficulty we find in pointing out any one particular doctrine as constitutive of the unique originality of Christianity.

For a Person came, and lived and loved, and did and taught, and died and rose again, and lives on by His Power and His Spirit for ever within us and amongst us, so unspeakably rich and yet so simple, so sublime and yet so homely, so divinely above us precisely in being so divinely near, — that His character and teaching require, for an ever fuller yet never complete understanding, the varying study, and different experiments and applications, embodiments and unrollings of all the races and civilizations, of all the individual and corporate, the simultaneous and successive experiences of the human race to the end of time.

CONCLUSION

APPRAISAL AND PROSPECTS

Appraisal

By way of conclusion we would like to insist that as our method indicated no thorough examination or understanding of von Hügel's religious philosophy can be obtained from a simple systematic exposé alone. To appreciate fully the origin, development and situational context of the baron's though, a concrete historial presentation is required as was evidenced by our first part. A break therefore was made with the traditional procedure in von Hügel research which offered the reader generalised treatments or sketches on a variety of Hügelian topics. In this manner we sought also to follow the baron's own procedure in his major work *The Mystical Element of Religion as studied in St. Catherine of Genoa and her Friends*. As the title indicates the book was not conceived as an abstract, general treatise on mysticism but a concrete study of the mystical element as it found expression in a particular historical person and her friends.

However, while lauding the baron's concrete approach in his *magnum opus* we must admit that the internal structure of the work itself left much to be desired[257]. This can be exemplified by recalling that the initial question about the secret of spiritual persuasiveness with which *The Mystical Element* opens on page 3 receives an answer only on pages 367-370. In the meanwhile, after labouring through the first volume of the work, some 370 pages, even so sympathetic and erudite a reader as Abbot Cuthbert Butler had lost the wood for the trees as is witnessed in a letter of his to von Hügel in 1909: "I have read every word of it — Vol. I of St. Cath.; and how interesting and instructive and truly edifying I found it all. Only p. 367-370 were beyond my ken; and if Vol. II is an enlargement of them, I don't know how it will be with it"[258]. The problem arose because between pages 3 and 367-370 von Hügel had become involved in so many historical details and disparate subjects, seemingly so unconnected with the initial question, that when

257. As Tyrrell reminds us: "What was originally intended for a critical life of St. Catherine of Genoa grew so overweighted with *scholia* and discussions that eventually the plan of the book was inverted, and the biography from being the substance became an appendage — an illustration of the theory of mysticism; and the structure bears some marks of this inversion". G. Tyrrell, *The Mystical Element of Religion (Review)*, p. 105.

258. E. C. Butler to von Hügel, 13 September 1909, Downside.

finally the conclusion emerges the original problem has long been forgotten and one is left wondering what it has all been in aid of. Furthermore, pages 367-370 do not explicitly state that the secret of spiritual persuasiveness lies in the existential appeal of the concrete embodiment of spiritual personality but, true to his method, the baron is content to allow the reader to draw this conclusion for himself as a result of the intervening study of the lives and doctrines of St. Catherine and her friends. While this approach is admirable the normal reader rightly expects to have the central conclusion of such a difficult work explicitly stated for him [259].

Furthermore, von Hügel's style does not always facilitate matters. Not simply on account of his Germanisms but more especially because of the long complex and condensed sentences with their many qualifying phrases and parentheses witnessing to the painstaking efforts the baron took in his determination to render faithfully all the evidence and to present all the various shades of truth in a delicate balance. However, if his work sometimes makes difficult reading, like all the great thinkers the baron realised that "there is no short cut to truth" [260] or as Tyrrell said: "It is easy to keep an empty room tidy" [261].

A distinctive feature of von Hügel's personality which finds an echo throughout all his work is his openness and tolerance to a variety of views and a plurality of expressions. This, coupled with his recognition of the danger of premature condemnations of what, after all, were possibly only temporary onesidednesses in other thinkers set him apart in an age and Church which was ready to condemn all deviations from the current orthodoxy [262].

The baron's openness to change and his readiness to sponsor advanced views in theology did not extend to moral, political or social matters. In these areas he was an eminent Victorian. As Maude Petre

259. Tyrrell's reaction to von Hügel's "Official Authority" paper may be applied to most of the baron's writings: "I think you might consider the common mind a little more. It was the same with your most wonderful synthetic paper [Experience and Transcendence] which you stuffed like a tight sausage. Solid, liquid, gas — ever the three forms in which thought can be presented; the last for an audience; the second for a book; the first, for an archangel in retreat". G. Tyrrell to von Hügel, 20 April 1904, BM.

260. A. N. WHITEHEAD, *Religion in the Making*, p. 77.

261. N. 257, ibid..

262. A striking example of the baron's open and fairmindedness can be found in an unpublished letter of Tyrrell to A. L. Lilley: "The Baron (who is here) cited me yesterday ad audiendum verbum remedievalism. I approached the tribunal like a guilty schoolboy with a half-learnt lesson. Of course he had it to his finger ends; — scored, analysed, numbered. To my agreeable surpise he was enthusiastic for every word of it. Where is he? Where are we all? However I ascribe it to his extraordinary docility and open-mindedness — the same that made him surrender on the subject of our recent controversies about 'apostates' — almost brings shame. I believe he would listen to the Devil and give him a perfectly fair hearing". G. Tyrrell to A. L. Lilley, 8 August 190[8], SAUL.

tells us: "He was not, so far as most of us knew him, open to any discussion of established moral laws, nor even conventions; any revolutionary inroads of tentative psychology into the moral domain, any easy-going resolution of moral restrictions, was to him objectionable, reprehensible, and inexcusably dangerous"[263].

In political affairs the baron was a Conservative. For example he stood on the platform of the Vestry Hall in 1886 to protest against the Irish Reform Bill and he believed that the British Empire had been "upon the whole greatly to the advantage of its subject races"[264]. With respect to the First World War, he accepted the allies' outlook unquestionably and as de la Bedoyère correctly notes: "The deeper layers of his spiritual insight, and consequently his deepest feelings, do not seem to have been reached by the moral and material catastrophy of the first world war, nor indeed, perhaps, by any of the socio-moral and politico-moral problems which since that war have so grievously tortured our generation and affected the whole Christian outlook"[265]. This was forcably borne out in a conversation the writer had in 1974 with Miss Juliet Mansel, a spiritual child of the baron who lived in his home for a number of years. During the war she worked as a nurse at the front but when she returned from the war in which her fiancé had been killed, the baron continued her spiritual direction just as before. As she related, he failed to discern the change the war had wrought on her since he had remained basically unaffected by the whole tragic event. Miss Mansel also recalled the squalor in which the baron's servants lived and she recounted that she had been particularly amused by von Hügel's references to the horse-busmen, washerwomen, etc. since she could not imagine him associating with their like. In these matters, it would seem, the baron was typical of the upper classes of his day and while he gave a substantial portion of his income to charity, he never fully appreciated the basic injustice of the times.

As a corollary we would just add that the purificatory role allotted by von Hügel to mathematical science within the spiritual life seems to us too intellectualistic and elitist. It results, we believe, from a misinterpretation of St. Catherine's symbolic expression and a somewhat positivistic conception of science on the baron's part. We ourselves would rather extend the possibility of this purificatory function to all man's routine human activities, believing that life itself offers sufficient barriers and opportunities for disciplining and overcoming man's egoism and selfishness if he will only avert to them[266].

263. M. D. PETRE, *Friedrich von Hügel: Personal Thoughts and Reminiscences*, in *The Hibbert Journal*, 24, 1925, pp. 78-9.
264. Bedoyère, p. 127.
265. Ibid., p. 280.
266. As Jean-Pierre de Caussade writes: "In order to reach the highest stage of perfection, the crosses sent by Providence, which are provided by their [men's] state at

In theology however, von Hügel's openness and tolerance towards other denominations and religions was far in advance of his time. From his earliest publications he referred to Protestants as "our separated brethren". And after his death Archbishop Nathan Söderblom wrote to his widow : "If you allow me to tell you from my far-off seat the impression and conviction that I got already in 1908 and that has been strengthened continually during the following years, that lay-Bishop in the Church of God was not only the foremost religious and theological thinker and writer of the Roman Church to-day, but no other man in our age has, as far as I can see, become a teacher and an initiator to seeking and believing souls in all the chief sections of the entire Church and communion of Christ, as von Hügel"[267]. In fact, the baron's home and his *London Society for the Study of Religion* became such a centre for enquiring souls of all denominations that von Hügel can be regarded as a kind of ecumenical movement in himself.

The baron's ecumenism extended beyond the limits of institutional Christianity and embraced all religions. For example, in his posthumous work *The Reality of God* he urged the Christian theologian "to enlarge Augustine's literary storehouse, and to bear in mind Indian and Persian, Egyptian, Greek, and Roman sighings after God"[268]. The breakdown and revision of the earlier unilinear and universalistic interpretation of history from Augustine to Bossuet necessitated by Voltaire's *Essai sur les mœurs* meant, even on the quantitative level, that the Christian theologian had to investigate the mass of new empirical documents, data and knowledge eminating from the study of other civilisations and religions. Von Hügel was one of the first Catholic theologians to recognise the necessity of this and to integrate the results of the historical and comparative study of religions within his theological work. In his brief history of the rise of the comparative study of religions Joachim Wach situates von Hügel alongside Max Scheler as one of the two Catholic thinkers who played a major role in the development of this new science[269].

Behind this scholarly interest in the study of the other religions lay von Hügel's belief in the intrinsic value of these religions as the vehicle and expression of God's love for the various peoples throughout history. His notion of the historical and graded character of God's revelation to all men allowed the baron, while recognising objective differences, to focus on the more general, unifying factor among the different

every moment, open to them a surer and far quicker road than extraordinary states and works". J.-P. DE CAUSSADE, *Self-Abandonment to Divine Providence*, London, 1972, p. 15.

267. S.L., p. 53.
268. R.G., p. 36.
269. Joachim WACH, *The Comparative Study of Religions*, London, 1969, pp. 5-6.

religions, namely, God's gift of love. Ultimately all barriers of race, colour and creeds are transcended and become secondary before the fundamental oneness and common sharing by each and every man in the One Divine Love of God. As in any love relationship this love is experienced as too strong and deep to allow individual differences to smother or quench it, but rather views the continual overcoming (not ignoring or eliminating) of genuine differences as a constant challenge and test to the everliving and deepening quality and purity of this love. Until religions learn and practise this lesson they will remain a sign of contradiction to everyone. Furthermore, unless the ecumenic movement among Christians today recognises and accepts this universal revelation and gift of God's love as a fundamental principle and framework within which their specifically Christian dialogue takes place and to which it must always return, there is a danger that the inner principle of all religion, the Holy Spirit, Whose activity knows no bounds, may be so cramped and stifled that the movement towards unity within Christianity becomes a legalised external unification of the major Christian institutions with very little meaning or consequence for the individual Christian. Consequently it may come to be regarded by the cynical as simply another ploy on the part of the institutional leaders to preserve their power by amalgamating at a time when their traditional power base is diminishing.

Furthermore, von Hügel's stress on the primacy of the interior, universalistic, mystical dimension of religion does not lead him to lose sight of the fact that in concrete existence, religion is always mediated and has an external historical component of God addressing his people in words and deeds, in flesh and blood. The barons mystically tempered incarnationalism respects man's condition as an embodied spirit-in-the-world-with-others and preserves the full interpersonal component which characterises the highest and deepest love relationship between the personal God and the human personality.

Within this context we would like to draw special attention to the fact that every doctrine of human spirituality must face squarely both the reality of God and the reality of man's condition in the world with others. Any exclusiveness here, any turning our back on the neighbour or flight from the world would be, as the baron says, "treason against both man and God"[270]. And although some of the most exclusive of the Christian mystics may seem, in their overzealous quest for the supreme reality, God, to deny the reality or value of all finite existence, they usually rectify this by their simultaneous recovery of the finite as a participant in the Divine reality and as such worthy of our respect and love[271]. In acknowledging both these factors and

270. E.L., p. 316.
271. As the baron remarks of the mystical élan: "It is essentially a plunge right away from all the other and lesser experiences — an act of abandonment into the *drawing*,

preserving a delicate balance between the legitimate demands of each the baron offers a spirituality which can be fully secular without being secularist and a secularity which can be spiritualised without becoming spiritualist. Ultimately man's spiritualisation and his humanisation proceed hand in hand.

The baron's balance is again evidenced in his conception of religion as a dynamic organic unity. And while he concentrated on the broader reality of religion, his insights are applicable to the Church also. For example by substituting Church for religion in the following passage of von Hügel we read: "If the Church turned out to be simple, in the sense of being a monotone, a mere oneness, a whole without parts, it could not be true; and yet if the Church be left too much a mere multiplicity, a mere congeries of parts without a whole, it cannot be persuasive and fully operative"[272]. The Church then should be a living unity and harmonic interaction of the traditional and institutional elements, the critical-historical, philosophical and theological elements and the mystical and operative elements. Only a view of the Church which recognises the relative, functional autonomy of each and all of these elements and which rejoices in their creative tension can be vital enough to allow the full reality of the Church to emerge anew appropriate to the conditions and needs of each time and place.

However, von Hügel's supreme contribution came in his decisive article "Experience and Transcendence" in *The Dublin Review* of April 1906 when he launched his programme of theological renewal by appealing for theology to abandon its abstract, deductive approach and instead to embrace the concrete, inductive, experiential method. By initiating a movement towards experience as the central locus of theological reflection the baron must be seen as an important forerunner of much of contemporary theology. But before experience could rise to its present preeminent place the narrow, fundamentally sense based notion of both the classical British empiricists and the neo-Kantians had to be broadened. In his recovery of a widened more empirical notion of experience in which reality, not simple sensa or phenomena, was immediately given the baron must be acclaimed a true innovator. Alongside such acquaintances and friends as Henri Bergson (France), William James (U.S.A.) and James Ward (England), von Hügel articulated a new notion in which experience no longer consisted of a pure manifold of sensa which had to be unified and ordered by the mind but rather that these existed together from the start as an in-

the attraction of God, and God, reached thus by this severance and by this plunge, then gives the soul a starting-point for such love of earthly things and persons as may be there to love". R.G., p. 92.

272. M.E.I, p. 50.

separable whole. Within this conception one is no longer caught in the vicious circle of attempting to derive either the subject from the object or vice versa. Both are simply there within experience from the beginning. Objective reality is immediately given and need not be inferred or proved. The subjective factor in experience is not a simple datum but rather recipiens. However, the connotation of passivity suggested by this expression is far from true. In fact our receptivity is always conative, active and even when non-voluntary it is never indifferent. This also holds true for religious experience. All man's experience is sensational, emotional, cognitional and volitional (fully personal) and within the ever-growing process of this more confused unity, discursive reason has the task of clarifying and differentiating the more obscure, compact whole. But the primordial unity of this lived experience can never be completely comprehended or exhaustively articulated by any participant within the process. And since there is no way of stepping out to have a look from outside, a sense of the unknowableness and mystery pervades all human knowledge and existence and this is especially evidenced in our relation and knowledge of the Divine transcendent reality.

Although the baron made the breakthrough to this notion of experience in 1906, he never developed his insights here systematically nor did he explicitly work out a general theory of experience as the epistemological basis and framework within which man's specifically religious experience could be situated. This must be our central criticism of von Hügel, for his failure here obscured the radically empirical roots of his thought and led to many misinterpretations. The lack of success among commentators in detecting this fundamental development in the baron's conception of experience is attributable also to the fact that almost the whole of his *magnum opus*, *The Mystical Element of Religion*, was written before he himself had become explicitly aware of this shift. The two epistemologies and conceptions of experience, that of the neo-Kantian Volkelt and of the radical empirical Ward, run alongside each other in the second volume of this work[273] while in the first volume Volkelt's reigns supreme[274]. The real transition occured only towards the completion of *The Mystical Element* and as the baron never revised this work in the light of his new insights, nor developed them systematically elsewhere the radically empirical notion of experience which forms the centre of his thought is not easy to unearth. Any originality claimed for this work stems from the fact that we discovered this key to von Hügel's thought and proceeded to construct a new synthesis of the baron's religious philosophy on this basis.

273. M.E.II, pp. 275-9.
274. M.E.I, pp. 55-7.

That von Hügel himself failed to follow up his breakthrough soon after 1906 can be attributed primarily to his involvement in the modernist crisis and to the mental anguish this controversy wrought on him. Nevertheless this omission has led some commentators to underrate his achievement. It also offered scholars the possibility of escaping from the difficult though essential task of penetrating to the motivating experiences and problems which underlay his thought and of concentrating instead on a variety of Hügelian topics. By elaborating systematically, at the beginning of our second part, the baron's insights on experience and interpreting these in a radically empirical fashion, the present work exposes and unfolds the first principles around which all the baron's thought revolves and so allows the often obscure, hidden unity and harmony inherent in the bewildering multiplicity of his ideas to appear. So, although von Hügel can be criticised for failing to develop and systematise his new insights and to a certain extent also for his lack of a technical vocabulary and precision in drawing distinctions, this is not a fundamental criticism of the man or his work. In his basic aim of re-establishing contact with reality, especially the Divine reality through recovering, unveiling and epistemologically grounding their engendering experiences the baron succeeded in erecting a new landmark in man's continual search, especially over the preceeding three centuries, for a safe ground of philosophising and theologising beyond dogmatism and scepticism in immediate experience[275]. Finally, in his determination to take all the data of human experience into account overlooking nothing, his analysis and explications are as adequate and as applicable to the immensity of reality as is possible in the achievement of any one man in this mysterious domain.

PROSPECTS

There are, we suggest, on the basis of what we have seen, two basic ways in which the divine may be experienced. On the one hand in a more general existential manner as mediated through each individual's own particular contact with the finitude and contingency of reality and secondly in a more specific and concrete way through the various historical religious institutions, traditions and communities which environ each individual from the very first moment of his birth.

Ideally these two modes of experience should supplement and complement each other combining to form a common source of harmonious

275. However precisely at this moment, and even more significantly since, the critiques of Marx, Nietzsche and more especially Freud were beginning to surface and the decisive questions about man, experience and reality were once again undergoing revolutionary shifts. But these would become the questions for another day and another generation more specifically, we would suggest, our own.

growth and creativity for the person. A major difficulty arises when society and culture no longer mediate the sacred but the secular and this is further compounded when the Church becomes identified or reduced to a structure and organisation and is no longer expressive, evocative or translucent of the deeper inner realities it should embody. Inevitably a socio-religious crisis develops.

Furthermore as part of this social process of secularisation modern man believes that to be honest to God he must be honest to himself, to others and to the world. In other words, he must respect the autonomy of other realities and areas acknowledging their rights to develop and work with their own specific methods, objects, limits, aims and ends. Gradually the god who accounted for the gaps in these areas has receded until he has been seen to be no longer necessary. To where we might ask has he gone? Has he been shunted out of every other sphere to find a final unassailable resting place in the private world of the individual need? Is it here that religion is to be located and where the churches will minister to the diminishing flocks of the future? We know how Bonhoeffer schoffed at such a prospect.

With the god who was never really God gone, the way should be open for the true God to emerge. But where, when, how etc. one cannot say. That there is a more in the midst of everything, a beyond amid the here and now, a depth disclosed in the heart of the ordinary which allows us to see the extraordinariness of it all, of this alone one can be confident. Not to have experienced this, even as a lack, is to have missed something of the real. It is to have failed to appreciate the most precious thing in life, the so-called ordinary relationships with family, friends and acquaintances in work and play, in health and sickness which if given a chance can generate such a source of meaning that the bland question of the meaning of life is seen for what it is — a pure abstraction.

This accords fully with a first principle of the religious philosophy developed throughout this work, namely that the Infinite is experienced only on occasion of and as a contrast to the finite. Consequently, we contend that the more really, fully and authentically we are involved in the world with others the more possibility there is of sensing the Beyond, More and Other in the midst of everything. Finite and Infinite are really two sides of the one coin — two poles held together in the closest tension — but it is the finite alone which we directly experience and which can mediate the Infinite. This is the essential point. We do not experience the two poles directly and live in a tension between them. Our immediate experience is of ourselves in a world with others. It is only by, in and through our personal experience, our relationships and our activities that the Divine becomes disclosed and discovered by each of us. Contrary to the neo-Platonic

mystic's belief that we must fly from the self, the world and others
to be alone with the Alone we suggest that complete involvement
in the world and engagement with others is the divine providential
purgative way through which each man purifies himself from his
selfish, egoistical self-attachment and self-interest and allows his selfless
altruistic, detached, disinterested, true selfhood to emerge.

These views, we suggest, extend a certain preference in theology
to the ancient mystical tradition and method of the *via negativa*. The
basis of a *Theologia negativa* resides in the fact that the ground of our
being is not to be found among the things of this world. A *Theologia
affirmativa* has been in ascendency for too long and has in a sense
tended to dull our sensitivity to the basic mystery which lies at the
centre of human existence. Instead of commencing with God and
affirming his highest attributes, the negative approach begins, as
Dionysius the Areopagite reminds us, with the concrete particular
realities of the world and through negation arrives at a stage or state of
openness to something beyond[276]. Describing this negative approach
Dionysius writes : "we mount upwards from below to that which is the
highest, and, according to the degree of transcendence so our speech
is restrained until, the entire ascent being accomplished, we become
wholly voiceless, inasmuch as we are absorbed in Him who is totally
ineffable"[277]. We suggest that this movement which results to a large
extent in silence before the ineffable mystery accords better with
modern man's experience than a knowledge and enumeration of God's
attributes which issues in a crescendo of many words.

---

276. As we read in Pseudo-Dionysius : "We ascend from the particular to the
universal conceptions, abstracting [negating] all attributes in order that, without veil,
we may know that Unknowing which is enshrouded under all that is known and
all that can be known, and that we may begin to contemplate the superessential
Darkness which is hidden by all the light that is in existing things". Dionysius the
Areopagite, *The Mystical Theology and the Celestial Hierarchies*, Surrey, 1965, p. 12.
277. Ibid., p. 14.

BIOGRAPHICAL INDEX

BERGSON, Henri (1859-1941). Professor of Philosophy at the Collège de France. His *Essai sur les données immédiates de la conscience* (1898) had considerable influence on von Hügel's development of a radically empirical notion of experience. Their only meeting took place in Paris on 14 April, 1907.

BISHOP, Edmund (1846-1917). Historian and liturgical scholar. A follower of Acton and a convert to Catholicism. Von Hügel valued his advice during the modernist crisis as coming from one who also belonged to a former generation — the era of the Syllabus. They met for the first time in Rome on 6 February, 1895.

BLONDEL, Maurice (1861-1949). Philosopher. His doctoral thesis *L'Action* (1893) inaugurated the new method of immanence which was highly appreciated by von Hügel but held suspect at Rome. In their prolonged philosophical discussions, especially in 1896 and 1899, both men seemed to be in fundamental agreement. Later they disagreed on the role of the historical critical method, cf. Blondel's «Histoire et Dogme» (1904) and von Hügel's response «Du Christ éternel» (1904). Their first meeting took place in Rome on 9 March, 1895.

BREMOND, Henri (1865-1935). A writer on spirituality and mysticism. He was a sympathiser of Tyrrell, Maude Petre and von Hügel during the modernist crisis. His positions on the quietist and pure love controversy and on mystical matters in his classical work *Histoire littéraire du sentiment religieux* (1916) were greatly influenced, even dictated by von Hügel. Their first meeting took place in Paris on 8 February, 1899.

BRIGGS, Augustus Charles (1841-1915). Scottish biblical exegete who later became Professor of Scripture at Union Theological Seminary, New York. In 1892 he was condemned by his own Presbyterian Church for his critical views and later reordained in the Episcopal Church. He collaborated with von Hügel in the publication of *The Papal Commission and the Pentateuch* (1906). They met for the first time in Rome on 19 November, 1897.

DUCHESNE, Louis (1843-1922). Professor of Church History at the Institut Catholique in Paris and Director of the French College in Rome. He founded the *Bulletin critique* to which von Hügel contributed and he represented the ideal of the historical critical scholar to which von Hügel aspired. They met for the first time in Paris on 12 May, 1884.

EHRHARD, Albert (1860-1920). Church Historian, Patrologist and Byzantinist. His *Der Katholizismus und das zwanzigste Jahrhundert* (1901) to which von Hügel subscribed, attempted to relate theology, religion and the Church to the modern insights of philosophy, history and the social sciences. They became acquainted for the first time in Rome on 14 December, 1897.

EUCKEN, Rudolf (1846-1926). The philosopher of the spiritual life. Eucken's *Lebensanschauungen* (1890), *Kampf* (1896) and *Wahrheitsgehalt* (1905) influenced von Hügel philosophically and it was Eucken who dissuaded him from all forms of faculty psychology. Von Hügel visited him for the first time in Jena on 11 May, 1898.

FOGAZZARO, Antonio (1842-1911). Politician, poet and writer. It was in response to his invitation that von Hügel journeyed to Caldonazzo on 26 August 1907 and thence to Molveno for the famous modernist meeting. Cf. *supra* p. 92. The following is von Hügel's unpublished diary account of the meeting:

27 August — Tuesday — Up at 6.30. With Fogazzaro and Scotti, in Church (a Mass finishing up) and back to Hotel Molveno. At 11, Don Brizio Casciola arrived, having walked over mountains ever since 6, — most strangely clad. After lunch arrived Casati (of Rinnovamento); Murri; Buonaiuti; Mari; Fracassini; and Piastrelli (Rome, — author of 'Quello che Vogliamo'), a young, round-blue-eyed, strong-chinned, thin-lipped, cropp-haired [sic] very clean, neat and composed man of 24 in lay dress. We all went into wood on mountainside, — discussing what Fogazzaro had better do about his 'Letture' in the case of fresh censures, and in matter of Le Roy. I engaged to send him opinions, and wishes of our group, the minute any fresh act appeared. We all 10 dined etc. at separate table throughout stay. I spoke a little to them in evening, about Anglicans and our movement.

28 August — Wednesday — Up at 6.30. To Molveno Parish Church. The priest already away on his turn among his parishioners in the mountains. Prayed in Church half an hour. After breakfast, with the nine into wood by lake-side: discussed the *Nachgeschichte* of Our Lord's life. I developed St. Paul's ideas. Continued meeting in large bed-room of our Hotel: discussed the *Vorgeschichte*: I developed the historico-critical position, and the moral and devotional questions involved. In afternoon, a further meeting in large bed-room: discussed practical matters: (1) what to do, if Enc. (or Pope otherwise) himself directly condemns 'Rinnovamento'; (2) what to do if subordination demanded of Priests to Decree *Lamentabili*; (3) as to the writing and circulating of 'Tracts', — I accepted one on N.T. (simply the critical methods and general results from these, illustrated by less disturbing cases) — Fracassini, Frederici, Semeria, Tyrrell to do others.

29 August — Thursday — Breakfast at 6.30. Made a little parting speech to our party, reading them Loisy's last letter, and dwelling on necessity of sincere, thorough critical work; of deep, self-renouncing Christian life; and of careful charity and magnanimity towards our opponents. Left, in one horse little open carriage, with Fogazzaro, at 7.30: reached Mezzo Lombardo at 11. Lunched with him at Hotel del Commercio there. In little train together to San Michele, and from thence to Trento. He on into Italy; I at 2.20 p.m. by Val Sugana line back to Levico. To Hotel on foot, — raining.

GENOCCHI, Giovanni (1860-1926). Professor of exegesis at the Apollinaire at Rome where he was an ally of the modernists and a moderating influence for them. Von Hügel received news of the loss of his Biblical Professorship from him on 26 July 1898. He is now considered to be the author of the "Lettres Romaines" (1904) which von Hügel had published.

HUVELIN, Henri (1838-1910). Abbé and spiritual director. He declined an offer of the Chair of History at the Institut Catholique preferring to "write in souls". He warned von Hügel of the abstractness of neo-scholasticism and guided him into the great Catholic tradition of the late 17th Century French spirituality. He was the supreme embodiment and ideal of sanctitity which von Hügel cultivated throughout his life. Apart from von Hügel he was also the spiritual director of Charles de Foucauld. Von Hügel visited him for the first time in Paris on 16 June, 1884.

JAMES, William (1842-1910). American Psychologist. He influenced von Hügel considerably in articulating a broader, more radically empirical notion of experience and in situating religious experience in the area of the pre-conscious. His "Reflex Action and Theism" (1897) added support to von Hügel's proposal of the three elements of religion. Von Hügel's only letter to him was written on 10 May, 1910.

KRAUS, Franz Xaver (1840-1901). Church historian and father of *Reform-katholizismus* which attempted to break out of the ghetto mentality of a narrow, political, absolutist neo-ultramontanism and return to a religious Catholicism à la Fénelon. Kraus also emphasised the necessity of a strong positive historical theology as a means of overcoming the neo-scholasticism of the time. Von Hügel met him for the first time in Rome on 22 November, 1895.

LILLEY, Alfred Leslie (1866-1947). Anglican vicar of St. Mary's Paddington Green (London). He was sympathetic to the modernist cause and of immense support to von Hügel during the crisis. After reading his *Modernism: A Record and Review* (1908) von Hügel was prompted to designate him as the providential historian of the movement. Von Hügel visited him for the first time at his vicarage on 20 April, 1903.

LOISY, Alfred Firmin (1857-1940). Biblical exegete. He held the Chair of Semitic Languages at the Institut Catholique which he lost in 1893. Von Hügel identified the struggle for the functional autonomy of the historical critical method within the Church with Loisy and defended him on this point continually. From 1908 onwards von Hügel began to suspect Loisy of immanentism and Loisy, for his part, felt that von Hügel's emphasis on the divine transcendence was too extreme. Von Hügel met Loisy in Paris for the first time on 18 October, 1893.

MIGNOT, Eudoxe-Irénée (1842-1918). Bishop of Fréjus and Archbishop of Albi. He was very well informed in biblical scholarship and sympathetic to Loisy and von Hügel. Loisy dated the beginnings of modernism from the first visit von Hügel paid Mignot at Fréjus on 22 November, 1893.

NEWMAN, John Henry (1801-1890). One of the leaders of the Oxford Movement, a convert to Catholicism and later a Cardinal. Von Hügel subscribed his early intellectual discipline to him and admitted that he spoke Newman even oftener than he knew. His Preface to the *Via Media* (1830) was instrumental in von Hügel articulating his conception of the three elements of religion. They saw each other for the first time on 13 June, 1876 when von Hügel and his wife spent a week with the Cardinal at Birmingham.

SEMERIA, Giovanni (1867-1931). A Barnabite, regarded by some as the leader of the Italian Modernists. In 1908 Pius X personally allowed him take the modernist oath with special reserves as to the rights of historical criticism. After a violent campaign against him he was released of all his functions and forced to leave Italy. Cardinal Mercier accepted him into his diocese in Belgium in 1912. After receiving a sad letter from Semeria, von Hügel visited him in Brussels on 16 October 1912 and spent 15 days with him. It was during this visit that von Hügel began to prepare his "Petite consultation sur les difficultés concernant Dieu" in answer to some enquiries from Semeria. The ultimate destination of von Hügel's answer is now believed to have been the baron's son-in-law, Count Francesco Salimei. Von Hügel met Semeria for the first time in Rome on 14 November, 1894.

TROELTSCH, Ernst (1865-1923). Evangelical theologian and philosopher. Von Hügel appreciated Troeltsch's historical knowledge, his metaphysical competence, his emphasis on the social aspects of religion and the polarity between human ethics and religious ethics. Their only meeting took place in Heidelberg on 3 May, 1902.

TYRRELL, George (1867-1909). An Irishman, a convert and later lecturer in Moral Philosophy at the Jesuit Scholasticate at Stonyhurst. He was a brilliant writer who became von Hügel's most intimate friend and confident and was considerably influenced by von Hügel especially in the critical study of the Scriptures. He corrected the manuscript of von Hügel's *Mystical Element*, adding immeasurably to its form. Von Hügel met him for the first time in London on 9 October, 1897.

VOLKELT, Johannes (1848-1930). Neo-Kantinian philosopher who had a considerable influence on von Hügel's epistemology until 1905 when von Hügel made the breakthrough to radical empiricism.

WARD, James (1843-1925). Professor of Psychology at Cambridge, England. He was the main influence on von Hügel adopting a radically empirical conception of experience especially through his decisive article "The Present Problems of General Psychology" (1904) which von Hügel read on 30 March 1905. They met for the first time in Cambridge on 27 May, 1902.

WARD, William George (1812-1882). Philosopher and theologian. A convert and early follower of Newman though he later differed from him in being fiercely anti-liberal, narrowly ultramontane and ardently scholastic. Von Hügel profited immensely from their discussions during the last nine years of his life.

INDEX OF NAMES

Bibliographical references are marked with an asterisk. Names listed in the Biographical Index are marked with a double asterisk.

BIBLIOTHECA EPHEMERIDUM THEOLOGICARUM LOVANIENSIUM

26. G. THILS et R.E. BROWN (éd.), *Exégèse et théologie* (Hommage J. Coppens, III), 1968. 328 p. FB 550.

27. J. COPPENS (éd.), *Ecclesia a Spiritu sancto edocta. Hommage à Mgr G. Philips*, 1970. 640 p. FB 580.

28. J. COPPENS (éd.), *Sacerdoce et Célibat. Études historiques et théologiques*, 1971. 740 p. FB 600.

29. M. DIDIER (éd.), *L'évangile selon Matthieu. Rédaction et théologie*, 1971. 432 p. FB 750.

*30. J. KEMPENEERS, *Le Cardinal van Roey en son temps*, 1971.

*31. F. NEIRYNCK, *Duality in Mark. Contributions to the Study of the Markan Redaction*, 1972.

*32. F. NEIRYNCK (éd.), *L'évangile de Luc. Problèmes littéraires et théologiques. Mémorial Lucien Cerfaux*, 1973.

*33. C. BREKELMANS (éd.), *Questions disputées d'Ancien Testament. Méthode et théologie*, 1974.

*34. M. SABBE (éd.), *L'évangile selon Marc. Tradition et rédaction*, 1974.

*35. *Miscellanea Albert Dondeyne. Godsdienstfilosofie. Philosophie de la religion*, 1974.

*36. G. PHILIPS, *L'union personnelle avec le Dieu vivant*, 1974.

37. F. NEIRYNCK, in collaboration with T. HANSEN and F. VAN SEGBROECK, *The Minor Agreements of Matthew and Luke against Mark with a Cumulative List*, 1974. 330 p. FB 800.

*38. J. COPPENS, *Le Messianisme et sa relève prophétique*, 1974.

39. D. SENIOR, *The Passion Narrative according to Matthew. A Redactional Study*, 1975; new impression, 1982. 440 p. FB 1000.

*40. J. DUPONT (éd.), *Jésus aux origines de la christologie*, 1975.

*41. J. COPPENS (éd.), *La notion biblique de Dieu*, 1976.

42. J. LINDEMANS – H. DEMEESTER (éd.), *Liber Amicorum Monseigneur W. Onclin*, 1976. 396 p. FB 900.

43. R.E. HOECKMAN (éd.), *Pluralisme et œcuménisme en recherches théologiques. Mélanges offerts au R.P. Dockx, O.P.*, 1976. 316 p. FB 900.

44. M. DE JONGE (éd.), *L'Évangile de Jean*, 1977. 416 p. FB 950.

45. E.J.M. VAN EIJL (éd.), *Facultas S. Theologiae Lovaniensis 1432-1797. Bijdragen tot haar geschiedenis. Contributions to its History. Contributions à son histoire*, 1977. 570 p. FB 1500.

46. M. DELCOR (éd.), *Qumrân. Sa piété, sa théologie et son milieu*, 1978. 432 p. FB 1550.

47. M. CAUDRON (éd.), *Faith and Society. Foi et Société. Geloof en maatschappij. Acta Congressus Internationalis Theologici Lovaniensis 1976*, 1978. 304 p. FB 1150.

48. J. KREMER (éd.), *Les Actes des Apôtres. Traditions, rédaction, théologie*, 1979. 590 p. FB 1600.

49. F. NEIRYNCK, avec la collaboration de J. DELOBEL, T. SNOY, G. VAN BELLE, F. VAN SEGBROECK, *Jean et les Synoptiques. Examen critique de l'exégèse de M.-É. Boismard*, 1979. XII-428 p. FB 950.

50. J. COPPENS, *La relève apocalyptique du messianisme royal. I. La royauté – Le règne – Le royaume de Dieu. Cadre de la relève apocalyptique*, 1979. 325 p. FB 848.

51. M. GILBERT (éd.), *La Sagesse de l'Ancien Testament*, 1979. 420 p. FB 1700.

52. B. DEHANDSCHUTTER, *Martyrium Polycarpi. Een literair-kritische studie*, 1979. 296 p. FB 950.

53. J. LAMBRECHT (éd.), *L'Apocalypse johannique et l'Apocalyptique dans le Nouveau Testament*, 1980. 458 p. FB 1400.

54. P.-M. BOGAERT (éd.), *Le Livre de Jérémie. Le prophète et son milieu. Les oracles et leur transmission*, 1981. 408 p. FB 1500.

55. J. COPPENS, *La relève apocalyptique du messianisme royal.* III. *Le Fils de l'homme néotestamentaire*, 1981. XIV-192 p. FB 800.

56. J. VAN BAVEL & M. SCHRAMA (éd.), *Jansénius et le Jansénisme dans les Pays-Bas. Mélanges Lucien Ceyssens*, 1982. 247 p. FB 1000.

57. J.H. WALGRAVE, *Selected Writings – Thematische geschriften. Thomas Aquinas, J.H. Newman, Theologia Fundamentalis.* Edited by G. DE SCHRIJVER & J.J. KELLY, 1982. XLIII-425 p. FB 1000.

58. F. NEIRYNCK & F. VAN SEGBROECK, avec la collaboration de E. MANNING, *Ephemerides Theologicae Lovanienses 1924-1981. Tables générales. Bibliotheca Ephemeridum Theologicarum Lovaniensium 1947-1981*, 1982. 400 p. FB 1600.

59. J. DELOBEL (éd.), *Logia. Les paroles de Jésus – The Sayings of Jesus. Mémorial Joseph Coppens.* 1982. 647 p. FB 2000.

60. F. NEIRYNCK, *Evangelica. Gospel Studies – Études d'évangile. Collected Essays.* Edited by F. VAN SEGBROECK, 1982. XIX-1036 p. FB 2000.

61. J. COPPENS, *La relève apocalyptique du messianisme royal.* II. *Le Fils d'homme vétéro- et intertestamentaire.* Édition posthume par J. LUST, 1982. XVII-272 p. FB 1000.

62. J.J. KELLY, *Baron Friedrich von Hügel's Philosophy of Religion.* 1983. 232 p. FB 1500.

In preparation:

63. G. DE SCHRIJVER, *Le merveilleux accord de l'homme et de Dieu. Étude de l'analogie de l'être chez Hans Urs von Balthasar.* 338 p. FB 1500.

64. J. GROOTAERS & J. SELLING, *The 1980 Synod of Bishops: «On the Role of the Family».* Preface by Prof. emeritus L. JANSSENS. FB 1500.

65. F. NEIRYNCK & F. VAN SEGBROECK, *New Testament Vocabulary. A Companion Volume to the Concordance.*